The Supreme Court
and Election Law

The Supreme Court and Election Law

Judging Equality from
Baker v. Carr to *Bush v. Gore*

Richard L. Hasen

NEW YORK UNIVERSITY PRESS

New York and London

NEW YORK UNIVERSITY PRESS
New York and London
www.nyupress.org

Library of Congress Cataloging-in-Publication Data
Hasen, Richard L.
The Supreme Court and election law :
judging equality from Baker v. Carr to Bush v. Gore / Richard L. Hasen
p. cm.
Includes bibliographical references and index.
ISBN 0–8147–3659–9
1. Election law—United States.   2. Equality before the law—United States.   3. Political questions and judicial power—United States.   4. Apportionment (Election law)—United States.
5. Presidents—United States—Election—2000.   6. Law and politics.   7. United States
Supreme Court.   I. Title.
KF4886.H37   2003
342.73'07—dc21   2003009365

New York University Press books are printed on acid-free paper,
and their binding materials are chosen for strength and durability.

Manufactured in the United States of America
10 9 8 7 6 5 4 3 2 1

To Lori
who inspires me every day with her
strength, intelligence, patience, and love

Contents

Preface

The idea for this book arose out of two events. First, Bill Marshall, who was working in the White House but planning a return to academia, called and asked if I would participate in a conference commemorating the fortieth anniversary of *Baker v. Carr*, the Supreme Court case opening the door to a variety of challenges to election laws in the United States. Second, the virtually tied presidential election of 2000 led to a dramatic intervention in the political process by the United States Supreme Court in the case of *Bush v. Gore*.

Thus, at the very time academics were turning their attention back in time to assess the role that courts should play in regulating elections and the political process, real-world events led to a court intervention in the political process beyond even the fanciful hypotheticals that law professors devise to torture students.

Much of the commentary in the immediate aftermath of the Supreme Court's decision in *Bush v. Gore* to halt the recount focused on that decision itself—its potential political motivations, its possible defensibility as a matter of pragmatism if not precedent, its effect on the legitimacy of the Supreme Court. But few who entered the fray in the heat of the moment reflected much on where *Bush v. Gore* fit into the larger picture of Supreme Court intervention in the political process since *Baker v. Carr*.

This book is an initial effort to examine the larger picture. I consider what role the Supreme Court has played and should play in regulating political equality in the United States. My work builds upon the emergence of election law as its own field of study, apart from, yet related to, its parents, constitutional law and political science. Dan Lowenstein of UCLA, one of the pioneers in the election law field, first enticed me to think about election law as its own subject when I was a student in his seminar in 1990. Since that time, Dan and I have worked together—through a casebook, a quarterly journal, and an electronic discussion group—to help the field grow. At this stage, election law scholars are beginning to confront major questions of how courts should (or should not) regulate politics.

An earlier version of chapter 2, "Judicial Unmanageability," appeared as "The Benefits of 'Judicially *Un*manageable' Standards in Election Cases Under the Equal Protection Clause," 80 North Carolina Law Review 1469 (2002), part of the symposium on *Baker v. Carr* organized by Bill Marshall and Melissa Saunders of the University of North Carolina. The rest of the material in this book is new.

Acknowledgments

This book is much stronger thanks to the insightful and challenging comments of many colleagues. Bruce Cain, Beth Garrett, Heather Gerken, Tom Mann, Chris May, Rick Pildes, Bob Pushaw, Roy Schotland, and Mark Tushnet had the patience to read and comment on the entire manuscript. I also received useful comments and suggestions from Ellen Aprill, Evan Caminker, Del Dickson, Sam Issacharoff, Pam Korland, Hal Krent, Dan Lowenstein, Michael McConnell, Dan Ortiz, Spencer Overton, Josh Rosenkranz, Peter Schuck, David Strauss, Stephen Wermiel, Richard Winker, Adam Winkler, and participants at a Loyola Law School faculty workshop.

I could not have written a book such as this without the support of Loyola Law School, particularly Dean David Burcham and Associate Dean Victor Gold. They made sure that whatever resources I needed to conduct my research were available, and, more importantly, they have created the environment for scholars and teachers to thrive.

Thanks also to Robert Nissenbaum, Paul Howard, and Renee Rastorfer of Loyola's law library for stellar support. Indeed, this book could not have been written without the support of research librarians. Much of the historical research conducted for this book relied upon the case files of Supreme Court justices. I am grateful to Del Dickson for helping me get started tracking down these materials. Jeff Flannery of the Library of Congress Manuscript Reading Room went above and beyond the call of duty in assisting me in examining the papers of Chief Justice Warren and Justices Brennan, Douglas, and Marshall. John Jacob, archivist of Justice Powell's papers at Washington and Lee University, was also generous with his time, as was Mike Widener of the University of Texas Law Library (Justice Clark's papers) and Nancy Shader of Princeton's Seely G. Mudd Manuscript Library (Justice Harlan's papers). Thanks also to the executors of

Justice Brennan's literary estate for permission to access his papers through 1985.

Peter Bartle, Sofya Bendersky, Amber Star Healy, Michael Kim, Trisha Ortiz, and Eugene Rome provided exemplary research assistance, and Betty Kinuthia and Thelma Wong Terre provided superb faculty support. Thanks to the editorial staff of NYU Press, including Alison Waldenberg, Deborah Gershenowitz, Ginny Wiehardt, Despina Gimbel, Jennifer Yoon, and Eric Zinner, for their thoughtful and careful work.

Finally, I thank my family. Thanks to my parents, for their support of my education and pride in my work; to my children, Deborah, Shana, and Jared, for the joy they bring me every day and for reminding me how much more there is to life beyond this book; and, most important, to my wife, Lori. I could not have asked for a better life partner. Lori's strength, intelligence, patience, and love inspire me every day to do my best work and to improve our world.

Introduction

Mighty Platonic Guardians

We would be mighty Platonic guardians indeed if Congress had granted us the authority to determine the best form of local government for every county, city, village, and town in America.
—*Holder v. Hall*, Justice Thomas, concurring.[1]

Supreme Court intervention in the political process has become a regular feature of the American political landscape. To give a few examples, the Court has required the reapportionment of virtually every legislative body in the country to comply with the principle of "one person, one vote"; ended the practice of political patronage employment; prevented local governments, states, and the federal government from limiting campaign spending in the name of political equality; curtailed the extent to which legislatures may take race into account in drawing district lines; and most recently (and, some would add, notoriously) determined the outcome of the 2000 presidential election.[2]

Though such intervention now seems commonplace, it was not always so common. In the period 1901–1960, the Court decided an average of 10.3 election law cases per decade with a written opinion. During the period 1961–2000, that number jumped to 60 per decade. Figure I-1 shows the trend.[3] The numbers are equally dramatic in Figure I-2, which displays the percentage of election law cases on the Court's docket. In the 1901–1960 period, on average only 0.7 percent of cases the Court decided by written opinion were election law cases. During the 1961–2000 period, that percentage increased seven and one-half times to an average 5.3 percent of cases.

The change in the 1960s is no mystery. In 1962, the Court decided *Baker v. Carr*,[4] determining that courts would now hear cases raising challenges to state apportionment plans (in court parlance, that such cases are "justiciable"). The Court did so despite Justice Frankfurter's strong protests that the courts should not enter into the political thicket for fear of harming the courts' legitimacy.

Perhaps encouraged by the Court's willingness to enter the thicket, and responding to the burgeoning civil rights movement, Congress passed the Voting Rights Act in 1965, beginning a dialogue between Congress and the Court over the contours and extent of voting rights. Congress passed major amendments to the act in 1982, partly in response to evidence of continued discrimination against racial minorities and partly in response to the Court's 1980 *City of Mobile v. Bolden*[5] decision that made it difficult for racial minorities to succeed in claiming that their votes were unconstitutionally "diluted." Congress created a statutory right to bring such a dilution claim under the new section 2 of the act, but it did so with exceedingly murky language—fully expecting the thorny statutory questions to be sorted out by the courts. The Court, in *Thornburg v. Gingles*,[6] did not disappoint, creating a three-factor threshold test, followed by a "totality of the circumstances" test, for judging claims of section 2 vote dilution.

Baker thus opened up the courts to a variety of election law cases, and the Court—with lower courts following its lead—has plunged forward in earnest to decide them. This book assesses how the Court has handled an important subset of these cases, those that regulate political equality, and sets forth some proposed methods and standards that the Court should employ in deciding such cases in the future. Especially given the controversy over *Bush v. Gore*, the Supreme Court case determining George W. Bush as the winner of the 2000 presidential election, the question whether the Court has been involved appropriately in regulating the political process is as timely as ever. Some see a rather straight line from *Baker* to *Bush*,[7] which should lead at least those critical of *Bush* to rethink *Baker*.

The Past and Future of Process Theory

Although *Baker* was controversial at the time, the case now has been canonized as an example of appropriate court intervention in the face of a failure in the political process. Tennessee had not reapportioned its legislative districts for sixty years, leading to a situation where rural voters, no

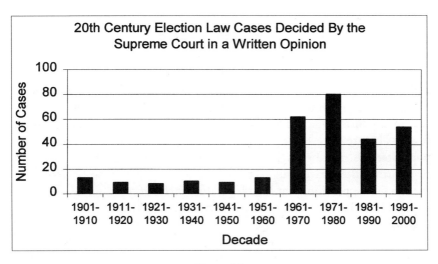

Figure I.1

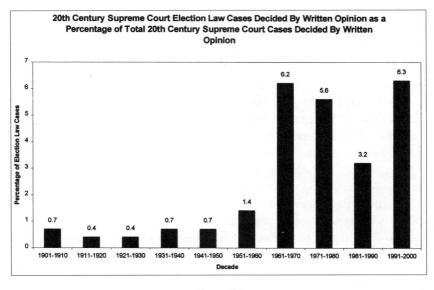

Figure I.2

Sources: Albert P. Blaustein and Roy M. Mersky, *The First One Hundred Justices: Statistical Studies on the Supreme Court of the United States.* Table 9 (1978) (data for 1901–1970); U.S. Department of Commerce, *Statistical Abstract of the United States.* (various years) (data for 1971–1999); Supreme Court of the United States, *2001 Year-End Report of the Judiciary* 5 (January 1, 2002) (available at www.supremecourtus.gov/publicinfo /year-end/2001year-endreport.html) (data for 2000)

longer a majority in the state, controlled a majority of the seats in the legislature: "37% of the voters of Tennessee elect[ed] 20 of the 33 Senators while 40% of the voters elect[ed] 63 of the 99 members of the House."[8] Other state legislatures were even more malapportioned; California, for example, had a 1,432 percent deviation between its largest and smallest districts before 1966.[9] The political market failed in the case of unequally populated districts because existing legislators could not be expected to reapportion themselves out of a job, nor would voters who benefit from the existing apportionment elect legislators inclined to do so.

John Hart Ely later argued in his important 1980 book, *Democracy and Distrust*, that "unblocking stoppages in the democratic process is what judicial review ought preeminently to be about."[10] Although much of Ely's theory of judicial review has been rejected by many constitutional law scholars,[11] the part that appears to have survived the test of time is his idea that courts should intervene in the face of political market failure. *Baker* was his poster child in crafting this argument.

Some observers describe Ely as having provided an after-the-fact justification for many of the activist decisions of the Warren Court, but the idea that courts should intervene to cure political market failure predates both Ely's work and the Warren Court. In the famous footnote 4 of Justice Stone's opinion in the 1938 case *United States v. Carolene Products Company*,[12] the Court endorsed more searching judicial review in three circumstances. In the second circumstance, the Court called for stricter review when the law at issue "restrict[ed] those political processes which can ordinarily be expected to bring about repeal of undesirable legislation."[13]

Most election law scholars have embraced process theory—at least that part focused on curing political market failures—almost as a matter of religious conviction. Samuel Issacharoff and Richard Pildes recently built upon Ely's work by advocating that the Court act to prevent political "lockups," primarily by the political parties.[14] I return in some detail to what has come to be known as "the political markets approach" in chapter 5, where I see it as a variant of recent (in my view, unwarranted) calls by both legal scholars and the Court to move away from adjudication of political equality cases on individual rights grounds and toward adjudication on "structural" or "functional" grounds.

Process theory has an intuitive appeal as a rule to apply in election law cases because it purports to provide both a reason for and a limit on judicial intervention in political cases, but it has proven to be problematic in three key ways.

First, the theory has not been successful in limiting judicial power: courts have not confined themselves to intervening in election law cases only in the face of political market failure. *Bush v. Gore* is the most recent example of this phenomenon. As Pamela Karlan and Elizabeth Garrett separately have argued, the Court in *Bush* had no need to intervene under process theory; the Florida legislature and the United States Congress were in a position to act if necessary to resolve disputes over Florida electors.[15] It is difficult to believe that even trenchant and well-argued criticism along these lines by prominent members of the legal academy such as Karlan and Garrett can serve to check the Court's desire to intervene in political cases when a Court majority wants to do so.[16] Thus, process theory may provide no meaningful constraint.

The second problem with process theory is that it masquerades as a purely procedural rather than a substantive basis for review of political cases.[17] A close consideration of the theory, however, reveals its implicit normative agenda. Return to the poster child for process theory, *Baker v. Carr*. Accepting the premise that the Tennessee political process was stuck in a position where a minority of rural voters controlled the state legislature, why should the Court intervene to "unblock" this "stoppage" in the political process?[18] The answer must be that there is some normative baseline—perhaps some rudimentary concept of equality that says the legislature should not be so far off from majority rule[19]—that allows us to conclude that unblocking the Tennessee stoppage is the right thing to do. If process theory operates in the world of substance, it must be weighed against other substantive arguments for intervention (or nonintervention) in political cases.

Daniel Lowenstein takes this point about the substantive dimension of process theory further, indeed too far. He believes process theory is a variant of "*Lochner*-era judicial interventionism," referring to the now-discredited approach of *Lochner v. New York*.[20] In *Lochner*, the Supreme Court struck down a state law setting maximum hours for bakers. Lowenstein agrees *Lochner* was decided incorrectly because it depended upon contested empirical and conceptual economic assumptions best resolved by legislatures, not courts. He then compares *Lochner* to process theories: "Tinkering with electoral and legislative procedures is no less subject to empirical imponderables than tinkering with the economy. What constitutes a democratic or impartial political procedure is just as conceptually contestable as what constitutes an externality in the economic realm." He concludes that "[i]f those who are aggrieved by an economic regulation ordinarily are consigned to the political arena to seek relief, why should not the same be true for those who disagree with some aspect of the political process?"[21]

One answer to Lowenstein is that those who are aggrieved by the political process—such as by being denied the right to vote—may have a more difficult time using the political arena to get relief than those who have the right to vote who are aggrieved by a particular economic regulation. Lowenstein denies that this claim is empirically correct, arguing that most political reforms in this country were carried out by political, rather than judicial, means.[22] He admits, however, that "the Supreme Court played a significant role in the extension of the franchise to blacks in the South."[23] Moreover, Lowenstein implicitly recognizes that his criticism goes too far, for even he believes that *Baker* and *Reynolds* were properly decided, all the while claiming that process theory is "in fact . . . very rarely applicable in our society."[24] So the difference between Lowenstein and most other election law scholars is one of degree as to how much process theory explains when the Court should intervene in the political process.

The third problem with process theory is that, despite its implicit substantive dimension, it is a shallow theory. It says nothing about how the courts should intervene in the face of political market failure.[25] *Baker* was a case of serious malapportionment of districts, and process theory provides a good reason for the Court to remedy the political market failure, if one accepts the weak equality rationale mentioned above. Should malapportionment have been remedied by requiring some "rational" apportionment, strict equality in the size of legislative districts, or something between these standards? Ely defended the one person, one vote standard that the Court adopted two years after *Baker* in *Reynolds v. Sims* as having the advantage of administrative convenience;[26] the standard in no sense flowed from process theory.

The shallowness problem of process theory is compounded by the fact that judges are not experts in political science, and even political scientists admit they sometimes have limited ability to predict how changes in rules governing elections and politics will affect political power. Judges, at least life-tenured federal judges such as those on the Supreme Court, often have every incentive to vote their values and not make self-interested decisions,[27] but impartiality does not cure competence concerns.

*Moving beyond Process Theory: Core and Contested Political Equality Rights in a Post–*Bush v. Gore *World*

Given the above three problems with process theory, this book looks beyond the theory and toward a broader view of how courts should decide election law cases. I concur with the aspect of process theory that says that courts generally should confine judicial intervention to cases of political market failure—in the face of a working political system of rudimentary equality, hands off by the judiciary makes sense—but I am not naive enough to believe that courts will in fact limit themselves. So part of this book is aimed at other devices that courts should use to experiment with various election rules that they might craft.

But procedural or mechanical fixes are not enough of a guide to decide such cases. Process theory's inability to provide substantive rules for curing political market failure proves the point. Thus, the next part of the book advocates a substantive theory of political equality to justify and limit the Court's role in regulating the political process.

The procedural and substantive arguments I make are intertwined, and both depend upon a critical assumption that I defend in this book: that the Supreme Court can (and should) distinguish between certain *core* political equality rights and other political equality rights that are *contested*.

Core political equality rights stem from two sources. The Court simply must accept a few of these core rights, such as nondiscrimination in voting on the basis of race or ethnicity, as minimal requirements of democratic government; they do not change along with public perceptions of the contemporary meaning of "democracy." But most core rights are *socially constructed*. The right to an equally weighted vote is now a core right (but was not when the Court decided *Baker*) because most people see it as a core right. Thus, most core political equality rights are the product of *social consensus*, or at least near-consensus. As my example of weighted voting shows, the Court itself can shape the social consensus with the rulings it makes.

On the other hand, some political equality rights are *contested*. For example, many but certainly not most people in the United States today believe that some groups, particularly members of racial minorities, should have the right to roughly proportional representation in legislative bodies. Contested political equality rights are neither a minimal requirement for democratic government (many democratic governments do not use proportional representation) nor the product of social consensus.

I use this distinction between core and contested political equality rights first in chapter 2 to make the procedural argument that when the Court chooses to craft a rule in an area of a contested equality right, it should do so with a murky (or vague) political rule. In contrast, when the Court chooses to craft a rule involving a core equality right, it is better suited to the use of a bright-line rule. The rationale is that the Court acting in an area of contested claims both has less reason to act decisively and also is in a greater danger of making poor policy choices.

In chapters 3 and 4, I make a stronger claim about core and contested political equality rights. Chapter 3 identifies three core equality principles and argues that if the government attempts to place a limit on the exercise of one of these three core political equality principles, the Court, with an eye on legislative self-interest and agency problems, must engage in a skeptical balancing of interests. In chapter 4, I argue that Congress or state and local legislative bodies (or the people, in those jurisdictions with an initiative process) should decide whether to expand political equality principles into contested areas. The Court should defer to legislative value judgments in such cases but, again, use searching scrutiny to control legislative self-interest.

A reader may accept my procedural and mechanical fixes described in chapter 2 without accepting the more controversial normative positions I put forward in later chapters. Before describing those normative positions in greater detail, I need to defend the constitutionalization of a substantive agenda of equality.

In making this move toward substance, I cannot avoid the charge that I am asking the Court to take on the role (or, more accurately, to continue in its role) as Platonic guardian of our political system.[28] The term "Platonic guardian" refers to Plato's allegory of the cave in *The Republic*.[29] In a dialogue between Socrates and Glaucon, Socrates describes a group of men who have been chained in a cave since birth so that they cannot turn their heads toward the light at the cave's opening. They see only shadows and attempt to discern which real objects cast the shadows. One man is freed, leaves the cave, and sees the real world. He returns to the cave, and before his eyes have adjusted to the dark his skills at discerning which real objects cast the shadows are poor compared to those of the men who stayed down in the cave. But after his eyes have adjusted, he is in a far better position to judge the shadows than are the cave dwellers to discern objects from shadows because he can rely upon the reality he observed on the surface.

Socrates explains that the cave is like the world, most people are like the prisoners in the cave, and philosophers are the ones who have seen the real world. The philosophers must be forced to return to the cave and to act as "guardians" or rulers of society. The philosophers should be told:

> "You have had a better and more complete education than any of the others; so down you go into the cave with the rest to get used to seeing in the dark. For then you will see far better than they do what these images are, and what they are of, for you have seen what the beautiful, the just and the good truly are." So our state will be ruled by minds which are awake, and not as now by men in a dream fighting with one another over shadows and for the power and office which in their eyes are the great good. Truly that state is best and most quietly ruled where the rulers have least desire to be such, and the state with the opposite sort of rulers is the worst. And will you name any other sort of man than a philosopher who looks down on political office?[30]

It is admittedly difficult for a liberal like me in the aftermath of *Bush* to argue in favor of the Court's role as Platonic guardian. The *per curiam* opinion in *Bush* disingenuously lamented, as Plato's philosopher might have, having to exercise its "unsought responsibility to resolve the federal and constitutional issues the judicial system has been forced to confront."[31] The lament was disingenuous because the Court could have declined to hear the case not once but twice.

But it is simply too late in the day to argue that *Baker* was wrongly decided and that the Court should promptly march out of the political thicket.[32] That argument carries no weight on the Supreme Court; not a single member of the Court has questioned *Baker* for decades. Even Justice Thomas, quoted at the beginning of this chapter from his concurring opinion in *Holder v. Hall,* has questioned only the scope of the grant of authority given by Congress to the Court in the Voting Rights Act. He has not questioned the general justiciability of election law cases. The last justice to have come close to calling for a return to nonjusticiability was Chief Justice Burger, who briefly quoted Justice Frankfurter's *Baker* dissent in his concurring opinion in the 1986 case *Davis v. Bandemer.*[33]

Even conservatives who once may have opposed *Baker* rarely question the case now.[34] Indeed, *Bush* may have convinced some conservatives that Court intervention in the political process is sometimes necessary, if only to stop a lawless or dangerous state court.[35]

Turning back the clock also ignores almost four decades of Congress depending upon the Court to fill in important gaps in legislation, such as the Voting Rights Act, regulating the political process. To be sure, the Court could continue to decide statutory cases and avoid constitutional ones. But the main lesson to be learned from the Voting Rights Act cases is that the Court has intervened frequently into the details of the political process with no apparent loss of popular legitimacy. Even the Court's unprecedented interference in the 2000 presidential election does not appear to have hurt its reputation among the public.[36] Justice Frankfurter's primary fear of loss of legitimacy has been neutralized by the facts.

Thus, for both practical and theoretical reasons, *Baker's* justiciability holding is unlikely to be reconsidered. With *Baker* in place, there is nothing else to do but to argue over *how* the Court should decide election law cases.

A Road Map

This book argues in favor of preserving room for Court intervention in the political process, but for intervention that is (1) tentative and malleable, (2) focused on individual (or sometimes group) rights and not on the "structure" or "functioning" of the political system, (3) protective of core political equality principles, and (4) deferential to political branches' attempts to promote contested visions of political equality. The chapters that follow define and defend these new proposed limits on Court intervention. I would like to think I would have made these recommendations had I been writing solely about the Warren Court, but perhaps I would not have;[37] certainly some of the more controversial election law cases of the Rehnquist Court have motivated my passion to write this book.

Other readers, with different visions, no doubt would argue for a different role for the Court in these political cases. But if the Court is going to continue to use the Constitution as a general grant of authority to make policy determinations about the proper workings of political process, it makes sense to steer the Court toward good policies. This book, then, begins a discussion that may be continued by others. It draws on insights from political science, economics, and legal theory in assessing how the Court should regulate the political process. It also considers in depth, for the first time in any published work, the internal papers of Supreme Court justices deciding many of these political equality cases. The papers show the extent to which the Court majority has consistently applied its own value judgments rather than deferred to precedent, social consensus, or any textual limitation of power in the Constitution.

To understand where the Court should go, I begin with where it has been. In chapter 1, I survey the Supreme Court's regulation of political equality since 1960 in four key areas: formal equality requirements, wealth, race, and political parties. Rather than canvass every case that arguably falls into each of these categories, the survey shows general trends. Not surprisingly, given that we are talking about a multimember body with shifting membership over a forty-year period, the Court's treatment is full of inconsistencies and changing rules over time. Nonetheless, the survey discerns some general patterns about the Court's treatment of political equality in each of these areas. The chapter concludes with a look at *Bush*, and considers how the case fits or fails to fit into the forty-year history of political regulation coming before it. Of all the criticisms that have been made of *Bush* (and I make many in this book), the idea that the case should be criticized as inconsistent with precedent turns out to be overblown.

Chapter 1 is primarily a descriptive chapter; to the extent it is normative, I try to limit myself to questions about whether cases show fidelity to precedent already set by the Court. In chapter 2, I turn more directly to the normative, arguing for the use of judicially *un*manageable standards in deciding election law cases. My claim is that the Court in cases involving contested political equality issues initially should use murky or unclear standards in articulating new political rights. Unclear standards lead to variations in the lower courts, and the Supreme Court can learn from such variations the best way to ultimately craft new political equality rules.

The substantive normative analysis of political equality begins with chapter 3. There I argue that the Court should play a central role in protecting the *core* of three equality principles: the "essential political rights" principle, the "antiplutocracy" principle, and the "collective action" principle. The three principles are *limits* on the government's power to treat people differently in the political process. The principles are derived primarily from social consensus (or near-consensus) about the contemporary understanding of political equality, and chapter 3 defends this basis for determining the scope of political equality claims.

The essential political rights principle prevents the government from interfering with basic political rights and requires equal treatment of votes and voters. The antiplutocracy principle prevents the government from conditioning meaningful participation in the political process on wealth or money. The collective action principle prevents the government from impeding through unreasonable restrictions the ability of people to organize into groups for political action.

I explain in chapter 3 that if the government attempts to place a limit on the exercise of one of these three core political equality principles, the Court, with an eye on legislative self-interest and agency problems, must engage in a skeptical balancing of interests. This kind of balancing is very different from the deferential balancing we have seen from the Court, particularly in recent years when it has acted to protect the Democratic and Republican parties from political competition.

Although the Court's role is to protect the core, the Court should not act on its own to take sides in cases involving *contested* equality principles. When a plaintiff raises such a claim, the Court should reject its constitutionalization.

Instead, as I explain in chapter 4, it is up to Congress or state and local legislative bodies (or the people, in jurisdictions with an initiative process) to decide whether to expand political equality principles into contested areas. The Court generally should defer to such decisions, if the Court can be confident that the legislature's intent is to foster equality rather than engage in self-dealing. Chapter 4 examines whether the Court's treatment of campaign finance laws and the Voting Rights Act is consistent with this idea. I argue that the Court was wrong to reject the equality rationale for campaign finance regulation in its initial campaign finance cases, and it appears poised to go down the wrong path in the Voting Rights Act cases as well, perhaps holding major provisions of the act unconstitutional as exceeding Congress's power to enforce the Fourteenth and Fifteenth Amendments.

Chapters 3 and 4 defend strict balancing tests as appropriate in the political equality cases. The balancing I call for differs significantly from the Court's balancing tests by requiring a close connection between legislative means and ends as an indirect way to police legislative self-interest. Nonetheless, balancing represents the typical way that the Court has (at least ostensibly) handled such claims in the past. A reader familiar with the Supreme Court's constitutional jurisprudence might not think balancing needs much defending. To the contrary, however, we are in the midst of a disturbing trend away from a focus on individual rights and toward "structural arguments" about workings of the political system.

In chapter 5, I consider these structural arguments, which have come from the Court in its racial gerrymandering cases such as *Shaw v. Reno*, and from election law scholars such as Issacharoff and Pildes, calling for the Court to promote a certain kind of political competition rather than engage in what they term "sterile" balancing of individual rights and state interests. I argue that far from being a sterile concept, equality claims, both individual and group, remain at the core of how the Court should evaluate election law claims. Structural arguments, whether made by the Court or commentators, are misguided and potentially dangerous. They evince judicial hubris, a belief that judges appropriately should be cast in the role of supreme political regulators.

Finally, the Conclusion chapter considers some remaining issues. First, can we get there from here? I argue that rational judges pursuing their self-interest might agree to the more minimal role for the Court I advocate as part of a tacit mutually beneficial agreement. I also consider how the lessons learned in the political equality cases may translate across other constitutional issues. I conclude by looking at how the Court has fared under my standards from *Baker* to *Bush*.

The Court remains well entrenched in the political thicket and is likely to remain there. This book is not an exit manual. Instead, it provides some possible minimalist strategies for the Court's forays into the forest to be successful, or at least not dangerous to the health of our democracy. It asks the Court to leave much of the future development of American democracy in the hands of those who are politically accountable.

1

The Supreme Court
of Political Equality

What Are Political Equality Cases?

In the 1970s, African-American voters made up about one-third of the Mobile, Alabama, electorate. Whites and blacks tended to prefer different candidates for each of the three city commissioners, a phenomenon voting experts have come to call "racially polarized voting."[1] Mobile conducted its elections for the city commission using an "at-large" system, meaning everyone in the city voted for each commissioner. Because of these three factors—whites heavily outnumbered blacks, voting was racially polarized, and the city used at-large voting—no candidate preferred by African-American voters had ever been elected city commissioner or was likely to be elected commissioner in the foreseeable future.

A change from the at-large election scheme to single-member districting likely would allow a majority of African-Americans to elect a commissioner of their choice. If one of the three new districts were to include a majority of African-Americans (a "majority-minority" district), that district likely would elect a candidate preferred by a majority of African-Americans. African-Americans likely could achieve such a result even if Mobile kept at-large districts if it adopted an alternative voting mechanism, such as cumulative voting, allowing residents to vote up to three votes for a single candidate.[2]

Does it violate principles of political equality to conduct Mobile's elections on an at-large basis, or, more focused for the purpose of this book, how should the Supreme Court decide a claim by Mobile's African-Americans that at-large voting under these conditions is unconstitutional? The Court confronted this question in its 1980 case *City of Mobile v. Bolden*,[3] holding that the Constitution did not require elimination of the at-large voting system absent proof the city intentionally used the system to deny Mobile's African-Americans a share of political power.

The question posed in *Bolden* nicely poses a choice between *individual* and *group* notions of equality.[4] From an individually oriented perspective, at-large voting in which each person is entitled to one equally weighted vote assures political equality. Under this view, Mobile's African-American voters' claim of a right to a majority-minority district lest their votes be "diluted" is no less than an attempt to elevate one cleavage among voters over others and institutionalize voting on racial lines.[5] Such an individually oriented thinker might ask why district lines should not be drawn to favor Republicans, or workers, or environmentalists (at least assuming it is geographically possible to do so).

The *Bolden* vote dilution claim may be more attractive to those who conceive of politics as primarily a competition among groups of voters with similar interests. To the extent that the interests of African-American and white voters differ, the persistent inability of African-Americans to have their interests represented through the election of a candidate of their choice offends at least some group-oriented notions of political equality.

According to these notions, the Court should take account of the racial cleavages in Mobile and provide for districting because racial divisions—unlike other divisions in society, say, between environmentalists and nonenvironmentalists—are *particularly salient and enduring* and—unlike the situation with Republicans or workers—result in a more or less *permanent class of political winners (whites) and losers (African-Americans)*. Until voting conditions change—in this case, until the end of racially polarized voting—districting to overcome vote dilution may be required to ensure that group interests get fairly represented.

The debate over the single question of when, if ever, at-large voting schemes in the context of racially polarized voting offend notions of political equality could take up this entire book. A number of books already have been devoted to it and related subjects.[6] The underlying issues are both theoretical and empirical. One could explore, for example, the nature of representation. What does it mean for African-Americans to elect a "candidate of their choice"? Did Mobile city commissioners elected at-large in fact "represent" the interests of the African-American minority as well? If the Court orders district lines to be drawn and a candidate for commissioner preferred by African-Americans is elected, will that commissioner be able to accomplish much legislatively, or might he or she be shut out by the other two white-preferred commissioners?[7]

Despite the complexity of these questions, they just scratch the surface of related issues. If the courts conclude that the Mobile at-large voting system indeed offends notions of political equality and must be scrapped, how far does the principle of interest representation go? What of a claim by African-Americans who make up 20 percent of the population of a city with racially polarized voting that the three-member city commission should be reconfigured to a commission of five members with one major-ity-minority district?[8] It was this type of claim for an increase in the num-ber of districts (brought under section 2 of the Voting Rights Act) that led to Justice Thomas's "mighty Platonic guardians" comment quoted in this book's introduction. What of a claim by these plaintiffs that they have the right to be "packed" into a single district so that they can have more "in-fluence" over the elected official? Or a claim that they should not be overly packed into one district so that they can have *some* influence over *more* commissioners?

My focus is not on these important, but narrower, questions. Instead, I aim to look at the larger picture of the Court's political equality jurispru-dence from 1962 to 2000. Douglas Rae has written that there are at least 108 independent theoretical conceptions of political equality.[9] The Supreme Court does not deal in high theory and its equality cases do not fit perfectly into Rae's categories, but we see just about as many permuta-tions of equality claims in the Court's rough-cut judgments. The ques-tions concerning the constitutionality of at-large elections raise just one set of political equality issues the Court has considered. Other Court cases have concerned very different equality issues such as whether a state may require a candidate for office to file a fee to run for election or whether a junior college district must run its elections so as to give everyone an equally weighted vote.

Theory or Doctrine?

Sometimes we may understand the Court's cases as posing a choice be-tween individual and group notions of political equality; sometimes that line does not divide the justices but another line does. Moreover, as we shall see, the doctrinal tools the Court uses sometimes drive the outcome of the cases. Most commonly, plaintiffs since *Baker* have framed political equality arguments as "equal protection" claims under the Fourteenth Amendment of the United States Constitution. That amendment provides in Section 1 that "[n]o State shall . . . deny any person within its jurisdiction the equal protection of the laws." Plaintiffs have also brought constitutionally based political equality claims under Article I, Section 2, providing for the direct election of members of the House of Representatives; the Guarantee Clause of Article IV, Section 4, providing that the United States "shall guarantee to every State in this Union a Republican Form of Government" (this clause is sometimes referred to as the "Guaranty Clause"); the First Amendment, preventing the government from abridging freedom of speech and association; and the Fifteenth Amendment, prohibiting discrimination in voting on account of race, color, or previous condition of servitude.

The Constitution contains other provisions bearing on the right to vote as well: the Seventeenth Amendment, providing for the direct election of members of the Senate; the Nineteenth Amendment, prohibiting discrimination in voting on account of sex; the Twenty-Fourth Amendment, prohibiting discrimination in voting in federal elections on account of failure to pay a poll tax or any other tax; and the Twenty-Sixth Amendment, lowering the legal voting age to eighteen. *Bush v. Gore* involved both the Equal Protection Clause and Article II of the Constitution, which gives state legislatures the power to set the qualifications for presidential electors.

It is not clear why doctrinal categories should drive the outcome of such political equality claims if the doctrine is mostly judge-made rather than dictated by the words of the Constitution itself: the justices of the Court ultimately interpret the meaning of vague phrases such as "equal protection of the laws" or "republican form of government" in the context of voting cases, and arguably the results in these cases should turn on consistent principles of equality rather than doctrine.

One illustration of doctrine prevailing over any theoretical understanding of equality is the divergent treatment of the one person, one vote standard in congressional elections and noncongressional elections, discussed in more detail below. The Supreme Court has said that under Article I, Section 2, congressional districting must just about exactly comply with the one person, one vote standard; a lower court recently followed Supreme Court precedent in striking down Pennsylvania's plan for congressional redistricting because one district (containing more than 646,000 people) had *19* more people in it than the others.[10] In contrast, the Court has upheld state and local districting with deviations up to 17 percent of the population against claims that such a population divergence violates the Equal Protection Clause.

Sometimes the Court decides political equality claims based on a statute rather than the Constitution. In a statutory case, the Court is not writing on a clean (or mostly clean) slate. It must contend with the words of the statute, often detailed and sometimes contradictory, written by Congress. It also does not have the last word when it comes to statutes; Congress can change a statute if a majority disagrees with the Court's interpretation.

Indeed, Congress can in some circumstances effectively override a constitutional decision. For example, after a majority of the Court rejected a constitutional vote dilution claim in the *Bolden* case, Congress amended section 2 of the Voting Rights Act in 1982 to allow a statutory vote dilution claim to succeed in the face of racially polarized voting even absent evidence of discriminatory intent.[11] Congress cannot impose in a statute a requirement that is itself unconstitutional, however. In recent years, some justices have suggested that the amended section 2 of the Voting Rights Act is itself unconstitutional, an issue I return to in chapter 4.

Four Kinds of Political Equality Cases

This chapter describes and seeks to organize the Supreme Court's major decisions on political equality since 1962. Rather than organize the cases by individual versus group equality claims, by doctrinal categories, or by constitutional versus statutory interpretation, I focus on four substantive areas of the law of political representation: formal equality, race, wealth, and political parties. My aim here is descriptive; I save for later chapters my views on whether many of these major cases were correctly decided.

Nor do I intend this chapter as a comprehensive look at every political equality case decided by the Court.[12] An exhaustive catalog would be difficult to compile because it would require judgment calls regarding which borderline cases properly concerned "political equality." Should such a catalog, for example, include *Rutan v. Republican Party of Illinois*?[13] *Rutan* considered whether a state government violated the First Amendment rights of government employees when it made firing, transfer, and promotion decisions on the basis of partisan affiliation. On the surface, the case concerned freedom of association, not political equality. Yet Justice Scalia in dissent argued—controversially—that *Rutan* and the other patronage cases banning the practice in most instances have dried up patronage opportunities that could have provided "social and political integration" for racial and ethnic minorities.[14] And if we include *Rutan* why not include the abortion decision of *Roe v. Wade*,[15] which many of its advocates see as a case promoting the political rights of women?

Comprehensiveness also is not necessary for my purposes. I aim to identify the types and scope of political equality claims that the Court has considered and the major cases it has decided. The discussion provides the background necessary for assessing both the procedural and normative arguments I make in subsequent chapters. It also serves the ancillary purpose of allowing evaluation of a criticism that has been made of the Supreme Court's decision in *Bush v. Gore*: that the case constituted a major deviation from equal protection election law cases that have come before it. The end of this chapter considers that question.

One final caveat: by focusing on cases since 1962, I do not mean to imply that the Court completely failed to regulate political equality before then. In fact, it had done so both to frustrate political equality claims and to foster (at least some versions of) political equality. An early example of Court frustration is *Giles v. Harris*,[16] a case that would be more notorious if more people paid attention to it.[17] In *Giles*, the Court refused to intervene to prevent wholesale disenfranchisement of African-Americans in Alabama, despite the unambiguous language of the U.S. Constitution's Fifteenth Amendment prohibiting discrimination in voting on the basis of race.

A brighter moment for the pre-*Baker* Court—at least as a political matter if not as a matter of legal reasoning—was its series of decisions in the *White Primary Cases*.[18] These cases struck down laws denying or interfering with the right of African-Americans to vote in Democratic primaries in the one-party South.

Despite the smattering of cases before *Baker*, the extent of Court involvement in political cases mushroomed in the 1960s (as evidenced in figure I-1), and the Court has created a huge amount of law in this area since then. The remainder of this chapter considers the four major categories of political equality cases decided by the Court beginning in the 1960s. The categories below are not in order of importance but account for a rough chronology of cases. The chapter ends with a look at how *Bush v. Gore* may fit into the context of these cases.

FORMAL EQUALITY

I begin by describing the Court's important formal equality cases since *Baker v. Carr*. By "formal equality," I mean the cases in which the Court considered questions about who gets to vote and the means by which jurisdictions aggregate votes, excluding cases (discussed in later sections of this chapter) in which the formal equality question is related directly to race, wealth, or party affiliation. Most formal equality cases concern the issues of voter qualifications and the weighting of votes.

Even before the justiciability revolution wrought by Baker as described in the introduction, the Supreme Court, with mixed results, on occasion had weighed in on some formal equality questions. In *United States v. Classic*,[19] for example, the Court held that the right to have one's vote counted in a congressional election extended to voting in a party's primary. The case concerned alleged criminal vote fraud in Louisiana, whereby election officials altered ballots to change the outcome of an election. The federal government charged the officials with violating federal statutes protecting citizens from infringements on rights or privileges secured under the Constitution—in this case, the right to vote for members of Congress guaranteed by Article I, Section 2.

The case turned out to be very important for African-American voting rights because the Court held that constitutional protections applied to primary elections. That precedent allowed the Court later to prevent racially discriminatory party primaries in the one-party South.[20] But the case itself was not about race; indeed, *Classic* established, among other things, that the right to cast a vote in a congressional election means the right to cast a vote that actually counts.

In contrast to the 1941 *Classic* case, which expanded political equality rights, the Court in the 1959 case of *Lassiter v. Northampton County Board of Elections* gave a less expansive interpretation of equality requirements.[21] In *Lassiter*, the Court upheld against an equal protection challenge a fairly applied literacy test.[22] The Court recognized the state's ability to set rational qualifications for voting, and concluded that the "ability to read and write . . . has some relation to standards designed to promote intelligent use of the ballot."[23] The decision had the effect of allowing states to discriminate in elections against would-be voters who were illiterate.

Weighting of Votes

After *Baker,* the trend in Warren Court formal equality cases pointed almost uniformly toward an expansive notion of political equality, beginning with cases requiring strict equality in the weighting of votes. First in *Gray v. Sanders,*[24] the Court struck down on equal protection grounds Georgia's system for conducting primary elections. Georgia used a "county unit system" in which it conducted popular elections for statewide office in each county, with the winner of the primary being the candidate who carried the plurality of the counties, not the plurality of voters. Georgia defended the system as analogous to the Electoral College used to choose the U.S. president and said it was designed to "achieve a reasonable balance as between urban and rural electoral power."[25]

Distinguishing *Lassiter* as a case involving voter qualifications, the Court held the constitutional infirmity in Georgia's system lay in the unequal weighting of votes. Though the holding was novel, Justice Douglas's *Gray* opinion treated the result as if it were self-evident:

> The Fifteenth Amendment prohibits a State from denying or abridging a Negro's right to vote. The Nineteenth Amendment does the same for women. If a State in a statewide election weighted the male vote more heavily than the female vote or the white vote more heavily than the Negro vote, none could successfully contend that that discrimination was allowable. How then can one person be given twice or ten times the voting power of another person in a statewide election merely because he lives in a rural area or because he lives in the smallest rural county? Once the geographical unit for which a representative is to be chosen is designated, all who participate in the election are to have an equal vote—whatever their race, whatever their sex, whatever their occupation, whatever their income, and wherever their home may be in that geographical unit. This is required by the Equal Protection Clause of the Fourteenth Amendment. The concept of "we the people" under the Constitution visualizes no preferred class of voters but equality among those who meet the basic qualifications.[26]

Although the Court in *Gray* stated that similar reasoning "underlies many of our decisions," it pointed only to cases such as *Classic* guaranteeing the right to vote and to have one's vote counted; none of those cases concerned voting strength and, in fact, *Gray* was literally unprecedented.

The *Gray* opinion ended with the strong statement that "[t]he conception of political equality from the Declaration of Independence, to Lincoln's Gettysburg Address, to the Fifteenth, Seventeenth, and Nineteenth Amendments can mean only one thing—one person, one vote."[27] The forceful rhetoric perhaps overshadowed the holding's novelty.

As attractive as the principle of an equally weighted vote may be to most contemporary readers, it is certainly true, as Justice Harlan argued in his *Gray* dissent, that the one person, one vote principle had never been "the universally accepted political philosophy in England, the American Colonies, or in the United States."[28] The Electoral College and the United States Senate are two longstanding American institutions that violate the principle by treating states—rather than people—as appropriate units for allocation of political power. Nor was there any language in the Equal Protection Clause itself or in the history of the adoption of the Fourteenth Amendment supportive of the one person, one vote rule. The Court majority simply made up this political equality rule out of whole cloth. We shall see a similar pattern of novel propositions being treated as self-evident in other political equality cases, in opinions written by both liberal and conservative justices.

The Court followed through on the logic of *Gray* in a series of cases on weighted voting. In *Wesberry v. Sanders,*[29] the Court struck down the election of members of Congress from unequally populated districts. The most populous district had more than 823,000 people; the least populous had about 272,000. The Court held that the practice of electing members of Congress from unequally populated districts violated Article I, Section 2 of the Constitution, requiring that representatives be chosen by "the People of the several states." The Court interpreted this provision to mean that "as nearly as is practicable one man's vote in a congressional election is to be worth as much as another's."[30]

The *Wesberry* opinion and the dissent by Justice Harlan both relied heavily on historical evidence about the adoption of the constitutional provision in Article I, Section 2. The majority took the position that the history supported the one person, one vote principle; Justice Harlan took the history to show that the Framers wanted equal population principles to govern apportionment of representatives *among* the states, but not as the means for electing representatives *within* each state.[31] Justice Clark, who argued in his concurring opinion that the Equal Protection Clause required equally weighted voting in congressional elections, stated that Justice Harlan "has clearly demonstrated that both the historical background and language preclude a finding that [Article I, Section 2], lays down the *ipse dixit* 'one person, one vote' in congressional elections."[32]

In *Reynolds v. Sims*, decided soon after *Wesberry*, the Court applied the Equal Protection Clause to invalidate unequally weighted voting in state legislative elections, reaching the issue that *Baker* opened up for the courts to consider. In *Reynolds*, the Court held that "as a basic constitutional standard, the Equal Protection Clause requires that the seats in both houses of a bicameral state legislature must be apportioned on a population basis."[33]

Echoing Justice Douglas's opinion in *Gray*, Chief Justice Warren, writing for the *Reynolds* majority, declared the one person, one vote principle applied to state legislative elections as the "clear and strong command of"[34] the Equal Protection Clause: "This is at the heart of Lincoln's vision of 'government of the people, by the people, [and] for the people.' The Equal Protection Clause demands no less than substantially equal state legislative representation for all citizens, of all places as well as of all races."[35]

The Court in *Reynolds* declared that "mathematical exactness" in districting was not required,[36] but it took a few years for the Court to settle on an acceptable range of deviation from such exactness. Three years after *Reynolds*, it unsurprisingly struck down Florida's redistricting plan on grounds the state failed to justify variations of 30 percent in state Senate district populations and 40 percent among House districts.[37] A few years after that, and after the Court had extended one person, one vote principles to local government apportionment in *Avery v. Midland County*,[38] the Court upheld a redistricting plan for Rockland County, New York, with population deviations of 11.9 percent. The Court held the county justified the plan "based on the long tradition of overlapping functions and dual personnel in Rockland County government and on the fact that the plan . . . does not contain a built-in bias tending to favor particular political interests or geographic areas."[39]

The Court soon thereafter approved a 16.4 percent deviation in Virginia's state reapportionment plans based upon Virginia's assertion that the plan followed political subdivisions. "While this percentage may well approach tolerable limits, we do not believe it exceeds them."[40] It similarly approved Connecticut's state redistricting plan with a maximum deviation of 7.83 percent, noting that such "minor deviations" required no justification by the state.[41] The Court later stated a general rule that population disparities under 10 percent generally required no justification from the state.[42]

In one of its most recent cases in this area of law, *Brown v. Thomson*, the Court upheld Wyoming's apportionment plan for its state House of Representatives that included a single district with a whopping 89 percent deviation from population equality.[43] The Court upheld the plan, which provided for each county in the state to have at least one representative in the House, because it was "justified on the basis of Wyoming's longstanding and legitimate policy of preserving county boundaries."[44]

In contrast, on the congressional redistricting front, the Court refused repeatedly to allow virtually any deviations from mathematical exactness. In *Kirkpatrick v. Preisler*,[45] the Court rejected Missouri's congressional districting where there was a 5.97 percent population deviation. Justice Brennan wrote for the Court:

> We reject Missouri's argument that there is a fixed numerical or percentage population variance small enough to be considered *de minimis*. . . . [T]he State must justify each variance, no matter how small. . . . We can see no nonarbitrary way to pick a cutoff point at which population variances suddenly become *de minimis*. . . .
>
> Equal representation for equal numbers of people is a principle designed to prevent debasement of voting power and diminution of access to elected representatives. Toleration of even small deviations detracts from these purposes.[46]

The Court similarly struck down a New York congressional districting plan with a 13.1 percent deviation,[47] and a Texas redistricting plan with about a 4 percent deviation.[48] By 1983, the Court confirmed in *Karcher v. Daggett* that a deviation of even less than 1 percent from population equality would not be sustained absent proof of a good-faith effort to achieve mathematically exact apportionment.[49]

Neither constitutional text nor theory appears to explain the Court's divergent treatment of deviations from perfect mathematical equality in districting depending upon whether congressional districting is involved. The result does not seem to flow from the different words or history of Article I, Section 2 compared to the Equal Protection Clause of the Fourteenth Amendment. Nor has the Court ever given a sustained political justification for the differences in treatment. In *Mahan v. Howell*, the Court rejected the use of a strict equality standard in state and local redistricting, weakly stating without elaboration that application of the "absolute equality" test "may impair the normal functioning of state and local governments."[50]

In fact, the divergence stems not from a deliberate choice by most of the justices but rather from occasional voting variations within a multi-member decision making body. Most justices stuck to their positions consistently. Justice Brennan, for example, consistently supported application of a strict standard in both the congressional and noncongressional contexts,[51] and Justice White's voting record was precisely the opposite. White dissented in *Karcher* "from the Court's unreasonable insistence on an unattainable perfection in the equalizing of congressional districts."[52]

In contrast, Justice O'Connor concurred in both *Brown* and *Karcher*, offering little explanation for her apparently inconsistent positions. Significant to the Justice was the fact that the 89 percent deviation in Brown involved only one county. She added that she had "the gravest doubts that a statewide legislative plan with an 89 percent maximum deviation could survive constitutional scrutiny despite the presence of the State's strong interest in preserving county boundaries."[53]

Voter Qualifications

Before the *Baker* revolution, the Supreme Court generally let the states set their own voter qualifications. Recall that in *Lassiter*, the Court upheld fairly applied literacy tests for voting as having "some relation to standards designed to promote intelligent use of the ballot."[54] The only notable exception the Court made was for voter qualifications whose purpose was to discriminate on the basis of race.[55]

In lockstep with the Court's decisions on the weighting of votes,[56] however, the Court in a series of post-*Baker* cases made it much more difficult for jurisdictions to impose voter qualifications other than the traditional qualifications of age, residency, citizenship, and nonfelon status.

The shift began in the 1965 case of *Carrington v. Rash*.[57] *Carrington* involved a provision of the Texas Constitution that prevented members of the armed forces from voting in any election in the state while remaining in the armed forces. Texas sought to justify the law on two grounds: first, to "immuniz[e] its elections from the concentrated balloting of military personnel, whose collective voice may overwhelm a small local civil community,"[58] and, second, to "protect[] the franchise from infiltration by transients."[59]

The Court, over the lone dissent of Justice Harlan, summarily rejected Texas's arguments. Citing *Gray*, it held that the state's first asserted interest was impermissible. The Court declared that military personnel who are in fact residents of Texas "have a right to an equal opportunity for political representation" regardless of their political views.[60] As for the state's interest in ensuring that only residents vote in its elections, the Court agreed that the state could limit voting to bona fide residents, but it held that "States may not casually deprive a class of individuals of the vote because of some remote administrative benefit to the State."[61] Rather than simply assume that military personnel did not intend to make Texas their permanent home, Texas had to determine residency on an individual basis.

By 1969, the Court characterized *Carrington* as standing for the proposition that "once the States grant the franchise, they must not do so in a discriminatory manner,"[62] and it followed through on the logical implications of *Carrington* soon thereafter in *Kramer v. Union Free School District No. 15*.[63] *Kramer* involved a New York law limiting the franchise in certain school district elections to owners and renters of taxable realty in the district (along with their spouses) and parents or guardians of children in public schools. An unmarried resident of the district who lived with his parents challenged the law as violating his equal protection rights.

The Court struck down the New York law on equal protection grounds. As I explain in the next chapter, the Court used a convoluted analysis to reach the result, without squarely holding that a state could never take into account anything other than the four traditional voter qualifications; the Court may have been opaque to avoid explicitly overruling Lassiter. But the upshot of *Kramer* is that jurisdictions have very little room to impose voting restrictions beyond the traditional categories. Indeed, outside the context of "special purpose districts" described below, the Court since Kramer has never upheld voter qualifications beyond the traditional categories of age, residency, citizenship, and nonfelon status.[64] And it is difficult to see how *Lassiter's* reasoning survives *Kramer*.

The Court since *Kramer* has considered a few cases involving the scope of voter qualifications within the traditional categories. In 1972, the Court in *Dunn v. Blumstein*[65] struck down a Tennessee "durational residency" law requiring that a person must live in the state for one year and in a county for three months before being allowed to vote in state elections. In *Dunn*, the Court strongly suggested that a thirty-day period would be sufficient for the state's administrative and antifraud purposes,[66] but the following year it upheld a fifty-day period.[67] In 1978, the Court held that those outside a formal municipal boundary but subject to many of its laws were not denied equal protection when they were excluded from voting in the municipality's elections.[68] The Court unsurprisingly concluded that a jurisdiction could limit voting to residents. Also unsurprisingly, the Court in the 1973 case *Richardson v. Ramirez*[69] upheld California's ban on voting by felons.[70]

The Court upheld the right of Congress in the Voting Rights Act to set the minimum voting age at 18 in federal elections, but not in state elections.[71] Following the decision, the Constitution was amended, adding the Twenty-Sixth Amendment prohibiting states from setting a voting age above 18. Finally, the Court in 1982 suggested, again unsurprisingly, that discrimination in voting on the basis of citizenship status comports with the Constitution.[72]

Special Purpose Districts as an Exception to Post-Baker Formal Equality Principles

With a few fits and starts, the trend in the post-*Baker* formal equality cases described above is clear: weighted voting and voting qualifications beyond the traditional categories violate the Equal Protection Clause of the Fourteenth Amendment.

The extension of the one person, one vote rule to local units of government in the *Avery* case may have put some pressure on both the weighted voting and voter qualification rules. In *Hadley v. Junior College District of Metropolitan Kansas City*,[73] the Court suggested a possible exception to the rules. *Hadley* applied the one person, one vote rule to elections for trustees of a junior college district. The Court squarely held that

> whenever a state or local government decides to select persons by popular election to perform governmental functions, the Equal Protection Clause of the Fourteenth Amendment requires that each qualified voter must be given an equal opportunity to participate in that election, and when members of an elected body are chosen from separate districts, each district must be established on a basis that will insure, as far as is practicable, that equal numbers of voters can vote for proportionally equal numbers of officials.[74]

But the Court followed up the general rule with the following statement: "It is of course possible that there might be some cases in which a State elects certain functionaries whose duties are so far removed from normal governmental activities and so disproportionately affect different groups that a popular election in compliance with *Reynolds* . . . might not be required."[75]

Soon thereafter, the Court applied the exception. In *Salyer Land Co. v. Tulare Lake Basin Water Storage District*,[76] the Court upheld provisions of the California Water Code providing for the election of directors of water storage districts. The plaintiffs—landowners, a landowner lessee, and residents within the area of the water storage district—challenged rules that allowed only landowners to vote in the district elections and that apportioned votes in the election according to the assessed value of the land. The Court held that neither the voter qualifications nor the unequal weighting of votes violated the Equal Protection Clause. Echoing the language of *Hadley*, the Court concluded that the "water storage district, by reason of its special limited purpose and of the disproportionate effect of its activities on landowners as a group" did not need to follow the usual rules.

The *Salyer* Court stressed the "relatively limited authority" of the district and the fact that the "costs of district projects are assessed against land by assessors in proportion to the benefits received."[77] The Court rejected the dissent's arguments that it was "grotesque" to give corporations voting rights and that it violated the Equal Protection Clause to deny residents the vote, including one resident whose home was 15.5 feet below the water level after a flood ordered by the district.[78] Five years after *Salyer*, the Court again applied the exception to voting in an Arizona agricultural improvement and power district.[79]

The Court did not define well which governmental entities could take advantage of the special purpose exception.[80] In recent years business improvement districts (or "BIDs") have argued that they fall into the *Salyer* exception, though the Court has yet to take a case considering the issue.[81] It is clear, however, that most local units of government do not fall into the *Salyer* exception.

In *Rice v. Cayetano*,[82] the Court rejected application of the *Salyer* exception to elections for the Office of Hawaiian Affairs. The election rules limited the franchise to voting by certain descendants of Native Hawaiians. Whether or not the voting scheme would fall into the *Salyer* exception, the Court held the rules violated the *Fifteenth* Amendment's prohibition on discrimination in voting on the basis of race.

RACE

Pre-*Baker* Race Cases

The Supreme Court considered claims that state and local voting laws discriminated on the basis of race well before the *Baker* revolution. But the Baker revolution coupled with the civil rights movement likely emboldened the Court to become more active in this area. The main vehicle for early challenges was not the Fourteenth Amendment's Equal Protection Clause but another amendment passed soon after the Civil War, the Fifteenth Amendment. That amendment prohibits discrimination in voting on account of race, color, or previous condition of servitude.

As early as 1884, the Court confirmed that the Fifteenth Amendment prohibits laws allowing whites only to vote.[83] But in the early twentieth century the Court in *Giles* backed away from enforcing the right of African-Americans to vote under the Fifteenth Amendment. In the meantime, many jurisdictions, particularly in the South, used a variety of devices to discriminate against voting by African-Americans, including the secret ballot (making it difficult for illiterate African-Americans to vote), poll taxes, literacy tests, and white-only party primaries.[84]

In the *White Primary Cases*, the Court once again more aggressively policed racially discriminatory voting. Following the *Classic* case holding that party primaries were governed by state constitutional law, the Court in the 1944 case *Smith v. Allwright*[85] held that discrimination in a party primary on the basis of race violated the Fifteenth Amendment. The Court went even further in *Terry v. Adams*,[86] holding that a private association whose views were often followed by the dominant Democratic Party in Texas violated the Fifteenth Amendment with its racially exclusionary straw poll.[87]

The final major racial voting case the Court decided before the *Baker* revolution was *Gomillion v. Lightfoot*.[88] In *Gomillion*, the Court struck down a law that changed the municipal boundaries of the city of Tuskegee, Alabama, to exclude all but four or five of its African-American residents but not a single white resident. The Court held the change in boundaries violated the Fifteenth Amendment because it deprived members of one race of their ability to vote.

Since the *Baker* revolution, the Court has considered racial voting cases under the Fifteenth Amendment, the Equal Protection Clause of the Fourteenth Amendment, and after 1965, the federal Voting Rights Act. The

Voting Rights Act in particular has proven remarkably successful in furthering the interests of minority voters.[89]

Equal Protection Race-in-Elections Cases after *Baker*

One of the first post-*Baker* race-in-elections cases was the 1965 case *Fortson v. Dorsey*.[90] In Fortson, plaintiffs challenged under the Equal Protection Clause Georgia's use of multimember districts for the election of state senators in some, but not all, Georgia counties.[91] The Court held the plan complied with one person, one vote principles, but suggested that there might be a constitutional violation in the use of multimember districts where, "under the circumstances of a particular case, [the apportionment scheme] would operate to minimize or cancel out the voting strength of racial or political elements of the voting population."[92]

Following *Fortson*, the Court flirted with holding multimember districts unconstitutional as violating the rights of members of minority groups in two cases,[93] and finally reached that result in 1973 in *White v. Regester*.[94] *Regester* involved challenges to two multimember districts in Texas. The Court focused on various factors, including the existence of other election rules that appeared to work against minority interests and the "historic and present" condition of minorities in the challenged districts. The Court appeared to endorse a "totality of the circumstances" approach to resolving claims that multimember districts violated equal protection.[95]

This doctrinal move permitting minority plaintiffs to use the Equal Protection Clause to achieve greater voting strength came to an abrupt halt in *City of Mobile v. Bolden*.[96] In *Bolden*, plaintiffs challenged the City of Mobile, Alabama's at-large voting system as violating the Equal Protection Clause, the Fifteenth Amendment, and section 2 of the Voting Rights Act (which at the time was regarded as duplicating constitutional requirements).

The plurality opinion in *Bolden* rejected the Fifteenth Amendment claim on grounds that there was no proof that African-Americans had been denied the vote. As for the claim under the Equal Protection Clause and section 2 of the Voting Rights Act, the Court held that such a case could not go forward without proof that the city had adopted at-large voting with the *intent to discriminate* against minority voters. The Court characterized *Regester* as a case where the Court had found such a discriminatory purpose. The dissent by Justice Marshall accused the plurality of changing the standard in *Regester* from one concerned only with discriminatory *effects*.[97]

Just two years later, the Court appeared to backpedal somewhat from the discriminatory intent standard of *Bolden* in *Rogers v. Lodge*.[98] In that case, the Court seemed to allow plaintiffs to prove discriminatory intent inferentially through proof of discriminatory effect, thereby resurrecting the totality of the circumstances approach of *Regester*. The Court has not had occasion to revisit this issue, however, because Congress amended section 2 of the Voting Rights Act after Bolden to create a statutory requirement modeled after *Regester's* totality-of-the-circumstances test. Cases that would have been brought as constitutional Equal Protection cases appeared instead as section 2 cases.

The story of the Equal Protection Clause and race in elections might have ended there had it not been for a shift in the Supreme Court toward a more conservative majority. Responding to state and local redistricting plans creating sometimes oddly shaped majority-minority districts—districts that the Justice Department's aggressive (but not necessarily incorrect) interpretation of the Voting Rights Act appeared to require—the Court in the 1993 case of *Shaw v. Reno*[99] recognized a new cause of action under the Equal Protection Clause: the "unconstitutional racial gerrymander." Before detailing the new "*Shaw* claim," I first review those Voting Rights Act cases decided by the Court that are essential to placing the new claim in context.

Voting Rights Act Litigation

The first Voting Rights Act case the Supreme Court considered was *South Carolina v. Katzenbach*,[100] a challenge to, among other things, the act's ban on literacy tests for voting. The Court upheld the ban under Congress's power to enforce the Fifteenth Amendment, even though *Lassiter* had held that literacy tests were not per se unconstitutional.

In 1969, the Court gave a broad reading to section 5 of the Voting Rights Act in *Allen v. State Board of Elections*.[101] Section 5 requires certain jurisdictions (primarily in the South) to obtain "preclearance" from the United States Department of Justice (or alternatively from a three-judge court in Washington D.C.) before making any changes in voting qualifications or any "standard, practice, or procedure with respect to voting." To obtain preclearance, the jurisdiction must prove that the change would have no racially "discriminatory purpose or effect."

In *Allen*, the Court held that a change from district-based to at-large elections fell under section 5 and therefore required preclearance. Similarly, the Court held that section 5 required preclearance of a change from the election to appointment of county officers; a change in the rules for an independent candidate to secure a position on the ballot; and a change in the procedures for casting write-in votes. Justice Harlan dissented, both on grounds that the majority misinterpreted section 5 to apply to questions such as the choice between at-large and districted voting and on grounds that there were no standards for judging discriminatory purpose or effect: "[I]t is not clear to me how a court would go about deciding whether an at-large system is to be preferred over a district system. Under one system, Negroes have *some* influence in the election of *all* officers; under the other, minority groups have *more* influence in the selection of fewer officers."[102] As for whether the Court properly interpreted the scope of section 5 of the act, Congress amended the Voting Rights Act a number of times without amending section 5, suggesting that at least subsequent Congresses were not dissatisfied with the Court's approach in *Allen*.

In 1976, the Court announced that in judging whether an election practice or procedure had a "discriminatory effect" under section 5, the Justice Department (or court) should consider whether the proposed change made the position of minority voters worse off.[103] This rule— dubbed the "nonretrogression standard"—took some of the steam out of section 5. In judging retrogression (at least as to districting claims), the Court appeared to use as a baseline the number of majority-minority districts. So long as a proposed plan has as many majority-minority districts as exist under the status quo, the plan is "ameliorative" (or nonretrogressive) and therefore passes muster under section 5.[104] The Court called application of this standard "straightforward,"[105] but it did not explain why it considered maximizing the number of majority-minority districts the appropriate baseline.

After Congress amended section 2 of the act to overcome the discriminatory intent standard in *Bolden*, the Justice Department took the position in section 5 preclearance cases that it would not grant preclearance to any plan that failed to meet the requirements of the amended section 2 regardless of whether the plan was nonretrogressive. In 1997, the Supreme Court rejected the Justice Department's interpretation and reaffirmed the nonretrogression standard as the only standard for judging discriminatory effect under section 5.[106] When that 1997 case returned to the Court in 2000, the Court held that the nonretrogression standard applied to discriminatory purpose claims as well, rejecting the Justice Department's argument that a jurisdiction's failure to comply with section 2 evidenced discriminatory effect.[107] The case is also notable for its footnote 3, which appears to provide that vote dilution claims may never be brought under the *Fifteenth* Amendment.

As for the amended section 2, the Court decided the leading case interpreting the act in 1986. In *Thornburg v. Gingles*,[108] the Court tried to walk a fine line between interpreting the act to require roughly proportional representation and a test that would make it difficult for minority groups to prove discriminatory effect. The Court interpreted the amended section 2 to require minority plaintiffs challenging a districting scheme to meet a threshold three-part test to prove vote dilution, followed by the "totality of the circumstances" test that had developed before *Bolden*.[109] The threshold test roughly required proof of racially polarized voting and that the minority group was sufficiently large and geographically compact to form a majority in a single-member district.[110]

Although the Court has decided a large number of cases under the amended section 2 since *Gingles*,[111] the *Gingles* framework has remained essentially intact. Yet the pressure section 2 creates on state and local jurisdictions to create majority-minority districts has been counterbalanced by the new *Shaw* cause of action.

Shaw v. Reno: The New Equal Protection Cause of Action for Unconstitutional Racial Gerrymanders

The Rehnquist Court in the 1990s was a very different court from the Warren Court of the 1960s that decided *Baker*, *Reynolds*, and *Fortson*. In the area of voting rights, no case better illustrates the point than *Shaw v. Reno*. *Shaw* involved a claim that even absent vote dilution, the very division of voters into districts on the basis of race violated the Equal Protection Clause.

Shaw was not the first time that the Court was faced with such a claim. In the first of such cases, *Wright v. Rockefeller*,[112] plaintiffs challenged a New York congressional districting plan that appeared to pack Puerto Rican voters into a single district in Manhattan. Among plaintiff's claims was that the plan unconstitutionally "segregate[d] eligible voters by race and place of origin." The Court sidestepped the issue, accepting the findings of the lower court that "appellants failed to prove that the New York Legislature was either motivated by racial considerations or in fact drew the districts on racial lines."[113]

The Court more squarely faced the claim in the 1977 case *United Jewish Organizations v. Carey (UJO)*.[114] The case, which the Shaw Court later characterized as "highly fractured," featured a number of less than clear opinions. Depending upon how one counts the votes, there was either a majority or a plurality of justices rejecting the argument that the creation of majority-minority districts somehow violates the Constitution in the absence of vote dilution.[115]

A decade and a half later, after some changes in the personnel on the Supreme Court, the Court by a 5-4 vote recognized a new cause of action for an unconstitutional racial gerrymander in *Shaw v. Reno*. The case arose out of North Carolina's redistricting for the United States House of Representatives after the 1990 census. In order to satisfy Justice Department preclearance requirements under section 5 of the Voting Rights Act as the Justice Department then understood it, the North Carolina legislature created a second majority-minority district, with an extremely odd shape. The Court held that the creation of such a district, even absent proof that such a district diluted anyone's voting rights, could violate the Constitution:

> [W]e believe that reapportionment is one area in which appearances do matter. A reapportionment plan that includes in one district individuals who belong to the same race, but who are otherwise widely separated by geographical and political boundaries, and who may have little in common with one another but the color of their skin, bears an uncomfortable resemblance to political apartheid. It reinforces the perception that members of the same racial group—regardless of their age, education, economic status, or the community in which they live—think alike, share the same political interests, and will prefer the same candidates at the polls. We have rejected such perceptions elsewhere as impermissible racial stereotypes. By perpetuating such notions, a racial gerrymander may exacerbate the very patterns of racial bloc voting that majority-minority districting is sometimes said to counteract.
>
> The message that such districting sends to elected representatives is equally pernicious. When a district obviously is created solely to effectuate the perceived common interests of one racial group, elected officials are more likely to believe that their primary obligation is to represent only the members of that group, rather than their constituency as a whole.[116]

The best reading of *Shaw* appears to be that the harm suffered by plaintiffs who claim an "unconstitutional racial gerrymander" is an *expressive harm*: the government harms the plaintiffs by sending a message that it is acceptable to separate people on the basis of race.[117]

Although the Court, by the same 5-4 margin, has steadfastly held to the central holding in *Shaw* recognizing this cause of action, much wrangling within the five-justice majority has occurred over the contours of the cause of action. Justice O'Connor, author of the *Shaw* opinion, has focused her attention on the *appearance* of the districts, characterizing the shape of the district at issue in *Shaw* "bizarre" and making the shape relevant to determining if a cause of action exists. Justice Kennedy, in contrast, has focused on the *motivation* of the legislature in passing the districting plan.

In *Miller v. Johnson*,[118] Justice Kennedy's majority opinion explained that the shape of the district was merely "persuasive circumstantial evidence" of a racial gerrymandering violation. *Miller* instead requires a plaintiff to prove

> that race was *the predominant factor* motivating the legislature's decision to place a significant number of voters within or without a particular district. To make this showing, a plaintiff must prove that the legislature subordinated traditional race-neutral districting principles, including but not limited to compactness, contiguity, respect for political subdivisions or communities defined by actual shared interests, to racial considerations.[119]

If plaintiffs prove that race is the predominant factor, the state must offer a compelling reason for making race such a factor and that its means of satisfying that compelling reason are narrowly tailored.

Other recent racial gerrymandering cases have considered which plaintiffs have standing to bring such suits;[120] whether compliance with section 2 or section 5 of the Voting Rights Act may serve as compelling interests to defeat a racial gerrymandering claim;[121] and how courts are to determine whether racial rather than political motivation explains the shape of districts.

The last point is very important because minority groups who may use the Voting Rights Act to counter vote dilution tend to vote for Democrats.[122] A plan that packs African-Americans into districts may be done for partisan reasons rather than racial or other reasons. In the most recent racial gerrymandering case, *Easley v. Cromartie*,[123] Justice O'Connor voted with the four usual dissenters in the racial gerrymandering cases to reverse a lower court determination that North Carolina used race as a "predominant factor" when it engaged in its latest round of redistricting. The Court held that

> [i]n a case . . . where majority-minority districts (or the approximate equivalent) are at issue and where racial identification correlates highly with political affiliation, the party attacking the legislatively drawn boundaries must show at the least that the legislature could have achieved its legitimate political objectives in alternative ways that are comparably consistent with traditional districting principles. That party must also show that those districting alternatives would have brought about significantly greater racial balance.[124]

It remains to be seen whether *Cromartie* represents a retreat from the racial gerrymandering cause of action or only a minor setback for those who support it. The reference to "greater racial balance" also will need fleshing out: "[t]o say that a plan with greater racial balance is necessarily superior to one with less seems directly contrary to the rationale . . . for the racial gerrymandering cases."[125]

WEALTH

Harper v. Virginia Board of Elections[126] was the first post-*Baker* case to consider the relationship between wealth and political equality. One of the devices commonly used to disenfrancishise African-Americans in the South during the first half of the twentieth century was the poll tax, a tax that must be paid in order to vote. Poll taxes intended to discriminate against African-American voting no doubt violate both the Equal Protection Clause of the Fourteenth Amendment and the Fifteenth Amendment's prohibition on abridgement of the right to vote on account of race. Before *Harper*, Congress passed and the states ratified the Twenty-Fourth Amendment, banning the use of poll taxes in federal elections.

Harper involved the constitutionality of Virginia's one dollar and fifty cent poll tax for state elections that the Court assumed for purposes of the case the Virginia legislature enacted without racially discriminatory intent. The *Harper* Court held "that a State violates the Equal Protection Clause of the Fourteenth Amendment whenever it makes the affluence of the voter or payment of any fee an electoral standard.[127] The Court reasoned that "[v]oter qualifications have no relation to wealth nor to paying or not paying this or any other tax."[128]

Although *Harper* again stated its principles as self-evident, the result in the 6-3 case reversing the lower court was hardly inevitable. The case began as a proposed a 6-3 *per curiam* summary affirmance (that is, without a written opinion) of the lower court decision upholding the poll tax. Justice Goldberg, joined by Chief Justice Warren and Justice Douglas, circulated a proposed dissent (reproduced in its entirety in Appendix 2). Relying on *Reynolds*, *Gray*, and *Carrington*, along with the Virginia poll tax's legislative history evincing intent to discriminate against both African-Americans and poor whites, Justice Goldberg would have held that "no reasonable state interest is served by barring from voting those citizens who desire to vote but who lack the requisite funds."[129]

Justice Goldberg sought to explain the limits of the equal protection principle that would bar the use of a poll tax in elections:

> The application of these principles obviously does not mean that Government—State or Federal—must equalize all economic inequalities among citizens. Nor does it mean that the Government cannot impose burdens or exactions which by reason of economic circumstances fall more heavily upon some than others. Nor however desirable it may be as a matter of social and legislative policy, does it require the State affirmatively to provide relief for all the incidents of poverty. The Constitution does not command absolute equality in all areas. It does mean, however, that a State may not frustrate or burden the exercise of the basic and precious right to vote by imposing substantial obstacles upon that exercise by a class of citizens not justified by any legitimate state interest. In particular it means that with respect to the fundamental right to vote, a reverse means test cannot be applied. A classification based upon financial means embodied in a voting statute is inherently not "reasonable in light of . . . [the statute's] purpose."

Justice Goldberg further rejected the long American history of tolerance for property qualifications and poll taxes as irrelevant for contemporary application of constitutional principles. "[W]e must consider voting rights in light of their full development, their 'present place in American life throughout the nation,' *cf. Brown v. Board of Education*, and our present conception of the meaning and application of the Equal Protection Clause."

Only one day after Justice Goldberg's dissent circulated, Justice Black circulated a memorandum to the other justices asking that the case be put for a full hearing.[130] Justice Black perhaps expected from the initial 6-3 vote for summary affirmance that the case would lead to a similar 6-3 vote on an opinion affirming the validity of the poll tax and distinguishing the cases cited by Justice Goldberg. If so, his expectations were dashed, because Justices Brennan, Clark, and White changed positions. Justice Black ultimately issued a dissent arguing the question of poll taxes should be left to the states unless Congress wanted to use its enforcement powers to ban the practice.

The Warren Court followed *Harper* by striking down laws allowing only property owners to approve bond measures.[131] But if *Harper* was a signal that the Warren Court would take steps to separate economic strength from political power, the Burger and Rehnquist Courts have been more ambivalent on the subject.

On the one hand, some later Court decisions have required strict separation of economic and political power. In *Bullock v. Carter*,[132] for example, the Court held that *Harper* required close scrutiny of laws requiring candidates for office to pay filing fees. It then struck down fees as high as $8,900 without alternative ballot access as violating equal protection:

> By requiring candidates to shoulder the costs of conducting primary elections through filing fees and by providing no reasonable alternative means of access to the ballot, the State of Texas has erected a system that utilizes the criterion of ability to pay as a condition to being on the ballot, thus excluding some candidates otherwise qualified and denying an undetermined number of voters the opportunity to vote for candidates of their choice.[133]

Two years later, in *Lubin v. Panish*,[134] the Court struck down a California law requiring candidates to pay filing fees of as low as $701.60. The Court held the law violated equal protection because it lacked an alternative means (such as petition signatures) by which indigent candidates could get their names on the ballot.

On the other hand, Burger and Rehnquist Court decisions have approved property-owner-only/weighted voting for "special purpose district" elections. Perhaps more significantly for the relationship between money and power, the Court in the landmark 1976 campaign finance case of *Buckley v. Valeo*[135] unequivocally rejected as "wholly foreign to the First Amendment" an argument that the government could limit spending on campaigns to promote political equality.

More recently, the Court may have signaled its interest in backing away from this strong stand in a 1990 case involving campaign expenditures by corporations, *Austin v. Michigan Chamber of Commerce*.[136] Since *Austin*, three justices have indicated they are sympathetic with the equality argument for greater campaign finance regulation. But *Buckley*'s square rejection of the equality rationale remains the strongest signal that jurisdictions may not impose generally applicable campaign finance laws to promote political equality.

POLITICAL PARTIES

The final equality area I consider is the law related to political parties and equality. A number of political party cases implicate equality concerns at least indirectly. In *Storer v. Brown*,[137] for example, the Court indicated it would uphold a state's right to impose a so-called sore-loser statute preventing losers in party primaries from running as a candidate in general elections. Laws that dictate who may be a party's candidate no doubt may serve to enhance some groups' or some individuals' political power at the expense of others.

Other political party cases more directly implicate equality. In *Davis v. Bandemer*,[138] the Court slightly left open the possibility that a major political party could challenge a redistricting plan that effectively shut it out of political power. In reaching the conclusion, the Court relied upon racial vote dilution cases such as *White v. Regester*.[139] Most recently, in *California Democratic Party v. Jones*,[140] the Court held that California voters could not force political parties to open their primaries to any registered voter. Both this case and *Bandemer* dictate the ground rules for political activity and thereby raise equality questions.

However, the political party cases with the most obvious implications for political equality concern the rights of third parties and independent candidates to ballot access and other government benefits. The leading Warren Court case here is *Williams v. Rhodes*.[141] In *Williams*, two minor political parties challenged Ohio's extremely restrictive ballot access laws that made it virtually impossible for a new political party to have its candidate's name placed on the ballot in presidential elections.

Ohio sought to justify its law to "validly promote a two-party system in order to encourage compromise and political stability."[142] The Warren Court rejected the argument, noting that the law favored the two major political parties: "There is, of course, no reason why two parties should retain a permanent monopoly on the right to have people vote for or against them. Competition in ideas and governmental policies is at the core of our electoral process and of the First Amendment freedoms."[143]

Although the Burger Court again rejected protection of the two major parties from political competition in *Anderson v. Celebrezze*,[144] in recent years the Rehnquist Court has moved dramatically toward greater protection of the two-party system. The trend began in *Munro v. Socialist Workers Party*,[145] where the Court rejected a First and Fourteenth Amendment challenge to Washington's new ballot access law that made it considerably more difficult than in the past for minor parties to qualify their candidates for a place on the general election ballot. Eschewing any kind of "litmus paper test" in favor of more ad hoc balancing, the majority rejected Justice Marshall's argument in dissent that minor parties deserved a place on the general election ballot. Marshall wrote: "The minor party's often unconventional positions broaden political debate, expand the range of issues with which the electorate is concerned, and influence the positions of the majority, in some instances ultimately becoming majority positions. And its very existence provides an outlet for voters to express dissatisfaction with the candidates or platforms of the major parties."[146]

If *Munro* allowed states to refuse measures to help minor political parties, two more recent cases have affirmatively allowed discrimination against them in the name of political stability and government neutrality. *Timmons v. Twin Cities Area New Party*[147] concerned the question whether the state of Minnesota could prevent a minor party from endorsing the Democratic Party's nominee for the state legislature. That practice, called "fusion," is a tactic minor parties use to increase their popularity and leverage their political power in the few jurisdictions, such as New York, that permit it.

The Supreme Court upheld the constitutionality of Minnesota's antifusion law. Among other arguments, the Court accepted the state's argument that "political stability is best served through a healthy two-party system." The Court remarked that the "traditional two-party system . . . temper[s] the destabilizing effects of party-splintering and excessive factionalism."[148] Thus, *Timmons* appears to overrule *William v. Rhodes* in allowing the government to favor the two major political parties over third parties and independent candidates.

Following *Timmons*, the Court in *Arkansas Educational Television Commission v. Forbes*[149] upheld against a First Amendment challenge the decision of a public television station to exclude an independent candidate for Congress from a televised debate. The Court held that the broadcaster's decision to exclude the candidate from the debate on grounds that his candidacy lacked public support "was a reasonable, viewpoint—neutral exercise of journalistic discretion" consistent with the First Amendment.[150]

Bush v. Gore

Among the many questions that commentators have raised about *Bush v. Gore* is whether the case flowed from election law precedent that came before it. That question is separate and apart from the question whether the reasoning in *Bush v. Gore* is sound or whether the Court reached the right result in the case even if the reasoning is unsound. The question of fidelity to precedent is important because some have called the opinion unprincipled and result-oriented, aimed at assuring that George W. Bush would be the new president and not Al Gore.[151] This chapter provides the relevant history of the Court's jurisprudence to answer the question; the answer, however, is not crystal clear.

Background Bush v. Gore grew out of the dispute between Democratic presidential candidate Al Gore and Republican presidential candidate George W. Bush over Florida's twenty-five electoral votes.[152] The initial results of the election in Florida were extremely close, leading Gore to take legal action in an attempt to reverse the results.

Following the certification of Florida's presidential election vote in favor of Republican George W. Bush, Democrat Al Gore contested the result of the election. Gore asserted that a recount of "undervotes" from certain Florida counties would show enough legally valid votes cast in his favor but not counted by the vote-tabulating machines to make up the extremely small difference in votes between himself and Bush. Undervotes are votes that vote-tabulating machines recorded as containing no votes in the presidential contest. The trial court held that Gore failed to meet the statutory standard for a contest,[153] and Gore appealed to the Florida Supreme Court.

The Florida Supreme Court, in a 4-3 vote, reversed the trial court. The court held that the trial court applied the wrong legal standards in judging the merits of Gore's claim.[154] Rather than remand the case for the trial court to apply the correct legal standard to the facts, however, the court ordered that certain recounts conducted after the deadline set by the Florida Supreme Court in an earlier case should be included in the totals and that a recount of undervotes go forward.[155] And rather than allow Gore to pick the counties for the recounts, the Florida court held that all Florida counties—and not just the counties singled out by Gore—had to conduct manual recounts of the undervotes.[156] The court failed to respond to Chief Justice Wells's observation in dissent that it was unfair to count only undervotes and not "overvotes," that is, votes that the machine recorded as containing more than one valid vote for president.[157]

The court further held that in examining the undervotes to determine if the ballots indeed contained a valid vote for a presidential candidate, the counters should judge the ballots using a "clear indication of intent of the voter" standard, as indicated in Florida statutes.[158] The court ordered that the trial judge manage the statewide recount,[159] which needed to be completed in short order.

The Florida court remanded the case to the original trial judge, who recused himself. Another trial judge ordered the manual recounts to begin of the Miami-Dade ballots (that had been shipped to Tallahassee for the election contest) and in counties across Florida. Meanwhile, Bush filed a petition for a writ of certiorari and a stay in the Supreme Court. As the recounts began on Saturday, December 9, the Supreme Court, by a 5-4 vote, stayed the Florida Supreme Court's order, thereby suspending the recount,[160] and agreed to hear a second case from the Florida controversy just days after it issued its first opinion.

The Supreme Court's Equal Protection Holding Late in the evening of Tuesday, December 12, the Supreme Court issued its opinion on the merits. Five justices (Chief Justice Rehnquist and Justices Kennedy, O'Connor, Scalia, and Thomas) joined in a *per curiam* opinion reversing the Florida court on equal protection grounds.[161] Chief Justice Rehnquist, joined by Justices Scalia and Thomas, issued a concurring opinion presenting as alternative grounds for reversal that the Florida Supreme Court's order violated Article II of the Constitution.[162] Four justices dissented (Justices Breyer, Ginsburg, Souter, and Stevens),[163] although Justices Souter and

Breyer expressed support for the equal protection rationale (though not the remedy).

In setting forth the equal protection standard to be applied in the case, the Court stated that "the right to vote as the legislature has prescribed is fundamental; and one source of its fundamental nature lies in the equal weight accorded to each vote and the equal dignity owed to each voter." The Court continued:

> The right to vote is protected in more than the initial allocation of the franchise. Equal protection applies as well to the manner of its exercise. Having once granted the right to vote on equal terms, the State may not, by later arbitrary and disparate treatment, value one person's vote over that of another. *Harper v. Virginia Board of Elections.* It must be remembered that "the right of suffrage can be denied by a debasement or dilution of the weight of a citizen's vote just as effectively as by wholly prohibiting the free exercise of the franchise." *Reynolds v. Sims.*[164]

The Court held that the recount mechanism adopted by the Florida Supreme Court did "not satisfy the minimum requirement for non-arbitrary treatment of voters necessary to secure the fundamental right"[165] to vote under the Equal Protection Clause for four related reasons: (1) Although the Florida court had instructed that the individuals conducting the manual recounts judge ballots by discerning the "intent of the voter," it failed to formulate uniform rules to determine such intent, such as whether to count as a valid vote a ballot whose chad is hanging by two corners. (2) The recounts already undertaken included a manual recount of all votes in selected counties, including both undervotes and overvotes, but the new recounts ordered by the Florida court included only undervotes. (3) The Florida Supreme Court had ordered that the current vote totals include results of a partial recount from Miami-Dade County. From this fact the Supreme Court concluded that "[t]he Florida Supreme Court's decision thus gives no assurance that the recounts included in a final certification must be complete."(4) The Florida Supreme Court did not specify who would count the ballots, forcing county boards to include team members without experience in recounting ballots. Nor were observers permitted to object during the recount.[166]

The Supreme Court then declined to remand the case to the Florida Supreme Court to order procedures satisfying these concerns, as Justices

Souter and Breyer urged.[167] The Court held that the Florida Supreme Court had recognized the Florida legislature's intention to participate fully in the federal electoral process. Under a federal statute, states that designate their electors by a certain date, in this election by December 12, cannot have their choice challenged in Congress when Congress later counts the electoral votes.[168] "That date [of December 12] is upon us, and there is no recount procedure in place under the State Supreme Court's order that comports with minimal constitutional standards. Because it is evident that any recount seeking to meet the December 12 date will be unconstitutional for the reasons we have discussed, we reverse the judgment of the Supreme Court of Florida."[169]

Did the Supreme Court Follow Precedent in Bush v. Gore? In considering whether the Court decided *Bush v. Gore* in line with precedent, we must first ask which precedents are closest to the facts of the case. The case is one that concerns formal equality, not wealth, race, or political parties. But even though *Bush* concerns formal equality, it does not pose a typical weighting of votes or voter qualification question. The Court had never before gotten itself involved in a nuts-and-bolts election dispute like the Florida dispute, leaving these questions to the lower courts.

The closest case on point appears to be the pre-*Baker* case *United States v. Classic*. As discussed above, *Classic* held that the right to vote included the right to have that vote counted. Arguably, such a precedent militated in favor of supporting Gore's position in the litigation, which would have led to the counting of more votes that might have been missed the first time through.

But the Court did not rely upon *Classic*. Instead, it grounded its equal protection language in *Reynolds* and *Harper*. As a matter of case analogies, *Reynolds* and *Harper* were far off the mark from the recount questions in *Bush v. Gore*. *Reynolds* involved malapportioned districts and *Harper* involved poll taxes, both cases concerning recurrent problems with the allocation of voting power having nothing to do with the nuts-and-bolts of conducting an election.

The Court in *Bush v. Gore* not only relied upon these cases but spoke the same "fundamental rights" language. Fundamental rights trigger "strict scrutiny," a very close review that usually leads the Court to strike down a state's actions.

The fundamental rights language in *Bush* is curious because the Court, on its view of the Florida Supreme Court's actions, could have struck down the Florida court's decision under the more deferential "rational basis" test, stating that there was no good reason for that court's failure to impose a uniform standard for the recounting of punch card ballots.[170] As the Court framed the issue, it suggested that strict scrutiny should apply to a host of nuts-and-bolts issues never thought to be of constitutional concern.

Perhaps the sweeping language and reliance on *Reynolds* and *Harper* demonstrate no more than the sloppy analysis of the Court working under tremendous time and political pressures. If so, the Court was especially sloppy to rely on these cases, which signal voting as a fundamental right and the application of "strict scrutiny" to review challenged voting procedures. If fundamental rights were really at stake, it is unclear why Florida's desire to take advantage of the federal "safe harbor" for its electors trumped the rights of all Florida voters to have their votes counted. For example, if the evidence had shown that Florida election officials had deliberately failed to count the votes of Miami residents and then certified the results without the Miami returns, it seems quite doubtful that the Court would have allowed the safe harbor to trump the right to have those votes counted.

Beyond the questionable reliance on *Reynolds* and *Harper*, we might ask whether the *Bush* decision is at least consistent with the trend shown in Rehnquist Court election decisions. On the one hand, the equal protection claim advanced by the conservative justices in the *Bush v. Gore* majority is a strong departure from the usual equal protection jurisprudence they have favored. Before the case, no Rehnquist Court opinion had ever relied upon *Reynolds* or *Harper* to expand the franchise or the scope of vote dilution claims. Instead, the leading voting case of the Rehnquist Court applying equal protection analysis is *Shaw v. Reno*, a case in which the Court *limited* the extent to which race may be taken into account in redistricting to benefit minority-preferred candidates for elective office.

On the other hand, Pamela Karlan has argued that *Bush* is in fact consistent with *Shaw*. She views both cases as demonstrating that the Court is moving away from individual rights and toward a "structural" view of equal protection: "Whatever interest the Supreme Court's decision [in *Bush v. Gore*] vindicated, it was not the interest of an identifiable individual voter. Rather, it was a perceived systemic interest in having recounts conducted according to a uniform standard or not at all. It was structural equal protection, just as the *Shaw* cases have been."[171]

Karlan's argument is provocative and worth exploring. In chapter 5, I return to the possible trend among both Court justices and some scholarly commentators to embrace "structural" arguments over individually oriented equality arguments. Here, it is enough to note as a matter of doctrine that the Court in Bush did not explicitly base its holding on the *Shaw* view of equal protection but, rather, grounded itself on the individual rights–oriented cases of *Reynolds* and *Harper*. If the Court saw *Shaw* as the authority for what it did, it never said so.

So returning to the central question posed in this section: Was Bush a great departure from applicable precedent? Yes and no. It was a great departure in the sense that the cases upon which the majority explicitly relied are too much of a stretch to provide a sound basis for arguing that the conclusion in *Bush* could be foreshadowed by those cases. Indeed, the closest case on point, *Classic*, suggests the Court should have reached the opposite result.

Nonetheless, the history of the Court's political equality jurisprudence from 1962 to 2000—through the Warren, Burger, and Rehnquist Courts— shows the Court consistently making new rules for election cases as it went along. There was no applicable precedent (or there was directly contrary precedent) when the Court decided *Baker*, *Reynolds*, *Harper*, and *Shaw*. In this sense, *Bush* continues the grand tradition of the justices as mighty Platonic guardians of our electoral process. So it is not unprecedented for the Court to make new law in this area.

This is not to say that *Bush v. Gore* was correctly decided. I conclude in chapter 3 that the Court was wrong to intervene, and, if it was to intervene, it erred in failing to give the Florida courts a chance to fix any equal protection problem. But criticism that the case deviates from precedent is not the strongest argument one can make against the decision.

Conclusion

My aim in this chapter is to give the reader a sense of the breadth and depth of the Court's political equality decisions from *Baker* to *Bush*. I set forth the major precedents, sometimes explaining obvious inconsistencies among them, but I have not delved into the their wisdom.

With this background, the next chapter begins by focusing on procedure: assuming the Court is going to make up its political equality jurisprudence as it goes along, what procedures should it follow in making decisions? The later chapters explore the substance of the political equality principles that should guide the Court.

2

Judicial Unmanageability and Political Equality

A Misplaced Focus on "Judicially Manageable" Standards[1]

The conventional story about the Supreme Court's decision in *Baker v. Carr*[2] to adjudicate disputes over legislative apportionment is that political market failure required judicial intervention. The market failed in the case of unequally populated districts because existing legislators could not be expected to vote themselves out of a job; nor would voters who benefit from the existing apportionment plan elect legislators inclined to do so.[3]

This market failure story makes an implicit normative judgment that unequally populated districts are improper, a judgment I consider in the next chapter. The story also evinces great trust in the judiciary, a point to which I now turn. If judges are to correct political market failures, their impartiality and general wisdom must make up for a lack of particular competence—as well as lack of accountability—in dealing with political matters.

Opponents of judicial intervention in politics doubted judicial competence in political cases, calling for nonjusticiability because "standards . . . for judicial judgment are lacking."[4] This concern over "judicial manageability" turned out to be seriously exaggerated in the legislative apportionment and districting cases, where the Court's adoption in *Reynolds v. Sims* of a strict "one person, one vote" standard required little more than knowledge of "sixth grade arithmetic,"[5] but it has proven more real in other cases, most recently, as I will explain, in *Bush v. Gore*.

The *Baker* Court majority and dissenters apparently failed to appreciate the benefits of judicial *un*manageability or initially murky standards for dealing with election cases regulating political equality. Precisely because these cases require the Supreme Court to make at least implicit normative judgments about the meaning of democracy or the structure of representative government, the danger of manageable standards is that they ossify new rules and enshrine the current Court majority's political theory. That enshrinement is precisely what happened in the one person, one vote cases.

Arguably, we cannot be surprised that the Court adopted the manageable standard of equally apportioned districts in *Reynolds*; manageable standards lower administrative costs, decrease the chances of lower court deviation from Supreme Court pronouncements, and increase reliance interests of those involved in the electoral process. But we must recognize the cost of manageable standards as well.

In contrast to *Reynolds*, where the Court does not articulate a manageable standard, it leaves room for future Court majorities to deviate from or to modify rulings in light of new thinking about the meaning of political equality in a democracy or about the structure of representative government, based on experience with the existing standard. It also allows for greater experimentation and variation in the lower courts using the new standard. Following modification and experimentation, the Court appropriately may articulate a more manageable standard. That new standard may be a flexible one or a bright-line rule, but either way it will be the product of less guesswork about its likely effects on the political process.

Initially, unmanageable standards no doubt come with costs as well: greater administrative costs, increased straying by the lower courts from Supreme Court majority pronouncements, and a decreased ability of political actors to rely upon Supreme Court precedent. But lack of Court competence in political matters suggests that those costs are worth bearing, at least for a time, as the Court and lower courts explore the contours of new equality rights.

Sometimes, as I argue in the next chapter, the Court should not create new equality rights at all. But once the Court—for good or ill—decides to create such rights, it must articulate *an appropriately precise* standard for judging similar equality claims: the more contested the Court's normative political theory underlying the claim in a particular case, the more the Court should strive to articulate legal standards that leave wiggle room for future Court majorities to modify.

My argument for initial judicial unmanageability draws upon the insights of judicial minimalist scholars such as Cass Sunstein. Sunstein proposes minimalism to "allow democratically accountable bodies to function,"[6] and his minimalism is somewhat open-ended. Like Sunstein, I will argue in the next two chapters that the Court should leave political equality decisions to politically accountable branches when dealing with contested equality claims. In this chapter, I propose a minimalist strategy so that the Supreme Court can gain valuable information before the Court *itself* settles upon the ultimate contours of a particular equality rule. My argument thus has some affinities to the "democratic experimentalism" theory of Michael Dorf and Charles Sabel, which envisions a division of labor and dialogue between political branches and the Court.[7]

Unsurprisingly, the Court sometimes has articulated unmanageable standards in political equality cases. *Bush v. Gore*'s new equal protection standard is the most obvious recent example. I do not claim that the Court in fact has articulated unmanageable standards as a means to acquire information about the ultimate contours of new equality rights. Just as likely, the articulation has been the product of political compromise, sloppy drafting, or unforeseen circumstances. My claim is that the Court *should,* at least initially, articulate unmanageable standards in certain equality cases.

Most scholars writing about *Baker v. Carr* and cases in its wake have extolled the virtues of manageability;[8] by contrast, I write here in praise of some unmanageability, at least in certain cases for a certain period of time. I begin by exploring whether the Court adopted an appropriately precise standard in the one person, one vote cases. I argue that the Court adopted the most manageable standard of all, which in retrospect has been too restrictive of political realities. I further consider how politics and jurisprudence might have been different had the Court adopted Justice Stewart's alternative, unmanageable standard for judging malapportionment claims. Justice Stewart's standard would have provided greater flexibility in dealing with apportionment problems and greater information to the justices as they refined the new constitutional standards.

I then turn to three additional areas in which the Court has adjudicated political equality claims: cases involving wealth tests for voting, voter qualifications, and vote counting. These three types of cases illustrate how the Court may increase the unmanageability of initial political equality standards as it faces more contested political equality claims.

Finally, I demonstrate how unmanageable standards may counteract the possibility of Court-imposed proportional representation, which lurks in the background of a number of political equality cases. Unmanageable

standards sometimes will be a better alternative than denying relief alto-
gether. Here I contrast two cases. In *City of Mobile v. Bolden,*[9] the Court rejected a claim that an at-large districting plan violated the Equal Protection Clause. It did so at least in part because it believed that to hold otherwise would have imposed a system of proportional representation on the
creation of legislative bodies. In *Davis v. Bandemer,*[10] the partisan gerrymandering case, the Court recognized a claim of an unconstitutional partisan gerrymander under the Equal Protection Clause, but did so using an
unmanageable standard.

Contrary to the predictions of justices not signing the plurality opinion
and of some commentators, the Court in *Bandemer* successfully avoided
imposing a proportional representation test on partisan gerrymandering
claims. Thus, the *Bolden* Court was incorrect that a decision under the
Equal Protection Clause inexorably would have led to proportional representation.

One Person, One Vote, One Manageable Standard

The one person, one vote standard was hardly inevitable. In 1946, Justice
Frankfurter's plurality opinion in *Colegrove v. Green* announced the
Court's refusal to enter the "political thicket."[11] Frankfurter explained that
the Court would not decide legislative apportionment issues because their
"peculiarly political nature" made them unsuitable "for judicial determination."[12]

The Court essentially overruled *Colegrove* in *Baker v. Carr,* thereby allowing challenges to legislative apportionment to go forward. Justice
Brennan, writing the majority opinion in *Baker,* described the contours of
the "political question" doctrine. He explained that the doctrine precluded
judicial intervention in six categories of cases, including the category of
cases in which "a lack of judicially discoverable and manageable standards
for resolving" the dispute existed.[13]

The majority and dissent in *Baker* disagreed about whether apportionment cases fell into this category. Over Justice Frankfurter's argument in
dissent that "standards . . . for judicial judgment are lacking,"[14] the majority stated that "[j]udicial standards under the Equal Protection Clause are
well developed and familiar, and it has been open to courts since the enactment of the Fourteenth Amendment to determine, if on the particular
facts they must, that a discrimination reflects *no* policy, but simply arbi-

trary and capricious action."[15] The *Baker* majority distinguished *Colegrove* as a Guaranty Clause case, and characterized that clause as "not a repository of judicially manageable standards."[16]

This move by the *Baker* majority was nothing short of a judicial sleight-of-hand. As Michael McConnell explained in a recent article:

> As an interpretation of the political question doctrine, this was nonsense. At the time of *Baker,* the Equal Protection Clause had never been applied to the districting question, and there were any number of possible interpretations, with no judicially manageable means of choosing among them. ("One person, one vote" is obviously a judicially manageable standard, but at the time of *Baker,* the Court had not embraced it.) Conversely, if the Court were inclined to develop judicially manageable standards under the Equal Protection Clause, it could do so equally well under the [Guaranty] Clause. The existence *vel non* of "judicially manageable standards" was inherent in the underlying issue, not in the constitutional label attached to it. Thus, it is hard to avoid the conclusion that the fateful decision to shift ground to equal protection was made for no reason other than to avoid the *appearance* of a departure from the nonjusticiability precedents.[17]

It may be, as McConnell argues, that the choice to use the Equal Protection Clause rather than the Guaranty Clause pushed the Court to choose particularly manageable standards in *Reynolds* and later cases.[18] McConnell argues that the Equal Protection Clause language committed the Court to a focus on equal populations while a Guaranty Clause claim could have allowed the Court to focus on preserving the right of a state not to be trampled by a permanent political minority.

But in other equal protection election cases the Court has not imposed any exacting requirement of strict equality such as in *Reynolds*. In cases such as *Bandemer,* the Equal Protection Clause has proven quite malleable. And, as a matter of Court politics, the Guaranty Clause route was impossible at the time of *Baker,* given that Justice Stewart simply refused to overrule any existing precedent.[19]

In any case, my concern here is not with the doctrinal question of *where* (if anywhere) in the Constitution standards for policing the apportionment process should come from but, rather, with the *ramifications* of *Baker's* holding that courts would find judicially manageable standards in the Equal Protection Clause to decide apportionment cases.

Justice Brennan's statement in *Baker* that standards to apply in this area were "well developed and familiar" was true only if taken to an unhelpful level of abstraction. During the drafting of the *Baker* opinion, Justice Douglas sent Justice Brennan a note calling the equal protection test articulated in the majority draft "a wholly new standard of Equal Protection."[20]

Thus, in *Baker,* the Court announced the existence of judicially manageable standards but left everyone to guess about what those standards should be. Would the Court require strict population equality, apportionment that was "rational" rather than "arbitrary and capricious," or compliance with some other standard? The Equal Protection Clause provided no answers on its face.

Justices' conference notes from the time reveal that the lack of an articulated standard in *Baker* apparently stemmed not from an oversight by the Court but from the political compromises necessary to get a majority vote in favor of justiciability. During the conference following the initial oral argument in *Baker,* Justice Harlan argued that the case should not be justiciable because "[t]his Court is not competent to solve this type of problem."[21] Justice Brennan responded, "I do not believe that the remedies are insoluble—I have worked it out with a judicial remedy."[22] At that point, Brennan obviously was contemplating some standard, perhaps the one person, one vote standard.

Justice Stewart, the swing vote, could not decide how to vote, and the case was set for reargument.[23] Following reargument, Justice Stewart expressed the view in conference that the case was justiciable, but he rejected the argument that "equal protection requires representation approximately commensurate with voting strength. States could give towns only one vote, whatever their size."[24] Justice Frankfurter asked, "What are the standards by which [a] remedy is to be fashioned[?]"[25] By this point, Justice Brennan had proposed asserting jurisdiction, but not directing a specific decree.[26] He hoped that the "assertion of power will cause the Tennessee legislature to act."[27] Chief Justice Warren similarly declared that "all we have to decide is that there is juris[diction.] [We] don't have to say states must give absolute equality."[28] Thus, the emergence of one person, one vote awaited future Court decisions, after some changes in Court personnel.

Meanwhile, the case appeared to divide the justices bitterly, as illustrated by a note that Frankfurter sent to Harlan just before Justice Frankfurter collapsed in his chambers. In the note, Frankfurter stated that the

Baker majority failed "to appreciate the intrinsic and acquired majesty of the Court's significance in the affairs of the country."[29]

Reynolds v. Sims,[30] establishing the one person, one vote standard for judging the constitutionality of state legislative apportionment, did not follow automatically from *Baker.* The Court moved there after *Baker,* first in *Gray v. Sanders,*[31] striking down unequal weighting of votes within a single constituency, and then in *Wesberry v. Sanders,*[32] requiring that congressional districts be drawn on an equal population basis. As late as the conference in *Wesberry,* Justice Brennan hesitated in imposing the one person, one vote standard. He stated, "On the remedy, I think that we would be wise only to reverse and let the district court fashion a remedy without giving any hints as to what it should do. There must be substantial equality. This one is way out of line."[33]

Nonetheless, first in *Wesberry,* then in *Reynolds,* the Court majority adopted the one person, one vote standard. In *Wesberry,* the Court held that "as nearly as is practicable[,] one man's vote in a congressional election [must] be worth as much as another's."[34] In *Reynolds,* the Court held that "as a basic constitutional standard, the Equal Protection Clause requires that the seats in both houses of a bicameral state legislature must be apportioned on a population basis."[35]

Chief Justice Warren, writing for the *Reynolds* majority, declared the principle as the "clear and strong command of"[36] the Equal Protection Clause: "This is at the heart of Lincoln's vision of 'government of the people, by the people, (and) for the people.' The Equal Protection Clause demands no less than substantially equal state legislative representation for all citizens, of all places as well as of all races."[37] The Court left the states with just a bit of wiggle room:

> So long as the divergences from a strict population standard are based on legitimate considerations incident to the effectuation of a rational state policy, some deviations from the equal-protection principle are constitutionally permissible with respect to the apportionment of seats in either or both of the two houses of a bicameral state legislature. But neither history alone, nor economic or other sorts of group interests, are permissible factors in attempting to justify disparities from population-based representation.[38]

The Court held that a state might justify minor deviations for the sake of keeping political subdivisions together in the state body.[39] But a state could not promote that interest if "population is submerged as the controlling consideration in the apportionment of seats in the particular legislative body."[40]

The Aftermath of the One Person, One Vote Cases, and the Problems of Judicially Manageable Standards

The Supreme Court's first foray into the political thicket required most states to reapportion both congressional and state legislative districts.[41] The one person, one vote standard announced by the Court was easy to understand and was popular among the public.[42] As Ely points out, once the reapportionment took place on an equal population basis, controversy over the cases died down: legislators elected from the newly apportioned districts had every incentive to preserve the new status quo.[43]

The only significant litigation regarding state or congressional apportionment to follow from these cases was the question of how much a state could deviate from exact mathematical equality for subordinate reasons, such as the desire to keep a political subdivision together in one district. The last chapter explains in detail that the Court has allowed virtually no deviation in the case of congressional districting, and allowed some, but not much, deviation in the case of state legislative districts.

More significant litigation arose out of attempts to apply the one person, one vote standard to local elections. Beginning in *Avery v. Midland County*,[44] the Court required local government entities to apply the standard, despite protests that an equally districted *state* legislature could use state law if desired to equalize any unequally districted local or regional entities.[45] *Avery* left open the possibility that the one person, one vote standard would not apply to special purpose districts whose burdens fell disproportionately on one group,[46] and in two cases, the Court applied this exception to exempt elections for special purpose water districts.[47] But these exceptions have not been applied widely. In practice, the lion's share of elections even on the local level is conducted using the one person, one vote standard.

Despite the popularity of the one person, one vote standard, some scholars recently have attacked it. Not all the attacks are strong; one weak argument claims that the standard has opened up the political system to all kinds of partisan and racial gerrymandering and incumbency protection.[48] According to this argument, once legislators became free to violate traditional "constraints" on redistricting such as adherence to the boundaries of political subdivisions in the name of one person, one vote, they were "liberated to snake lines all over the map to achieve their own purposes."[49]

This claim is weak because no such "constraint" ever existed in the sense of a pre-*Reynolds* legal obligation on legislators to draw district lines conforming to the boundaries of political subdivisions. Although many pre-*Reynolds* districts conformed to such subdivisions, conformity resulted from neither legal constraint nor civic motivation. Self-interested legislators looking to protect their interests did not *need* to violate political boundaries because they had a much more potent weapon to protect themselves: the drawing of vastly unequal districts or simply preserving districts that had become increasingly malapportioned over time.[50] Indeed, adherence to the boundaries provided some political cover for legislators to draw or retain grossly malapportioned districts.

Another, more convincing line of attack has focused on the *Avery* branch of these cases. Critics have argued that the one person, one vote standard sometimes works to prevent the formation of regional governments to deal with problems that appropriately are handled on a regional, rather than local, basis. As Bruce Cain explained, the Court's decision to apply the standard locally

> deprived the American people of an entire class of institutional mechanisms for compromise which could be used to solve collective action problems. For example, when the San Francisco Bay area considered establishing a regional government to cope with problems of growth and traffic management, its lawyers informed the planners that they could not design a confederation which did not conform to the principle of one person, one vote. Since the smaller cities were unwilling to join into any arrangement that would allow their suburban votes to be swamped by the more numerous votes of the larger, urban cities, the governance problem proved to be insurmountable. What the Bay Area cities wanted was to replicate the logic of the original compromise that induced smaller states to join the large states in the union at the founding of the country. In effect, the courts made it impossible for modern legislators to do what the Founding Fathers had been able to do.[51]

The Bay Area cities were correct in believing the courts would not uphold a regional compromise that violated the one person, one vote principle. The Supreme Court rejected a one borough, one vote rule for a regional government body in New York City in *Board of Estimate v. Morris*.[52] As Richard Briffault explained in his careful examination of this problem, "The inability to create a federal structure in which the principle of population equality is tempered by a concern for some parity among the pre-existing units [of local government] may render the regional unit politically impossible."[53]

The Road Not Taken:
Justice Stewart's Judicially Unmanageable Alternative

The regional government argument advanced by Cain and Briffault suggests a number of responses. First, one could argue that the one person, one vote standard's effect of hampering regional government is unfortunate, but it is a small price to pay for the fundamental gains in equality that the Court worked in *Wesberry* and *Reynolds*. Second, one could echo Justice Fortas's dissent in *Avery*, agreeing that the one person, one vote standard was necessary on the state level but disagreeing with its application on the local level. Reversal of *Avery* but not *Reynolds* would eliminate the de facto Court prohibition on regional governments, and an equally districted state legislature could block unequal and unfair regional government plans.

Both of these responses to the regional government problem are reasonable ones, and choosing between the two today is difficult. But perhaps the problem could have been avoided from the beginning. Despite Justice Brennan's reassuring rhetoric in *Baker* that equal protection standards were "well developed and familiar,"[54] when the Court decided *Baker, Wesberry, Reynolds,* and then *Avery*, it was in uncharted territory.

At first the Court proceeded cautiously, refusing in *Baker* to articulate particular standards to judge the equal protection claim, with at least Justice Brennan hoping that the threat of Court action would lead to a political solution. But then the Court in *Wesberry* and *Reynolds* committed itself to the one person, one vote principle, and, with the exception of an allowance for minor deviations in state legislative districting, it has remained behind this principle for nearly forty years. In *Avery*, despite protests of Justice Fortas and others, the Court extended the one person, one vote rule to local government bodies.

In hindsight, the Court may have been wiser to adopt initially Justice Stewart's alternative test, which he articulated in one of the companion cases to *Reynolds, Lucas v. Forty-Fourth General Assembly*.[55] Stewart agreed the cases were justiciable,[56] but he disagreed with the one person, one vote standard. He stated that the *Reynolds* majority was wrong in seeing the principle as rooted in a universally accepted representational theory or historical practice in the United States.[57] He disagreed that unequal districting "debased" a citizen's votes: "I find it impossible to understand how or why a voter in California, for instance, either feels or is less a citizen than a voter in Nevada, simply because, despite their population disparities, each of those states is represented by two United States Senators."[58]

Stewart rejected reliance on population equality alone in view of what he saw as the legitimate differing needs of different states. He then put forward his alternative:

> The fact is, of course, that population factors must often to some degree be subordinated in devising a legislative apportionment plan which is to achieve the important goal of ensuring a fair, effective, and balanced representation of the regional, social, and economic interests within a State. . . . What constitutes a rational plan reasonably designed to achieve this objective will vary from State to State, since each State is unique, in terms of topography, geography, demography, history, heterogeneity and concentration of population, variety of social and economic interests, and in the operation and interrelation of its political institutions. But so long as a State's apportionment plan reasonably achieves, in the light of the State's own characteristics, effective and balanced representation of all substantial interests, without sacrificing the principle of effective majority rule, that plan cannot be considered irrational.[59]

Justice Stewart further explained that his proposed alternative test for compliance with the Equal Protection Clause had two attributes: the plan must be rational in light of the state's own characteristics and needs, and it must not "permit the systematic frustration of the will of a majority of the electorate of the State."[60] Using this standard, Justice Stewart would have upheld the unequal districting plans in Colorado and New York,[61] but he agreed with the majority's result in *Reynolds* to strike down Alabama's scheme, which he deemed irrational.[62]

Justice Stewart's proposed alternative is an homage to judicial unmanageability.[63] Among the terms he did not define carefully in his alternative are "subordination," "fair, effective and balanced representation," "rational," "reasonably designed," "reasonable achieve[ment]," "effective and balanced representation," "substantial interests," "effective majority rule," and "systemic frustration of the will of the majority."

Long and protracted litigation over virtually every state's apportionment likely would have followed from the adoption of Justice Stewart's alternative standard. Perhaps the litigation would have boiled down to a question whether the challenged scheme looked more like Alabama's scheme, which fails Justice Stewart's test, than New York's scheme, which passes Justice Stewart's test. More likely, lower courts would have developed more specific tests for judging the constitutionality of state plans, and likely those courts' tests would conflict. The Court then would have been asked to bring some order to the chaos.

This description may appear to have little to commend it; we are all to a greater or lesser extent drawn to political order over chaos.[64] But a period of uncertainty and experimentation in this area would have been a positive, rather than a negative. Prior to *Reynolds,* judges had no experience engaging in this massive redistricting enterprise. Perhaps judicial intervention would be for the good; perhaps it would not. Perhaps there would be ways to police egregious malapportionment but give leeway to the states. But the one person, one vote rule was a single, decisive step in one direction; Justice Stewart's alternative test would have allowed for initial baby steps in different directions by lower-level decision makers who did not have to speak definitively for the nation.

Perhaps a manageable standard was necessary in *Reynolds* because it was the Court's first real entry into a state's political processes. Briffault argues that Stewart's position "could have been seen as an apologia for the perpetuation of malapportionment," and that the Court's decisive one person, one vote standard may have "enhanced the legitimacy of judicial intervention . . . by indicating that questions of representation could be resolved by a relatively simple formal rule, rather than a complex analysis."[65] But my main point is a more general one about how the Court should handle political equality cases.

Critics feared that Justice Stewart's test, which would have required the courts to delve into the details of political power in each state, would have unduly burdened the courts and undermined their legitimacy. For example, Jan Deutsch argued that the test

> would indeed require the Court to canvass the actual workings of the floor leadership in the legislative branches, the mechanisms of party control not only over voters and the city government but also over elected

representatives—in short, the details of the petty corruption and net-
works of personal influence that all too often constitute crucial sources of
power in municipal politics. . . . Even assuming that the evidence was
available and would be forthcoming, is it likely that our society could accept, as a steady diet, the spectacle of the judiciary solemnly ruling on the
accuracy of a political boss's testimony concerning the sources of his
power over voters and the degree of control that he exercised over elected
officials?[66]

Deutsch's argument raised a genuine concern, though one that appears
in hindsight to be unwarranted in light of current litigation under section
2 of the Voting Rights Act, which requires the courts to engage in exactly
this kind of analysis.[67] The concern could have been tested in the lower
courts as they struggled with the new unmanageable standard. This period
of experimentation would have not only benefited the development of
standards for Supreme Court policing of the districting process but aided
the Supreme Court's thinking about further entries into the political
thicket, such as its later forays into policing of racial or partisan gerrymandering.

Nor would it be fair to characterize Justice Stewart's standard as one
that would have promoted more result-oriented judging.[68] Once the
Court entered into this thicket, the choice was not one between judging
based upon objective standards and result-oriented judging. Rather, the
choice was whether to have all the results dictated at the front end through
the one person, one vote rule, or to allow for variation on the back end
through Justice Stewart's flexible standard. Arguably, the latter is a more
satisfactory solution, at least initially, and at least in situations like the apportionment cases where highly disputed normative principles are involved.

That is not to say that the Court should never have refined Justice Stewart's test into a more manageable standard, perhaps even eventual use of
the one person, one vote standard. But the Court lost valuable information by moving decisively, rather than incrementally.

Of course, nothing now formally prevents the Court from backpedaling
from a decisive standard like the one person, one vote standard. But my
sense is that a move from a mushy unmanageable standard to a more
manageable standard is easier for the Court than to overrule existing
precedent or even to make an unannounced switch from a firm manageable standard to mushiness. The point is illustrated by the criticism that

the Court has faced for its inconsistent willingness to allow slight deviations in district populations depending upon whether the districting is congressional or whether it is state or local.[69] Had this distinction developed incrementally out of an unmanageable standard based on a real need for disparate treatment, it would have been more defensible.

In addition, the Court sometimes will not get valuable information about the effects of its decision when it adopts a manageable standard in the first instance, and therefore will not know about the need to backpedal. For example, the problems with regional government formation perhaps were not appreciated adequately at the time the Court decided *Avery*. With a Stewart-like standard applied on the local level, the Court could have observed whether state legislatures responded to regional government plans that failed to comply with one person, one vote. Perhaps the legislatures would have blocked such plans with great population disparities; or perhaps the legislatures would have approved of such plans, finding that the "federal" model was politically desirable on the regional level. Perhaps also the Court could have observed the success or failure of political pressure on the state government from people in malapportioned regional government districts. This information would have proved valuable to the Court in considering the ultimate constitutionality of unequally apportioned regional government schemes.

Calibrating Controversy to Unmanageability: Wealth Qualifications, Voter Qualifications, and Vote-Counting Standards

Unmanageability is not an unmitigated good in political equality cases. As noted earlier, unmanageability imposes greater administrative costs, increased straying by the lower courts from Supreme Court majority preference, and a decreased ability of political actors to rely upon Supreme Court precedent.

These concerns are mitigated, however, when the Court calibrates the unmanageability of its standard to the novelty or controversy of its equal protection holding: the greater the novelty or controversy surrounding the holding, the more unmanageable the standard that the Court should articulate. I illustrate this approach using three cases of increasing novelty or controversy: *Harper v. Virginia Board of Elections*,[70] *Kramer v. Union Free School District No. 15*,[71] and *Bush v. Gore*.[72] *Harper* involved a poll tax for voting in state elections; *Kramer* involved a law limiting the franchise in a school district election to owners and renters of taxable realty in the district, along with their spouses, and parents or guardians of children in public schools; and *Bush v. Gore* concerned the standards over a recount of votes for Florida's electors in the 2000 presidential election.

Before proceeding with this analysis, I offer a significant caveat. I argue in the next chapter that *Kramer* may have been a case, and *Bush v. Gore* surely was a case, where the Supreme Court should have declined to create a new political equality rule at all. By talking about the use of unmanageability in these cases, I do not mean to imply my agreement with the decision to craft a new right.

Core Equality Claim/Highly Manageable Standard

Harper fits into the category of cases in which the Court's political equality holding had little novelty and therefore it was appropriate for the Court to articulate a highly manageable standard. In *Harper*, Virginia residents sought to have Virginia's poll tax, which required an annual payment of one dollar and fifty cents as a precondition to voting, declared unconstitutional.[73] The Court (unlike the initial dissent discussed in the previous chapter) chose not to rely upon history indicating that the tax originally was devised to disenfranchise African-Americans,[74] instead asking whether a *fairly applied* poll tax could violate the Equal Protection Clause.[75]

The Court, in holding that a fairly applied poll tax violated equal protection, announced a bright-line manageable rule: "We conclude that a State violates the Equal Protection Clause of the Fourteenth Amendment whenever it makes the affluence of the voter or payment of any fee an electoral standard."[76] The Court's rationale was similarly simple: "Voter qualifications have no relation to wealth nor to paying or not paying this or any other tax."[77]

The Court did not need to announce such a bright-line rule in striking down Virginia's poll tax. For example, the Court could have said something more opaque, adopting language from Justice Goldberg's proposed *Harper* dissent a year earlier: "[A] State may not frustrate or burden the exercise of the basic and precious right to vote by imposing substantial obstacles upon that exercise by a class of citizens not justified by any legitimate state interest."[78]

The Court was correct in articulating a highly manageable standard. The reason is not that the doctrinal case under the Equal Protection Clause for the rule was stronger than the doctrinal case for the one person, one vote rule in *Reynolds*. As Ely explained, despite the *Harper* Court's calling the poll tax "irrational," "[i]t may also be true, or at least it is not irrational to think so, that persons of some wealth tend to be more 'responsible' citizens or, more plausibly still, that willingness to pay a fee for voting is some reflection of serious interest in the election."[79] Instead, the Court was correct in using the manageable standard because a near–social consensus existed in the United States against the poll tax by the time the Court decided *Harper*.

The case for this social consensus was made, somewhat ironically,[80] by Justice Harlan in his *Harper* dissent. Justice Harlan explained that poll taxes in *federal* elections had already been banned by the Twenty-Fourth Amendment, which had passed very quickly.[81] Most states had abolished poll taxes for state and local elections, leaving only four states (including Virginia) still using them.[82] After setting forth the old argument that the poll tax encourages the "right" kind of voters to vote, Justice Harlan explained that such "viewpoints, to be sure, ring hollow on most contemporary ears. . . . Property and poll-tax qualifications, very simply, are not in accord with current egalitarian notions of how a modern democracy should be organized."[83]

The Court's position was thus neither novel nor particularly controversial. Indeed, it was in line with an emerging view of political equality that excluded wealth considerations.[84] In such circumstances, the Court properly articulated a manageable standard eliminating all wealth qualifications for voting.

Somewhat Contested Equality Claim/Less Manageable Standard

Kramer fits into the category of cases in which the Court's equal protection holding was somewhat more contested than in *Harper* and therefore it was appropriate for the Court to articulate a somewhat less manageable standard. In *Kramer*, the plaintiff, an unmarried district resident who lived with his parents, brought a class action suit challenging a New York law limiting the franchise in his school district's election to owners and renters of taxable realty in the district, along with their spouses, and parents or guardians of children in public schools. The plaintiff did not challenge the age, citizenship, or residency requirements imposed by the district.[85]

By the time the Court decided *Kramer* in 1969, it had understood its earlier cases such as *Reynolds* and *Harper* to require application of strict scrutiny to voting classifications because voting constituted a "fundamental right." Strict scrutiny requires that the state provide a compelling state interest to justify its discrimination and that the means be narrowly tailored to meet that interest. The Court held that the state failed to meet its burden under strict scrutiny and that the New York law therefore was unconstitutional. Of particular interest here is that the Court articulated a fairly unmanageable standard to apply in future cases.

The state argued that it had a legitimate interest in limiting the franchise in school district elections to those "primarily interested in such elections" and that the category of those persons allowed to vote were those primarily interested in school affairs.[86] The Court understood the argument as one limiting the franchise to those "directly affected" by school affairs, rather than those "subjectively concerned" about school matters.[87] As the Court wrote: "The State apparently reasons that since the schools are financed in part by local property taxes, persons whose out-of-pocket expenses are 'directly' affected by property tax changes should be allowed to vote. Similarly, parents of children in school are thought to have a 'direct' stake in school affairs and are given a vote."[88]

The Court declined to reach the question whether the state's interest was compelling. Instead, the Court held that the classification was not narrowly tailored to meet the interest. "The classifications [of the state law] permit inclusion of many persons who have, at best, a remote and indirect interest in school affairs and, on the other hand, exclude others who have a distinct and direct interest in the school meeting decisions."[89] The Court elaborated in a footnote:

> For example, appellant resides with his parents in the school district, pays state and federal taxes *and is interested in and affected by* school board decisions; however, he has no vote. On the other hand, an *uninterested* unemployed young man who pays no state or federal taxes, but who rents an apartment in the district, can participate in the election.[90]

As Briffault has noted, the Court in *Kramer* (as it had in *Baker*) engaged in a judicial sleight-of-hand.[91] It wrote that it understood the state's argument as one about an *objective* interest in elections, but its analysis switched to the plaintiff's *subjective* state of mind and the subjective state of mind of fictional unemployed counterpart in holding the provision was not narrowly tailored.[92]

Thus, the Court enunciated a fuzzy rule when it could have enunciated a manageable standard. The Court failed to define what "constitutes an 'interest' sufficient to justify a claim to the franchise"[93] in the school district election. The Court could have simply and clearly held that the franchise may not be limited except on the basis of age, citizenship, and residency. That would be an exceedingly manageable rule to apply in future cases.

Perhaps the Court did not so hold because to do so would have contradicted directly the Court's earlier decision in *Lassiter v. Northampton County Board of Elections*.[94] In *Lassiter*, the Court upheld a fairly applied literacy test on grounds that the "ability to read and write . . . has some relation to standards designed to promote intelligent use of the ballot."[95] A rule that limits voter qualifications to age, citizenship, and residency has no room for literacy tests. Despite the fact that Justice Stewart focused his *Kramer* dissent on his inability to distinguish the case from *Lassiter*,[96] the *Kramer* majority did not even cite *Lassiter*.

In retrospect, the Court's articulation of a less manageable standard may have been wise. As Briffault argues, the disenfranchisement in *Kramer* was not especially troubling—it did not disenfranchise traditionally victimized groups, no entrenchment of a territorial minority existed, and no class discrimination existed.[97] Thus, the extension of equal protection law in this direction was somewhat novel. Moreover, unlike the situation in *Harper,* there was no evidence of a societal consensus that voting qualifications like the ones in *Kramer* or *Lassiter* were improper. The Court faced a situation where the equal protection issue was more novel, and thus the Court was correct to be less than crystal clear on the rule to apply in future cases.

The fuzziness of the *Kramer* standard gave room for the Court to further refine franchise standards. It carved out an exception for special purpose districts in which the franchise could indeed be limited to classes of persons disproportionately impacted by the district's decisions. Indeed, in such elections, votes could be allocated other than on a one person, one vote basis.

What emerged from *Kramer* and the cases involving special election districts is a more nuanced set of rules that prohibits additional voter qualifications in most elections but allows such qualifications in a special class of elections. That regime would have been much harder to create if the *Kramer* Court had simply said "no additional voter qualifications in any elections." Still, the difficulty of satisfying the exception for special purpose district elections suggests that the Court should have created an even murkier standard in *Kramer*.

Contested Equality Claim/Unmanageable Standard

Bush v. Gore fits into the category of cases in which the Court's equal protection holding had great novelty and therefore the Court properly articulated an unmanageable standard. The end of the previous chapter explored one question in connection with the case: whether the case followed existing election law precedent. Here, I focus on a very different aspect, the unmanageability of the case's equal protection standard.

The Supreme Court began its equal protection analysis with the following words:

The right to vote is protected in more than the initial allocation of the franchise. Equal protection applies as well to the manner of its exercise. Having once granted the right to vote on equal terms, the State may not, by later arbitrary and disparate treatment, value one person's vote over that of another. *See, e.g., Harper.* It must be remembered that "the right of suffrage can be denied by a debasement or dilution of the weight of a citizen's vote just as effectively as by wholly prohibiting the free exercise of the franchise." *Reynolds.*[98]

After noting that "[t]he question before us . . . is whether the recount procedures the Florida Supreme Court has adopted are consistent with its obligation to avoid arbitrary and disparate treatment of the members of its electorate,"[99] the Court answered the question in the negative. It held that the recount mechanism adopted by the Florida Supreme Court did "not satisfy the minimum requirement for non arbitrary treatment of voters necessary to secure the fundamental right"[100] under the Equal Protection Clause for a number of reasons. No doubt, the most important reason to the Court was the fact that the Florida Supreme Court had instructed the individuals conducting the manual recounts to judge ballots to discern the "intent of the voter," but it had failed to formulate uniform rules to determine such intent, such as whether to count as a valid vote a ballot whose chad is hanging by two corners.

So what precisely is the equal protection holding of *Bush v. Gore*? Commentators have noted that the case's judicial standard is muddled. Michael Dorf and Samuel Issacharoff, for example, write that "[w]here *Baker v. Carr* and *Reynolds v. Sims* spawned a judicially-enforceable rule that is, if anything, unduly mechanical, the *per curiam* opinion in *Bush v. Gore* was perfectly opaque as to what impact, if any, its decision would have on future challenges to election procedures."[101] Similarly, Spencer Overton noted that the Court avoided the "articulation of a clear, workable rule."[102]

By including language in the opinion limiting its precedential value to the "present circumstances,"[103] perhaps the case means nothing for the future development of equal protection law. On the other hand, by including vastly broad language indicating that it violates the Equal Protection Clause to "value one person's vote over that of another," the opinion has potentially broad implications. Indeed, elsewhere I have explored how the equal protection holding in *Bush v. Gore* might—and I emphasize *might*—apply to a host of other "nuts and bolts" election questions.[104]

The opacity of the equal protection holding is actually the best feature of a very bad opinion. Overton noted the Court "left lower courts and others without manageable tools to determine equal protection violations in the political context"[105]—precisely, and all for the good. Now, as myriad cases make their way through the federal courts raising a *Bush v. Gore* equal protection claim (for example, is punch-card voting, with its relatively high error rate, now unconstitutional?), the courts will try different approaches to deal with the claims. *Bush v. Gore* will be viewed by lower court lenses in Rashomonic fashion and the Court will eventually sort it out. If the Court does its job well (a big "if," no doubt), it can refine its new equal protection standard in light of what works and does not work in the lower courts.

The Court was right to articulate an unmanageable standard because its holding was unprecedented and not in line with any social consensus about the proper standards to use in the recounting of ballots, an issue about which the public had no opinion before the 2000 controversy. Chapter 1 showed how the majority could not properly rely upon *Reynolds* or *Harper* in support of its novel holding. Neither case involved the mechanics of elections, what had heretofore been seen to be a matter for local officials. Indeed, the Court in recent years had expressed great deference to local officials who wished to structure their elections in the ways they see fit.

The Court in *Bush v. Gore* moved in a new direction, without societal consensus or precedential reason to do so. Opacity made sense. The same may be said of the line of cases beginning with *Shaw v. Reno*,[106] establishing the "unconstitutional racial gerrymander." Although I am quite critical of *Shaw* for reasons developed in chapter 5, once the Court decided to adopt the new, unprecedented cause of action, some struggle over the correct standard to apply is appropriate. Indeed, we might view the conflict between Justice O'Connor's "bizarreness" standard and her focus on the shape of districts and Justice Kennedy's "predominant factor" standard focused on legislative motivation as a struggle over how unmanageable a standard should be applied to this new constitutional claim.

Unmanageable Standard or No Standard: The Court and Fear of Proportional Representation

Lurking in the background of many of these political equality cases decided under the Equal Protection Clause is what Sanford Levinson has called the "brooding omnipresence of proportional representation."[107] Levinson explained that courts and commentators would not be concerned with thorny issues such as the constitutionality of partisan gerrymandering if the Warren Court in *Baker* "had not embarked on what was widely (and perhaps correctly) perceived as a radical intervention into long-established modes of apportioning legislative seats."[108] Once the Court opened the door to claims of inequality in a system that granted everyone a vote, it opened the door as well to claims that the Constitution demanded greater proportionality in the voting rules employed to choose elected officials. This fear of proportional representation goes all the way back to *Reynolds*, where Justice Stewart in dissent in the companion *Lucas* case warned that the majority's position would lead to proportional representation.[109]

The fear that political equality arguments, pushed to the extreme, might lead to court-imposed proportional representation is not laughable.[110] Assuming the justices have this fear, the question becomes what strategy the Court should use to block this development. The Court appears to have used two strategies: refusing to extend its political equality precedents to new types of claims and using unmanageable standards as a bulwark against extreme cases of political inequality.

City of Mobile v. Bolden[111] is an example of the Court's use of the first strategy. In *Mobile,* African-American residents of Mobile, Alabama, brought a class action suit challenging the constitutionality of the city's at-large method of electing its three city commissioners.

The Court rejected the argument that the at-large method violated the Equal Protection Clause. A four-justice plurality stated that plaintiffs' claim failed because the plaintiffs lacked evidence that the electoral system was designed with a racially discriminatory *purpose.*[112] Justice Blackmun concurred in the result on grounds that the relief afforded by the trial court "was not commensurate with the sound exercise of judicial discretion."[113] Justice Stevens concurred essentially on grounds that a contrary ruling would be impossible to administer.[114]

Three justices dissented.[115] Justice Marshall, joined by Justice Brennan, relied explicitly on *Reynolds v. Sims* in arguing that the at-large system constituted a denial of equal protection:

> *Reynolds v. Sims* and its progeny focused solely on the discriminatory *effects* of malapportionment. They recognize that, when population figures for the representational districts of a legislature are not similar, the votes of citizens in larger districts do not carry as much weight in the legislature as do votes cast by citizens in smaller districts. The equal protection problem attacked by the "one person, one vote" principle is, then, one of vote dilution: under *Reynolds,* each citizen must have an "equally effective voice" in the election of representatives. In the present cases, the alleged vote dilution, though caused by the combined effects of the electoral structure and social and historical factors rather than by unequal population distribution, is analytically the same concept: the unjustified abridgment of a fundamental right. It follows, then, that a showing of discriminatory intent is just as unnecessary under the vote-dilution approach . . . as it is under our reapportionment cases.[116]

The plurality rejected Justice Marshall's reliance on *Reynolds.* It saw his dissent as an endorsement of proportional representation and "not the law. The Equal Protection Clause . . . does not require proportional representation as an imperative of political organization."[117]

Regardless of whether Justice Marshall's position should properly be characterized as an endorsement of proportional representation, it seems no more a stretch to extend the equal protection analysis of *Reynolds* to the means of aggregating votes, what Marshall refers to as "electoral structures," than to the mechanics of voting. In other words, the principle of promoting political equality has no natural stopping point, even if we can draw distinctions among the cases.

Thus, a plurality of justices wished to stop the equality precedents from going so far as proportional representation, while two other justices saw Justice Marshall's test as an unmanageable one. In retrospect, the plurality's fears appear unfounded. Congress essentially codified Justice Marshall's position in *City of Mobile v. Bolden* through an amendment to section 2 of the Voting Rights Act in 1982.[118] Although section 2 has moved "electoral structures" toward greater proportionality, it does not appear to have created any general right to proportional representation. The Court has been careful not to interpret section 2 so broadly, even if lower courts have latched onto language from the Court's 1994 *Johnson v. De Grandy*[119] case to elevate proportionality to a key factor in assessing compliance with section 2.[120]

If indeed it was primarily fear of proportional representation, rather than some concern on the merits, that led the *Bolden* plurality away from a holding in favor of the plaintiffs, the Court should have considered imposing an unmanageable standard to see if lower courts could develop satisfactory ways to adjudicate these claims. The Court appears to have (perhaps unwittingly) adopted this type of approach in another election case from the 1980s, *Davis v. Bandemer*.[121] *Bandemer* involved whether a political party could raise a claim of unconstitutional partisan gerrymandering. A majority of the Court concluded that the Indiana Democrats' claim that the 1981 redistricting plan violated their rights under the Equal Protection Clause was justiciable.[122] Then, speaking for a plurality of the Court, Justice White articulated an unmanageable standard for judging when an unconstitutional partisan gerrymander has occurred.

The plurality's analysis began by stating that to make such a claim, proving both "intentional discrimination against an identifiable political group and an actual discriminatory effect on that group" is necessary. The plurality summarily upheld the district court's finding of discriminatory intent, noting that one party's control of the districting process often will have the intent of discriminating against the other party.[123]

The big question in *Bandemer* was how a political party could prove "actual discriminatory effect." The plurality's analysis on this point began by recognizing that there is no constitutional right to proportional representation[124] and that "mere lack of proportional representation will not be sufficient to prove unconstitutional discrimination. . . . Rather, unconstitutional discrimination occurs only when the electoral system is arranged in a manner that will consistently degrade a voter's or a group of voters' influence on the political process as a whole."[125] Applying this test, the Court concluded that the Indiana Democrats failed to prove discriminatory effect.

Commentators have disagreed on the meaning of *Bandemer* since it was decided. Bernard Grofman, for example, construed the case to mean that partisan gerrymandering is unlawful when it is "(1) intentional, (2) severe, and (3) predictably nontransient in its effects."[126] Daniel Lowenstein, in contrast, believes that the Court imposed an extremely high bar for proving partisan gerrymandering, but did so in a way to "retain the option to intervene." He suggests that perhaps members of the plurality did so because they "recogniz[ed] the complexity of the subject, [and they] may have been uncertain what abusive practices might be brought to light in the future."[127]

Lowenstein seems closest to what at least some of the justices intended. Justice Brennan wrote the following in a memorandum sent to Justice White about an early White draft opinion:

> Should not the opinion encourage a reading that will discourage the bringing of suits alleging partisan gerrymandering? If that is desirable (and I definitely think that it is), would you consider expanding the statement of facts . . . to include a fuller description of the evidence introduced by the Democrats to demonstrate the effects of the Indiana law? The object would be to discourage lower courts from too readily relying upon a supposed paucity of such evidence as a reason to distinguish the case. . . . Should we not also be careful to use . . . language that avoids making it more difficult than it already is to prove racial gerrymandering?[128]

Laurence Tribe contends that the plurality opinion did not give "any real guidance to lower courts forced to adjudicate this issue."[129] In other words, *Bandemer* is a case of unmanageable standards. Since *Bandemer*, lower courts have struggled with *Bandemer*, and allegations of partisan gerrymandering thus far have met with little success.[130] Indeed, Michael

McConnell has called the *Bandemer* standard "so toothless that [the Court] might as well have held partisan gerrymandering nonjusticiable."[131]

These historical developments belie the strongly voiced concerns at the time of *Bandemer* that the case likely would lead to a constitutional right to proportional representation. Justice O'Connor, in her *Bandemer* concurrence, stated that the plurality's "standard will over time either prove unmanageable and arbitrary or else evolve toward some loose form of proportionality."[132] Peter Schuck developed these arguments further, purporting to demonstrate that "*Bandemer,* despite the Court's disclaimer, will encourage proportionality as the standard against which partisan gerrymandering claims will tend to be measured."[133]

For good or not, *Bandemer*'s unmanageability has served as a bulwark against proportional representation. Had lower courts more aggressively interpreted *Bandemer* to create such a right, the Supreme Court was ready to reinterpret its standard in *Bandemer* to reverse the trend. In the meantime, as Lowenstein suggests, *Bandemer* serves as a backstop (and perhaps as a deterrent) to police the most egregious forms of partisan gerrymandering. The unmanageability solution, rather than the path taken in *Bolden,* provides the Court with the greatest flexibility as it ponders these political questions about which it sometimes has little more to go on than intuition.

Conclusion

Unmanageability in the pursuit of political equality is no vice. Indeed, unmanageable judicial standards have much to commend them in certain circumstances. If we think about the overused metaphor of the Court making its way through the political thicket, we might imagine a few ways that the Court could reach its destination. We begin with the Court stuck in a deep forest. Manageable standards are the equivalent of the leader using all of her resources to clear the path in a particular direction. That strategy is appropriate if one has a very good sense of where one wants to go, but dangerous if one does not.

When unsure of the correct direction, the leader's best strategy might be to stay in a single location and send a few scouts out along different paths. Each scout then reports to the leader with updated information on the paths available. The leader, after receiving this information, can then make a more informed decision on the ultimate path to be taken. If the Court, as is likely, will remain in the political thicket, unmanageability may be one of the best tools available for finding the right paths.

The next chapter turns to the related and much more substantive question: How should the Court choose among the alternative paths before it? In other words, What *substantive decisions* should the Court make when faced with political equality claims?

3

Protecting the Core
of Political Equality
Core versus Contested Equality Principles

Harper v. Virginia Board of Elections[1] and *Lubin v. Panish*,[2] decided just eight years apart from one another, on the surface appear to be similar cases. *Harper* is the poll tax case described in detail in the previous chapter. In *Lubin*, following the Supreme Court's decision in *Bullock v. Carter*[3] (a decision itself relying on *Harper*), the Court struck down on equal protection grounds a California law requiring candidates to pay filing fees as low as about $700. Both decisions limited the role that wealth or money may play in the allocation of political power, an idea I will refer to as *the antiplutocracy principle*.

Although both decisions stem from the antiplutocracy principle, there is a large gap between them. *Harper* aimed at the very *core* of the principle. A poll tax may deter people of different wealth levels from voting, but because of the declining marginal utility of money, the tax will have its strongest effect on the poor, who might have to choose between voting and eating. The right at issue in *Harper,* the right to vote, is central to any well-functioning democracy. Finally, as we saw from Justice Harlan's *Harper* dissent, by 1966 a near–social consensus had developed against the use of poll taxes.

Lubin's filing fee is a far cry from *Harper*'s poll tax. The filing fee prevented no one from *voting*. It only marginally limited the choices of candidates available to voters. A filing fee of $700 (in 1976 dollars; worth about $2,200 in 2002 dollars) seems unlikely to deter serious candidates from running for election (except perhaps in the smallest local elections); even candidates who would be popular with poor voters need to raise substantially larger sums than $700 in order to run an effective campaign even in a moderately sized jurisdiction. Nor was there any consensus or near-consensus in 1974 or today that candidates should be entitled to full public financing of their campaigns. *Lubin* thus is a case in which the Court recognized a *contested* political equality right. Both *Harper* and *Lubin* concern the antiplutocracy principle, but only *Harper* goes to the core of that principle.

Following the arguments in chapter 2, at the very least the Court in *Lubin* should have used an initially unmanageable standard in crafting the political equality right. My claim in this chapter is bolder and more substantive. I use the distinction between core and contested political equality claims to delineate the proper and respective roles of the Court and legislatures in deciding such questions. In particular, I argue that the Court should play a central role in protecting the *core* of three equality principles set forth below. When faced with government claims that a limitation on core equality is necessary to serve an important government interest, the Court, with an eye on legislative self-interest and agency problems, must engage in a skeptical balancing of interests.

Although the Court's role is to protect the core, the Court should not constitutionalize *contested* political equality principles.[4] Instead, as I explain in the next chapter, it is up to Congress or state and local legislative bodies (or the people, in jurisdictions with an initiative process) to decide whether to expand political equality principles into contested areas. The Court generally should defer to such decisions to accept contested equality principles, assuming that the Court is confident that the legislature's intent is to foster equality rather than engage in self-dealing. Chapter 4 applies these tools to the Court's treatment of campaign finance laws and the Voting Rights Act.

Returning to the distinction between core and contested political equality rights in *Harper* and *Lubin,* the Court was right to strike down Virginia's poll tax, but it erred in striking down California's relatively low filing fees as a violation of equal protection. It should have left the determination of fees, within reason, to the legislative body charged with setting them. That is not to say that the Court was incorrect in *Bullock* in striking down Texas's considerably higher fees (as high as $8,900 then; as high as $38,600 in 2002 dollars). The question is whether such fees indeed would prevent serious candidates from running for office and, if so, whether that undermined the core of the antiplutocracy principle. The tools in this chapter should help answer this more difficult question.

I begin this chapter by defending the argument that the Court should constitutionalize core equality principles but not contested ones. I then describe the core and contested applications of three equality principles:

(1) the essential political rights principle
(2) the antiplutocracy principle
(3) the collective action principle

I use Court cases from *Baker* to *Bush* to illustrate application of these principles. I conclude by looking at how the Court should balance equality and other state interests when the state argues against protecting a core equality principle.

Why Should the Court Protect the Core and Only the Core?

At least since *Colegrove,*[5] courts and commentators have struggled with the appropriate level of judicial intervention in the political process. Liberals who in 2000 decried the Court's intervention in *Bush v. Gore* saw perhaps for the first time what conservatives have complained about since *Baker v. Carr:* an apparently result-oriented Court using the Equal Protection Clause of the Fourteenth Amendment to achieve a result that a majority of justices believed was substantively fair.

Most observers agree that Court intervention in the political process is dangerous (because it leaves important decisions about the structuring of democracy in the hands of unaccountable judges) yet sometimes necessary (because the courts are the only bodies able to police fundamental unfairness in the allocation of political power).

The dominant scholarly answer to this dilemma has been process theory, the idea that courts should intervene when, and only when, the political process is failing. The prime example offered by process theorists is apportionment. Legislators had no incentives to reapportion districts to make them more equal in size, and voters in many states had no way to bypass such legislative decisions.

As the introduction noted, process theory is problematic in at least three respects. First, it has provided no meaningful limit on court intervention in practice, perhaps because of the difficulty of determining whether "political market failure" exists. Second, process theory masquerades as a non-normative theory, when in fact it is normatively based. How do we know that grossly malapportioned districts need "correcting"? Process theory just begs that question. Finally, as a normative theory, process theory is very shallow, providing no answer, for example, to the question whether the strict one person, one vote principle or Justice Stewart's more amorphous standard would be the most appropriate remedy for a claimed malapportionment.

Rather than hide behind the alluring label of "process theory," we would be much better off if courts acknowledged more forthrightly the fundamental value judgments inherent in deciding to intervene in political cases. Better for the Supreme Court to say (as in fact it did in *Baker* and *Reynolds*) that there is something fundamentally undemocratic about malapportioned districts than to hide behind a technocratic and ostensibly neutral application of process theory.

There are at least three advantages to having the Court focus on substantive equality principles rather than on the political process. First, the Court's focus on substance rather than process clarifies for both members of the Court and the public at large what normative value judgments the Court is making, value judgments the Court would make in any case under process theory. If the justices continue in their role as "mighty Platonic guardians" of the political process—and all indications are that they will continue to do so for the foreseeable future—the Court should confront those choices directly, and the public should be informed of the breadth and depth of the equality principles the Court applies in these cases.

The apportionment cases provide a good example. Viewing *Reynolds* as a process case does not tell us how far its equality holding should go. Should it apply to local districting issues? To other political claims within equally apportioned districts, such as a claim of vote dilution by minorities? If the Court instead identifies the substantive principle at stake in apportionment, that principle can be applied to similar, though not identical, situations.

Second, by requiring the Court to focus on the substantive equality principle at stake, the Court is more likely to consider whether the case's holding might have unintended consequences on other political issues. If such a problem is apparent from a clear articulation of the substantive principle behind the case, the Court will be positioned, using the tools developed in chapter 2, to use an initially murky statement of the principle to move slowly into defining the principle's borders.

Using the apportionment example again, if the Court is worried about broad application of its substantive principle, it may state that principle vaguely. In a sense, that is what the Court in *Reynolds* did. Although the *standard* the Court announced in *Reynolds* was the extremely manageable one person, one vote standard, the *underlying equality principle* that the Court articulated in *Reynolds* was quite murky. Courts and commentators were left to guess what the Court meant in stating that the Equal Protection Clause guarantees "fair and effective representation."[6]

Third, a focus on substance is more honest than a focus on process, because the Court will not always provide process protection absent a threat to a substantive equality principle recognized by a Court majority. Consider first how a Court using process theory and a Court focused on substantive equality principles would analyze *Harper*. A process theorist would ask whether the poor voters in *Harper* could effectively organize for political action to overturn the poll tax, while the question for someone concerned with substantive equality principles would be whether a state may condition voting on wealth or property ownership. In the case of *Harper*, the result is likely the same under either analysis: poll taxes must fall—because, under process theory, such voters cannot organize effectively for political action, or because, under some substantive equality principle, wealth conditions for voting are normatively improper.

Now consider how both analyses apply to the question whether a state may prevent *nonresidents* from voting. A process theorist might well conclude, as in the analysis of *Harper*, that nonresidents may not be denied the vote because nonresidents likely would have a difficult time organizing for political action to gain the vote in a jurisdiction in which they are not residents. By contrast, a substantive focus would ask whether voting by nonresidents is at the core of any political equality principles. As we will see, the Court has said that jurisdictions may exclude nonresidents from voting. Whether that conclusion is a good one or not, it seems that a substantive, rather than the process-oriented, analysis focuses our attention in the right place; it is hard to see how process theory helps very much.

The same may be said of a consideration whether *ex-felons* should be allowed to vote: Process theory certainly supports their inclusion, for what group has less political power than a group of convicted felons?[7] But the Court is unlikely to extend the vote to ex-felons as a matter of constitutional right. And the reason is substantive.

One criticism some may level at a shift to substance is that it simply replaces the question whether the process is working with the unquestionably normative question of what constitutes the core of political equality. That latter determination will depend at least in part upon the value

judgments of the justices. The criticism is absolutely correct, but its consequences are far from clear. If the import of the criticism is that process
theory is somehow more "neutral" than focusing on substance, my earlier
analysis should have put the idea to rest: there is nothing neutral or natural about deciding that the political process must be "fair" to protect the
"outs" from the "ins," or that an administrable way to achieve fairness in
the apportionment context is one person, one vote.

If, on the other hand, the criticism is that a substantive focus allows the
Court to make value judgments about equality unmoored to the text or
history of the Constitution[8] (the same criticism that has been made
against process theory), that argument is simply too late. From *Baker* to
Bush, the Court has indicated its intent to remain in this realm for the
foreseeable future. As long as the Court continues to make such value
judgments, it should not be encouraged to mask them behind a veil of
process.

But are there means that we might use to cabin the Court's intervention
in such cases? Even those who, like me, believe it is appropriate for the
Court to make value judgments in order to protect some political equality
principles might look for a way of limiting the Court's regulation of political equality. I argue that the Court should intervene only to protect *core*
political equality rights.

Intuitively, it seems less objectionable that the Court constitutionalized
the core of the antiplutocracy principle as it did in striking down *Harper*'s
poll tax than that it struck down the low filing fee in *Lubin*. The Court also
seemed to stray far when it constitutionalized the one person, one vote
standard on the local level in *Avery,* or proscribed some race-conscious redistricting in the *Shaw* line of cases.

If we may meaningfully distinguish between *core* rights that the Court
should protect and *contested* rights that the Court should not constitutionalize, the Court's political equality jurisprudence would markedly improve. It would provide a strong limit on judicial intervention in politics,
while still preserving that "backstop" role to police fundamental unfairness in the political process.

Limiting intervention to the core makes sense. When the Court acts to
constitutionalize contested political equality rights, it runs a greater danger of unintended political consequences. *Harper* may be read narrowly as
a case about the use of wealth in voting because it is at the core of the antiplutocracy principle. We can imagine a stopping point in *Harper,* one
that bans property or wealth tests for voting but does no more. But

Lubin—recognizing a contested equality right—may be read much more broadly; if it violates the antiplutocracy principle to require candidates for office to pay relatively low fees, many other political activities requiring money become equally subject to attack, including this country's entire system for private financing of elections.

Moreover, there is less to be gained from constitutionalizing contested equality principles. *Harper* served to prevent states in the South from resurrecting and maintaining poll taxes that discriminated against African-Americans and poor whites. But it is difficult to see that the holding in *Lubin* has done anything to expand the pool of candidates for whom poor voters would wish to vote.

This is not to say that extending equality principles to contested areas is a bad thing. We may do very well as a society to have all publicly financed elections, to honor the one person, one vote standard in all local elections, and to put an end to race-conscious districting. But those choices should be made by legislative bodies, not by the Court. The next chapter considers when the Court should allow legislative bodies to embrace contested equality principles in the face of competing interests, such as the protection of free speech and association guaranteed by the First Amendment. For now, I turn to identifying the core equality rights.

Identifying Core Political Equality Rights

The limiting principle I have identified depends crucially on being able to distinguish between core and contested political equality rights. How is the Court to do so?

A few basic political equality rights are absolutely essential for any government to function as a democracy. These include the right to speak on political issues and nondiscrimination on the basis of race or ethnicity in the right to vote. I also place in this category the right to organize for political action unfettered by laws passed by elected officials intended to insulate the officials from political competition. Justices would identify this narrow class of rights by examining the text or history of the Constitution, or basic political theory about the meaning of representative government. I envision a small universe of such rights, rights that hardly would be controversial.

The Court should protect these core political equality rights regardless of current social views. Imagine what I hope is a very unlikely scenario: in the ongoing "war on terrorism" public opinion shifts in a dramatic and antidemocratic fashion so that jurisdictions started passing popular laws denying the right to vote to Arab-Americans. The Court should unequivocally strike such laws down, regardless of popular opinion and regardless of the consequences for the justices on the Court.

Most core political equality rights, however, are *socially constructed*. Even the idea of nondiscrimination in voting on the basis of race or ethnicity is socially constructed: "universal suffrage" is a relatively recent phenomenon (as well a misnomer, because excluding children, nonresidents, noncitizens, and ex-felons remains the rule). Much of what constitutes the core of political equality rights depends upon a social consensus or near-consensus about the ground rules for contemporary democratic governments to function.

To identify the socially constructed core, the Court must examine contemporary attitudes about practices alleged to infringe upon political equality rights. Recall Justice Harlan's *Harper* dissent describing social consensus against the poll tax. Harlan chronicled the swift passage of the Twenty-Fourth Amendment barring poll taxes in federal elections, the repeal of poll taxes in most states and localities, and contemporary attitudes about the poll tax in the public. Harlan concluded: "Property and poll-tax qualifications, very simply, are not in accord with current egalitarian notions of how a modern democracy should be organized."[9] The analysis pointed to social near-consensus in the United States about the inappropriateness of the poll tax, leaving just a few outlier states such as Virginia that needed policing by the Court.

The Court thus could define most core political equality rights by identifying social consensus (really "social near-consensus," but I use "social consensus" as a shorthand throughout the rest of this book). The practice of identifying social consensus about core political equality rights is analogous to the Court's deciding in the criminal context that under "evolving standards of decency," it is cruel and unusual punishment to execute the mentally retarded but not juveniles.[10] In such cases, the Court takes the pulse of the nation in imposing minimum constitutional standards in the Eighth Amendment context. The same issues recur in new cases as social values—reflected in public opinion and legislative action—change.

One wrinkle present in the political equality context but not the Eighth Amendment context is that legislatures comprise politicians whose careers are affected rather directly by the laws they pass. Thus, legislatively enacted election laws may not always express contemporary public attitudes about political equality.

Undoubtedly, my proposed new test is subject to manipulation by disingenuous justices. The Court could "find" or not "find" social consensus and rule as it wishes in political equality cases. The focus on social consensus should provide some restraint, however. It would have been difficult for a justice in 1966 to deny that there was social consensus about the inappropriateness of the poll tax to modern democratic thought. The standard may be no less malleable than the "political market failure" standard of process theory, but at least it asks the right, substantive question that process theory begs: What does basic political fairness require in contemporary society?

When the court fails to defer to social consensus, it runs the risk of *forming* it. When the Court decided *Reynolds*, it appears that there was no social consensus for the one person, one vote rule, though perhaps there was consensus that electoral systems that consistently defeated majority rule violated contemporary democratic norms and that the Court had to fix the problem somehow. As Jonathan Still has shown, there are many ways besides strictly equally weighted voting to structure a democratic government.[11] But now, more than three decades after *Reynolds*, the one person, one vote rule has become broadly accepted, with the term "one person, one vote" being seen as synonymous with basic political equality rights.

Core and Contested Visions of Three Principles of Political Equality

I turn now to identifying three core equality principles. I derive these principles from my view of the few basic rights essential to a contemporary democracy as well as from my observation of social consensus on political equality as a citizen of the United States at the beginning of the twenty-first century. No doubt many readers from other times and places—and certainly some readers from my time and place!—would or will disagree with the principles as I set them forth and with my placing certain rights at the core. I do not claim to possess the incontrovertible Truth on political equality issues. Instead, I intend this analysis as a means of starting a dialogue about which political equality principles belong in the core.

THE ESSENTIAL POLITICAL RIGHTS PRINCIPLE

The first of the core equality principles is the essential political rights principle. It may be succinctly stated as follows:

Each person has basic formal political rights, including the right to speak on political issues, to organize for political action, and to petition the government. The government may not deny the right to vote on the basis of gender, literacy, national origin, race, religion, sexual orientation, or on any other basis absent compelling justification. Voters have the right to have their votes counted and weighed roughly equally to the votes of other voters.

Most elements of the essential political rights principle, at least stated in the abstract, should hardly be controversial. Various provisions of the Constitution embody the principle, including the First Amendment's prohibition against the government's abridging freedom of speech, assembly, and association, the Fifteenth Amendment's prohibition against discrimination in voting on account of race or previous condition of servitude, and the Nineteenth Amendment's prohibition against discrimination in voting on account of gender.

Some aspects of the principle had been recognized by the Supreme Court in cases well preceding the *Baker* revolution, some of which are described in the introduction. As far back as 1886, the Court in *Yick Wo v. Hopkins* recognized that the right to vote is fundamental because it is "preservative of all rights."[12] Similarly the Court in the 1944 case of *Smith v. Allwright* held that discrimination in a party primary on the basis of race violated the Fifteenth Amendment.[13] Today, no credible speaker in the public sphere would contend that the right to vote should be denied, for example, to African-Americans or Jews. Recently, the Court in *Romer v. Evans*[14] made it clear enough that discrimination in voting on the basis of sexual orientation would violate the Equal Protection Clause as being wholly irrational.

The right to a roughly equally weighted vote is of new vintage, the product of *Baker* and *Reynolds*. Perhaps in the early 1960s, social consensus would not have recognized equally weighted voting as an essential political right, meaning that perhaps the Court should not at that time have constitutionalized the principle, leaving it instead to Congress—if it chose—to impose reapportionment through its powers under Section 5 of the Fourteenth Amendment. Or the Court could have recognized a narrower right against continued frustration of majority rule. However, the public quickly embraced the one person, one vote rule after *Reynolds*, and it now is part of conventional thinking about the requirements of a good democracy. At least today, we can recognize the principle at the core of the essential political rights principle.

Three pre-*Baker* cases stand out as violating the core of the essential political rights principle, at least as I understand it today. In *Giles v. Harris*,[15] the Court refused to intervene to prevent wholesale disenfranchisement of African-Americans in Alabama. If the guarantee of the equal political rights principle means anything, it is that the right to vote cannot be denied on the wholly arbitrary ground of race. Another early example is the Court's failure in *Minor v. Happersett* to hold that the denial of the right to vote to women violated the Fourteenth Amendment's Privileges and Immunities Clause.[16] Finally, in the 1959 case of *Lassiter v. Northampton County Board of Elections*,[17] the Court upheld a state's use of a literacy test for voting. Although a literacy test is not wholly irrational if one views voting as a means for choosing the best candidates, the test is unacceptable under the essential political rights principle, which recognizes that politics is about the division of power among political equals; it is not a "test" to find the "best" candidate.

Since *Baker,* the Court has generally protected the core of the essential political rights principle. As chapter 2 explained, the Court essentially overruled *Lassiter* in cases such as *Kramer v. Union Free School District No. 15*,[18] making the imposition of voter qualifications beyond the traditional qualifications usually unconstitutional. *Dunn v. Blumstein*,[19] limiting discrimination against new residents in voting, also fits into the category of protecting the core of the essential political rights principle.

If anything, the Court has overprotected against voter qualifications rules, going well beyond core equality principles to protect contested visions of political equality. Despite urging by their clerks who wanted to preserve the ability of states and localities to impose voter qualifications in less important elections, Chief Justice Warren and Justice Brennan in *Kramer* thus refused to apply anything less than a "compelling state interest" test to restrictions on the right to vote.[20] The Court instead should have examined more closely whether there was social consensus for universal suffrage *in the type of election* at issue in *Kramer,* a school board election in which some people are no doubt more affected by decisions than others. It would have been very useful to know, for example, the common practices in school board elections before *Kramer*: Was the trend toward universal suffrage in these elections or not?

The Court ultimately examined the relevance of the *type* of election at issue in the cases involving special election districts such as a California water district in the *Salyer Land* case.[21] *Salyer Land* would be difficult case for a Court committed to protecting core and only core political equality rights. On the one hand, it appears to violate the core of the equal political rights principle to deny the right to vote in district elections to district residents whose property might be flooded or who could face physical injury from the decisions of the district's elected board. On the other hand, perhaps the Court was right to view the boards as not really government bodies at all.[22] If so, social consensus to protect core political equality rights in elections for *governmental bodies* simply would not apply.

The most egregious modern example of the Court's failure to protect the core of the essential political rights principle is *Bush v. Gore*.[23] There, the Court majority began by recognizing a contested equality right to have votes recounted according to a uniform standard. More important, the Court crafted a remedy that violated a core element of the essential rights principle: the right to have all votes *counted*. The Court did so by refusing to remand the case to the Florida courts for a recount in accordance with a uniform standard. The Court instead allowed the "safe harbor provision" of a federal statute regarding the inability of Congress to challenge a state's electoral votes as trumping the right to have all votes counted.

That core right goes back to the pre-*Baker* case of *United States v. Classic*.[24] When the *Bush* Court prevented the recounting of votes in Florida using a uniform standard, it essentially decided the presidential election, rather than allowing the decision to be determined by votes cast where the voter's intention was clear. This was a serious violation of the core of the principle.

In other cases, the Court has correctly refused to constitutionalize contested claims under the essential political rights principle. Many of these cases challenged traditional voter qualifications such as ex-felon status or residency. The Court in the 1973 case of *Richardson v. Ramirez*[25] thus upheld California's ban on voting by felons. There is a strong argument that the Court's textual analysis of the Fourteenth Amendment does not support the ruling in *Richardson*.[26] Nonetheless, the Court was correct in its result. Felons had traditionally been excluded from voting, and societal views on felon voting in 1973 had not progressed to the point that there was a social consensus that felons constitute competent members of the community who should be entitled to vote.

Attitudes on felon disenfranchisement may be changing, however slowly, with more states moving away from a lifetime ban on ex-felon voting. As Pamela Karlan noted in 2002, "At the time *Richardson v. Ramirez* was decided, a majority of the states disenfranchised nearly all felons for life. Today, by contrast, only eight states permanently disqualify first-time felons and only thirteen states disqualify significant numbers of individuals who have finished serving their sentence."[27]

Perhaps one day the Court should look to such statistics to hold that a lifetime ban on ex-felon voting violates core equality principles. Until that time, the decision should be made (as it has been thus far) by the political branches—Congress, state or local legislative bodies, or citizens through the initiative process—not by the Court. The same may be said of the extension of voting to noncitizens, nonresidents, or those under a certain age. Citizens may well believe that citizen and residency limits are necessary to prevent manipulation of the political processes by those who may bear none of the consequences of voting decisions. Age requirements are justified by a parallel concern that voters must have a basic cognitive capacities and a rudimentary understanding of their interests.

This is not to say that there are no cases close to the line. In *Holt Civic Club v. City of Tuscaloosa*,[28] the Court held that those outside a formal municipal boundary but subject to many of its laws were not denied equal protection when they were excluded from voting in the municipality's elections. The Court viewed the case as a simple one of allowing a "government unit [to] legitimately restrict the right to participate in its political processes to those who reside within its borders."

But the case is more complicated. There is at least some measure of inequality in denying the vote to those subject to a jurisdiction's laws. Any fear of manipulation of the process by the nonresidents is lessened in the *Holt* context: unlike nonresidents from a distant town who potentially could be bused in to vote for a particular candidate but who bear none of the consequences of the voting decisions, the nonresidents in *Holt* bore some of the consequences because they were subject to the municipality's laws.

The problem with recognizing a right of *Holt's* nonresidents to vote is finding a stopping point based on the extraterritorial effects of a jurisdiction's decisions. As the *Holt* majority noted, "the indirect extraterritorial effects of many purely internal municipal actions could conceivably have a heavier impact on surrounding environs than the direct regulation contemplated by" the state statutes imposing the police jurisdiction over the surrounding areas. It is unclear why the non-residents in *Holt* should get the franchise but others seriously affected by the municipality's actions should not. Should New Jersey residents get to vote for New York City's mayor, given the strong effects that New York City policies have on New Jersey? This same stopping point problem could explain why courts should reject challenges to voting restrictions by 16- or 17-year-olds.

Conceivably, the Court in *Holt* could have employed an unmanageable standard to calibrate the right to vote with the extraterritorial effects of a jurisdiction's actions on those who seek the vote.[29] Probably the Court made the right decision by instead leaving the question of voting rights for nonresidents to the political branches, despite the apparent unfairness in the particular case.

THE ANTIPLUTOCRACY PRINCIPLE

The second of the three principles, the antiplutocracy principle, may be stated succinctly as follows:

The government may not condition the ability to participate fundamentally in the electoral process on wealth or the payment of money.

Harper represents the strongest application of this principle's core, which can be stated in the simplest terms—conditioning the vote on the payment of money discriminates against the poor. The Court should equally forbid other voter qualifications closely associated with wealth, such as property ownership.

The core of the antiplutocracy principle has remained essentially unchallenged since *Harper,* except in the special election district cases such as *Salyer Land* approving a "one assessed acre, one vote" principle. The exception, however, has remained cabined there, and given the *Salyer Land* rule limiting the exception to districts that do not have general governmental purposes, the core principle seems safe enough.

Moving from the core *Harper*-like case toward more contested versions of the antiplutocracy principle, things get much more difficult. The central problem is that political participation costs money and therefore those who are poor may argue under the antiplutocracy principle for a *subsidy* to engage in political activity. *Lubin* presents one manifestation of the argument: a poor candidate asked for relief from a government-imposed candidate fee to conduct elections. In particular, the candidate wanted the option of collecting signatures on a petition in lieu of having to pay a filing fee. Moving to a further extreme, some scholars have argued that the antiplutocracy principle requires that government publicly finance candidate election expenses.[30]

One way of drawing a bright line between core and contested antiplutocracy arguments is to use the distinction between *payments* and *subsidies* for political activity. Under this line of argument, the government may not *charge* you to engage in political activity, but the government need not *subsidize* privately financed political activities. With that bright line, *Harper* and *Lubin* are correctly decided, but the claim of a constitutional right to public campaign financing should be rejected.

On closer inspection, this argument fails. When the government prints ballots and opens polling places in general elections, it subsidizes the act of voting. Before the adoption of the secret (or Australian) ballot, voters had to come up with their own ballots, and usually used a ballot printed at private expense by a political party.[31] When the government runs party primaries, it subsidizes not only voting but also acts of political association with the political parties. Certainly the government could not simply stop holding general or primary elections or quit printing ballots on the grounds that it is simply refusing to subsidize political activity. There is certain political activity that we expect the government to subsidize.

Because the payment/subsidy line does not work in delineating the core and contested elements of the antiplutocracy principle, there is no substitute for a close evaluation of the nature of the political activity, the burden that the cost of that activity places on those without adequate resources, and social consensus over the appropriateness of public subsidy of the activity.

The beginning of this chapter contrasted *Harper* and *Lubin* using these tools. At bottom, it is hard to believe that reasonably set candidate filing fees would appall most Americans in the way that poll taxes certainly would today. Claims that the Constitution should require full public financing of electoral campaigns likewise go too far. Again, campaigning is important political activity. But a government decision not to finance campaigns does not prevent campaigns from going forward. Most candidates with a chance of success should be able to raise at least some funds, and there are some methods of campaigning that are, or are nearly, costless. To the extent a candidate is successful initially using modest funds, her success should attract additional funds. In addition, there is no consensus (or near-consensus) that private financing of political campaigns is *constitutionally objectionable* like a poll tax, even if (as is sometimes claimed) a majority of Americans would support public financing of congressional campaigns.

THE COLLECTIVE ACTION PRINCIPLE

The third of the principles, the collective action principle, may be succinctly stated as follows:

The government must not impose, and must remove if imposed, unreasonable impediments on individuals who wish to organize into groups to engage in collective action for political purposes.

To understand the third equality principle, I begin with insights of economic theory concerning the ability of individuals to come together to organize for political action. Economists conceive of politics as taking place in a political "market" in which organized interest groups compete with one another to demand goods, services, and the implementation of their ideological agendas. The outcome of this struggle is determined by relative group strength, as expressed through the resources, or political capital, available for political competition: the greater a group's political capital, the more it secures from the state.[32]

Political capital depends not so much upon intensity of belief as upon the ability to marshal political resources, be it money, participation in a march, or something else. Marshaling resources, however, is often difficult. People in large groups tend to "free ride," rather than contribute to provide a public good (such as a political outcome) that is shared by all.[33] Consider a poor person deciding whether or not to participate in a government rally demanding greater government benefits for the poor. The individual may reason that her individual participation in a mass rally is not likely to affect the chances that the benefits to the poor will be provided. If the government provides the benefits to the poor, she will enjoy it whether she participates in the rally or not. It therefore does not appear individually rational for her to participate in the rally. The problem, of course, is that if enough people follow this "logic of collective action," the rally never takes place and the government benefit is not provided, making the individual and others like her worse off.

Organizers of unorganized or poorly organized diffuse groups face this built-in disadvantage in organizing for political action. Even absent legal impediments, it is extremely difficult to organize into an effective political group, much less into a new political party to challenge the Democrats and Republicans.[34] But on top of such difficulty, government laws may

make it much more difficult for nascent or latent political groups or organizers of a new political party. The most important example here is a law
imposing tough requirements on new parties desiring to be listed on gov-
ernment-printed election ballots.

The government may advance all sorts of reasons for requirements that
impede collective political action. For example, the government may claim
that tough ballot access requirements are justified on grounds that long
ballots confuse voters. Sometimes, however, the real reason "the government" imposes laws burdening collective political activity is to forestall
political competition. "The government" is made up of elected officials
who might act in their own self-interest to preserve or further their own
political power. To the extent a new political party could threaten the existing power structure, government officials have a self-interest in discour-
aging it.

The third equality principle—what I term the collective action principle—recognizes these self-interest concerns and requires the government
not to impose, and indeed to remove if imposed, unreasonable impediments on individuals who wish to organize into groups to engage in collective action for political purposes. It is essential to a democracy that
takes equality seriously that those who are in power not pass laws for the
purpose of protecting their own positions through a stifling of political
competition. This is a position that the Court should recognize regardless
of current social views, though I believe most Americans in any case
would recognize that self-dealing by politicians in crafting the rules for
electoral competition is improper.

The "ballot access cases" are at the core of the collective action principle. The leading case here is the 1968 case of *Williams v. Rhodes*.[35] In
Williams, two minor political parties challenged Ohio's extremely restrictive ballot access laws that made it virtually impossible for a new political
party to have its candidate's name placed on the ballot in presidential elections. Ohio sought to justify its law as a means to "validly promote a two-
party system in order to encourage compromise and political stability."[36]
The Warren Court rejected the argument, noting that the law favored "two
particular political parties—the Republicans and the Democrats—and in
effect tend[ed] to give them a complete monopoly"; "[t]here is, of course,
no reason why two parties should retain a permanent monopoly on the
right to have people vote for or against them. Competition in ideas and
governmental policies is at the core of our electoral process and of the
First Amendment freedoms."[37]

Yet new parties have not always prevailed in the ballot access cases. For example, in *Jenness v. Fortson*,[38] the Court upheld a Georgia law requiring a candidate for office who did not win a major party primary to obtain the signatures of 5 percent of the number of registered voters at the previous general election for the office in question in order to get his name on the general election ballot. The Court recognized "an important state interest in requiring some preliminary showing of a significant modicum of support before printing the name of a political organization's candidate on the ballot—the interest, if no other, in avoiding confusion, deception, and even frustration of the democratic process at the general election."[39]

Jenness does not necessarily violate the collective action principle. The principle, as I have stated it, prevents imposition of only *unreasonable* impediments to collective political action; the question in *Jenness* is whether Georgia's ballot access requirements were unreasonable. As I explain in the next section, answering that question requires a weighing of equality interests against other interests.

Moving away from the core of the collective action principle toward more contested claims, the cases get much more controversial relative to the heart of issues related to race and elections. Some argue for a contested version of the collective action principle, what we might call the "fair fight corollary":

In the face of strong evidence that a law governing the political process has consistently prevented a politically cohesive and sizable group from gaining a non-trivial share of political power, the government must change the law to allow conditions for more proportional representation of the group's interest in the political process.

The collective action principle requires that the government *remove impediments* to collective action; the fair fight corollary moves more controversially by requiring the government to take steps to *actively encourage* groups to engage in political collective action. *City of Mobile v. Bolden*[40] featured plaintiffs advancing just such an argument.

To the extent that the *Bolden* plaintiffs could prove that the City of Mobile adopted at-large voting to *intentionally* discriminate against African-American residents by making it harder for them to organize for political action, the case fits comfortably within the collective action principle: the Court must remove the government-imposed impediment to effective political action by requiring districting or some other method (such as cumulative voting) that allows for effective collective action.

But if we take the case as the Court took it—as one where the plaintiffs could not prove that the City of Mobile instituted at-large voting *with the intent* to discriminate against African-American residents—the question posed was whether the Constitution requires that the government take affirmative steps to undo *unintended effects* that leave a political group with much less than a proportional share of political power.

As noted in chapter 2, the Court need not have decided against the plaintiffs in *Bolden* out of fear that the opinion would require proportional representation across the board. Using a sufficiently murky standard, the Court could have required *more* proportionality without *strict* proportionality.

But the Court was right in *Bolden* not to constitutionalize the fair fight corollary. In the first place, there was not in 1980 and there does not appear today to be any consensus that rough proportionality among interest groups (or, more narrowly, among racial and ethnic groups) is required as a condition of political equality. Democracies widely vary as to the extent their electoral systems use proportional representation. Facing highly contested claims of equality that go beyond core principles, the Court should not impose a solution favoring for the foreseeable future one side in this contentious debate.

Justice Marshall argued otherwise in his *Bolden* dissent, calling the imposition of an intentional discrimination standard for constitutional vote dilution cases "an attempt to bury the legitimate concerns of the minority beneath the soil of a doctrine almost as impermeable as it is specious."[41] He concluded by suggesting that the decision could lead minorities not to "respect political channels seeking redress."[42] But as strong a moral argument as Justice Marshall may have had that the creation of a black majority district was normatively desirable, his views certainly did not represent a consensus about the meaning of equality in the United States in 1982.

Second, and more important, there is a great danger that the constitutionalization of racial or ethnic politics could have serious unintended negative consequences for society later on down the line. The extreme example here is Lebanon.[43] The Lebanese constitution fixed power relations at the 1940 level. It mandated that the prime minister must be a Sunni Muslim, the president a Maronite Christian, and so forth. As Muslim, particularly Shiite, population growth outstripped that of the Christian population, the entrenched powers blocked any change to the constitution or other political arrangements. This "consociational" arrangement has led to societal breakdown, civil war, and foreign invasion.

I have great sympathy with the claim of plaintiffs for some proportionality in the *Bolden* context and with the fair fight corollary generally. But the decision to impose highly contested views of equality not at the core of equality principles should be left to the *legislative bodies*, where the political process can work to craft a solution that is more easily reversible. Indeed, following *Bolden*, Congress amended section 2 of the Voting Rights Act in effect to legislate the fair fight corollary in the context of banning at-large voting when it served to dilute minority voting strength. The next chapter argues in favor of the Court's deferring to Congress's decision to pass and amend the Voting Rights Act to provide for rough proportionality.

Legislative rather than Court imposition of the fair fight corollary will be easier to reverse if it is desirable to do so. Indeed, the Voting Rights Act has a built-in sunset provision that in 2007 that will end some important provisions of the act unless Congress reenacts them. The provisions should be reenacted assuming the persistence, at least in some places, of racially polarized voting,[44] but the sunset provision forces an appropriate close and contemporary reexamination of the issue.

Balancing Core Equality Rights with Government Interests

Table 3-1 sets forth examples showing how the Court has ruled in core and contested applications of the three equality principles. The pattern shows a good deal of inconsistency with the ideas set forth in this chapter. Cases in which the Court constitutionalized the core and failed to constitutionalize contested claims are consistent with this chapter. On the other hand, had the ideas in this chapter been followed, cases in which the Court constitutionalized contested claims were wrong. As for cases in which the Court failed to constitutionalize the core, the analysis remains incomplete. In such cases, identifying an equality interest as in the core is just the first of two steps. The second step is a careful balancing of interests, to which I now turn.

Cases raising political equality issues come in three basic varieties. In the first kind of case, plaintiff challenges a law on equality grounds and the government defends the law on the basis that plaintiff's claimed equality interest is not entitled to protection. For example, in *Reynolds*, the

TABLE 3–1
Core and Contested Equality Principles

Equality Principle	Supreme Court Action			
	Constitutionalizing Core	Not Constitutionalizing Core	Constitutionalizing Contested Claim	Not Constitutionalizing Contested Claim
Essential political rights	*Classic, Reynolds*	*Bush v. Gore* (failure to remand)	*Bush v. Gore* (uniform counting)	*Holt*
Antiplutocracy	*Harper*	*Salyer Land* (if viewed as gov't.)	*Lubin*	
Collective action	*Williams v. Rhodes*	*Timmons, Munro*		*City of Mobile v. Bolden*

states whose reapportionment plans were challenged argued that the Constitution did not mandate population equality. The City of Mobile made a similar argument in *Bolden* in the context of the challenge to the city's at-large voting scheme.

In the first kind of case, the Court should identify whether the equality claim is in the core or is contested. If the equality claim is in the core, the Court should reject the state's argument and accept plaintiff's argument by constitutionalizing the principle. If the equality argument is contested, the Court should reject plaintiff's argument but leave room for Congress or other legislative bodies to impose the contested equality concept through legislation.

In the second kind of case, plaintiff challenges a law on equality grounds and the government defends the law on the basis that plaintiff's equality interest is outweighed by some other government interest. *Jenness* is a case along these lines; the state of Georgia asserted an interest in preventing "confusion, deception, and even frustration of the democratic process at the general election" in asking the Court to uphold its ballot access requirements. When the plaintiff's equality claim is at the core of equality principles, the Court must engage in a careful balancing as I describe below. When the equality claim is contested, the Court should not engage in balancing but should simply reject plaintiff's claim, again leaving room for the government to later enact the contested equality principle. This is how the Court should have dealt with *Lubin*.

In the third kind of case, plaintiff challenges a law that the government claims to have enacted to promote political equality. Plaintiff may claim that the legislature lacked authority to pass the law or that the law violates some other constitutional or statutory right of the plaintiff. The next chapter considers the third type of case in detail. When the government acts to protect the core, plaintiff can raise no successful argument against the law to the extent that it is constitutionally *required*. As for government action promoting a contested equality principle (as in a case such as *Bolden* or the campaign finance case of *Buckley v. Valeo*), the Court must again engage in a skeptical, careful balancing, a balancing that differs from the careful balancing I call for in the second case in that it sometimes defers to legislative value judgments about the meaning of equality.

Table 3-2 summarizes the three kinds of cases and the Court's proper response in each case. In the remainder of this chapter, I consider the careful balancing the Court should employ in the second kind of case, where a plaintiff raises an equality claim in the core and the government argues that some other interest trumps that core equality right.

Invading the Core: State Interests or Self-Interest?

The careful balancing that I call for in these cases differs significantly from the balancing that the Court has engaged in thus far in its election law cases. The Court's balancing in this second category of cases has been deferential to the government, particularly in its failure to require any proof that the government's interest is genuine and significant enough to trump a core equality principle. My proposed balancing is skeptical because of the self-interest problems that arise when government officials set the rules for electoral competition. It requires strong proof of the need for and significance of the government interest.

I illustrate the contrast by focusing primarily on ballot access cases and related cases involving the government's providing different benefits to the Democrats and Republicans on the one hand, and minor parties or independent candidates on the other. I begin with what the Court has done, and then explain how the balancing that I propose differs from the Court's approach.

The Court reached different results in *Williams v. Rhodes* and *Jenness v. Fortson*, even though the same core equality principle—the collective action principle as manifested in the claim of a minor party or independent candidate to ballot access—was at play. In both cases the Court engaged in

TABLE 3–2

Types of Cases Raising the Equality Issue and the Court's Proper Response

Type of Claim	Court's Proper Response if Equality Issue	
	Is in Core	Is Contested
Plaintiff claims equality right/ government disagrees	Constitutionalize (*Harper*)	Reject constitutionalization (*City of Mobile v. Bolden*)
Plaintiff claims equality right/government advances competing interest	Careful balancing (*Munro, Timmons*)	Reject constitutionalization
Plaintiff challenges law the government claims promotes political equality	Reject plaintiff's claim	Careful balancing, deferential to value judgments but skeptical of legislative self-dealing

a balancing of interests, but the Court in *Jenness* distinguished *Williams* based upon both the interests asserted by the state and the magnitude of the burden on the party or individual seeking ballot access.

In *Williams,* the Court rejected as illegitimate any protection of the two-party system and gave little credence to the argument that the Ohio access requirements promoted political stability. It also viewed the Ohio rule as making it very difficult for either new popular parties or old small parties to obtain ballot access. In *Jenness,* by contrast, the Court viewed the Georgia ballot access restriction as less onerous and simply supposed—with apparently very little thought[45]—that the restrictions there could be justified as preventing "confusion, deception, and even frustration of the democratic process."[46]

If *Williams* represents skepticism about ballot access requirements, *Jenness* represents deference to legislative decisions. There is no question that deference has won out in the Court's subsequent ballot access decisions. Cases such as *Anderson v. Celebrezze*[47] and *Munro v. Socialist Workers Party*[48] firmly establish that there is "no litmus-paper test" for judging the constitutionality of ballot access and related restrictions. In rhetoric, the Court states that the level of scrutiny rises on a sliding scale with the extent of the burden placed upon the minor party or independent candidate.[49] In fact, the Court shows considerable deference to barely defended or defensible state interests.

But the deference the Court has recognized in this area extends far beyond the sliding scale approach. If *Jenness* was implicit in not requiring evidence that ballot access restrictions were necessary to prevent "confusion, deception or frustration of the democratic process," *Munro* made the holding explicit. In the face of an argument that Washington State's new ballot access restrictions at issue in *Munro* were justified to prevent voter "confusion," plaintiffs argued that the state failed to prove that a longer ballot containing the names of minor party candidate would in fact cause any confusion. The Court flatly rejected the need for some evidence: "To require States to prove actual voter confusion, ballot overcrowding, or the presence of frivolous candidacies as a predicate to the imposition of reasonable ballot access restrictions would invariably lead to endless court battles over the sufficiency of the 'evidence' marshaled by a State to prove the predicate."[50]

As if the Court could not get more deferential to state interests in this area, it did so in 1997 in a way that implicitly overruled part of *Williams v. Rhodes*. In *Timmons v. Twin Cities Area New Party*,[51] the Court considered whether the state of Minnesota could prevent a minor party from endorsing the Democratic Party's nominee for the state legislature. That practice, called "fusion," is a tactic minor parties use to increase their popularity and leverage their political power in the few jurisdictions, such as New York, that permit it.

The Supreme Court upheld the constitutionality of Minnesota's antifusion law. Among other arguments,[52] the Court accepted the state's contention that "political stability is best served through a healthy two-party system."[53] The Court remarked that the "traditional two-party system . . . temper[s] the destabilizing effects of party-splintering and excessive factionalism."[54] Six justices signed this opinion, and a seventh expressed his willingness to entertain such an argument in a case where he believed the issue was presented properly.

The common thread that the above cases share is that although the Court appears to have "balanced" in the ballot access context, the "balancing" lowered the level of scrutiny to be applied whenever the Court viewed the ballot access rules (or related rules governing minor parties) as imposing only a small burden on the parties. In such cases, the state need merely assert amorphous interests such as "preventing confusion" or self-serving interests such as protection of the two-party system in order to justify the infringement on the minor party's or independent candidate's equality interests. Moreover, the state need do no more than simply posit a plausible connection between the interest it asserts and the need for the restriction without having to prove the challenged measure actually furthers the state's purported goal.

Careful Balancing as the Better Alternative

I agree with the Court's jurisprudence that a balancing of interests is required when a plaintiff's assertion of a political equality right is defended by the state's assertion of a government interest.[55] This is no small concession, for there is a strong movement among election law scholars (chronicled in chapter 5) to eschew balancing in favor of "structural" or "functional" approaches to the political process.

But beyond agreeing that some "balancing" is permissible, I believe there is very little to commend the balancing as it currently takes place. Although the "no litmus-paper" sliding scale approach has an aura of flexibility—a trait I praise in chapter 2's discussion of judicially unmanageable standards—it is flexible in the wrong place. I advocate flexibility in chapter 2 in *how* the Court articulates the particular equality interest it creates in a new line of cases; flexibility there allows the Court to learn from future lower court decisions varied ways of regulating the political process without causing unintended consequences. In contrast, flexibility here means that the Court automatically affords *less protection to a core equality right* (here, the collective action principle) whenever it concludes that the government has not infringed "too much" on the right. The Court would almost surely not tolerate such a sliding scale in other election contexts involving core equality rights. For example, would it allow a poll tax lower than $8.33 (the 2002 equivalent to the $1.50 poll tax in Virginia in 1966) on grounds that the payment is not "too much"? The answer is almost certainly no.

More important, the Court is wrong in failing to require *evidence* of some causal connection between the restriction on ballot access and the government's asserted interest. It may well be that a long ballot could confuse voters. The revelations coming out of the Florida 2000 election bear this out to some extent. In Duval County, for example, instructions told voters to vote every page. Because the number of candidates on the ballot for president was large, the list extended to two pages. The result: 26,000 voters of that county cast invalid votes for president, most of them overvotes.[56]

Of course, the Duval County confusion resulted from *the combination* of the long ballot and the incorrect instruction. There is a good argument for eliminating the instruction over curtailing the right to ballot access. My point is simply that a concern over confusion cannot be dismissed out of hand but must be examined by a court. In the face of strong evidence that a law impinging on a core equality right is necessary to serve an important interest put forward by the legislature, the Court will have to make a difficult judgment call. And in making that call the Court will have to consider the strength of the competing claims.

A legislative body imposing a ballot access restriction might officially list "confusion prevention" as the rationale for the law but really have in mind self-interest concerns. It is not so much that minor parties have the real potential in most jurisdictions to gain seats in the legislature; they usually do not, although Jesse Ventura's win in the 1998 gubernatorial race in Minnesota (home of the antifusion law) proves that third party prospects are not inevitably hopeless. But minor parties can upset the balance of power between the parties, sometimes with a minor party drawing enough votes away from one major party candidate to give the win to the other major party candidates. Because this possibility that the minor party could be such a "spoiler" (as Ralph Nader is asserted by some Democrats to have been in 2000), legislators from one or both parties may wish to make ballot access rules difficult for minor parties purely out of self-interest.

More generally, the problem of self-interest potentially lurks behind legislative actions that deal with the electoral process. Courts have to distinguish election laws that impinge on core equality values to serve an important government interest from those in which the asserted government interest is feigned in order to serve legislative self-interest. The Court cannot delve into the heads of legislators to discern their "real" motivations; sitting legislators may have different motivations in passing the same law. Instead, the Court must take a close look at the objective evidence supporting the stated rationale.

Some rationales are simply improper. By definition, the government does not get to trump a core equality right on grounds that it seeks to elevate the interests of those already in political power over those who would seek a share of that power. Sadly, however, this is exactly what the Court has blessed in the *Timmons* case. The Court said it was legitimate to enact laws to favor the "two-party system," which *Williams* aptly described as simply code words for such laws that favor the Democrats and Republicans.[57]

Nor in the absence of convincing evidence can it be argued that a two-party system is necessary for stability or to prevent factionalism. Despite the repeated claim that the two-party system promotes political stability, the contention remains unproven. It is true that the United States is a two-party system and that politics here has been relatively stable, if stability means orderly transitions between governments. But it is not clear that the two-party system *causes* stability. Proof of instability in countries with many parties does not itself prove that the two-party system leads to stability. Indeed, Ronald Rogowski, examining the empirical evidence across countries, concludes that proportional representation, which tends toward multiple-party systems, "best guarantees the *stability* of democratic policy."[58]

Similarly, the claim that the two-party system prevents interest group politics fares poorly in the era of capital-intensive campaigns. The Democratic and Republican parties' activities in raising unprecedented amounts of largely unregulated "soft money" donations belie the antifactionalist contention. The system we have seen in current years has been little more than legalized money laundering in which candidates for federal office, who otherwise would be limited by the Federal Election Campaign Act from raising more than $1,000 from individuals or $5,000 from a political action committee per election, raise huge amounts of soft money from corporations, unions, and wealthy individuals. The parties serve as the conduits for the sale of access by politicians for money to benefit their campaigns.[59] At the very least, the prevalence of soft money raises serious questions about whether the parties are in fact all-encompassing coalitions that prevent interest groups from seeking their narrow agendas.

In sum, cases such as *Jenness, Munro,* and *Timmons* may have been wrongly decided. I say "may have been" rather than "were" because we do not have enough evidence of (1) whether the interests put forward in the case to trump the equality right are adequately supported by the evidence; and (2) if so, how the Court should have engaged in the careful balancing of the rights. Without a doubt, there is good cause for concern that these cases were wrongly decided and have had negative effects on the political equality rights of third parties and independent candidates.[60]

Conclusion

Stripping away the facially neutral label of "process theory" reveals that the Court is making important normative value judgments about the requirements for political equality. These determinations have something of an ad hoc character to them, and the first part of this chapter aimed at defining an alternative normative framework for adjudicating political equality claims.

The chapter began the task of delineating a division of labor between the Court and legislative bodies over rules that promote political equality. The Court will serve the country best by constitutionalizing core, and only core, political equality rights. The core will perhaps grow over time, and part of the Court's task will be to consider whether ideas about equality have changed over the years so as to expand our notions of core political equality. Just as the one person, one vote standard has moved from a contested fringe to the very core of the essential political rights principle, we may some day see the fair fight corollary of the collective action principle also move into the core. Until that time, however, it is best for the Court to leave such a contentious issue to the political process, which, as we will see in the next chapter, appears to have worked very well in this area.

Finally, in cases where a plaintiff asserts a core equality right and the state asserts a countervailing government interest, the Court has erred in engaging in deferential balancing favoring the state. Balancing is required, but it must be a skeptical balancing that realistically recognizes the self-interest problem that inheres in government laws being passed by those whose livelihoods are affected directly by the laws.

4

Deferring to Political Branches on Contested Equality Claims

Who Decides the Validity of Contested Political Equality Measures and Why?

Voters in Missouri pass a law limiting individual campaign contributions to state officials to amounts as low as $100.[1] Congress decides to suspend state-imposed literacy tests for voting in state and local elections six years after the Supreme Court holds that such tests, if fairly administered, do not violate the Equal Protection Clause of the Fourteenth Amendment.[2] The New York legislature, in order to comply with the U.S. Justice Department's interpretation of the Voting Rights Act and to satisfy demands of its members to protect themselves and gain partisan advantage during the redistricting process, draws majority-minority districts that split a cohesive religious group into two districts.[3]

At first glance, these three actions have little in common beyond embracing the field of election law. In the first case, voters act through the initiative process to curb the role of money in elections. In the second case, Congress acts to impose a national standard for voter qualifications. In the third case, a state legislature pursues its own self-interested goals in redistricting while complying with federally imposed districting standards.

The common thread running through each action is that political actors have come together—at least arguably—to impose a contested version of political equality. There is (or *was,* in the case of literacy tests) no consensus or near-consensus that political equality requires very low campaign contribution limits, a ban on literacy tests in voting, or the creation of majority-minority districts.

If my argument in chapter 3 is correct, the lack of social consensus means that a plaintiff should not be successful in a constitutional challenge to a jurisdiction's failure to impose such measures. The question posed in this chapter is how the Court should approach challenges to political actors' *voluntary* decisions to impose a contested version of political equality.

It appears initially that the Court should not have a basis for striking down such legislation. The fact that a government action imposing political equality is not constitutionally *required* in no way indicates that it should be constitutionally *prohibited*. The problem, however, is that sometimes such legislation may run afoul of certain constitutional provisions. For example, the Missouri campaign finance law might be held to violate the First Amendment's protection against government abridgement of free speech and association. Congress's imposition of restrictions on states' voter qualifications may exceed congressional power. And a state's creation of a majority-minority district might impinge upon the political equality rights of others, such as by diluting the votes of other groups of voters. Moreover, in all cases where a legislative body acts (as opposed to the people acting through the initiative process), there is a danger that the legislature will take action for self-interested reasons but purport to act in the name of political equality.

The competing constitutional values at stake when a legislative body enacts a contested version of political equality suggest (as in the case of core claims) that the Court must engage in a *careful balancing* of interests. The balancing here is somewhat different, however, from balancing the Court should conduct when the state comes forward with a reason not to impose a *core* equality condition. In the case of a legislative body's voluntary imposition of a *contested* vision of political equality, the Court should be *deferential to (but not a rubber stamp of) the value judgments about the balance between equality and other interests* made by the legislative body while at the same time be *skeptical about the means by which the legislative body purports to enforce the contested political equality right.*

Court deference to value judgments about the balance between political equality and other interests is appropriate for reasons suggested by the previous chapter. Because of fears of ossification and entrenchment, it is unwise for the Court to constitutionalize contested equality claims.

But those fears of ossification and entrenchment are much less severe when such measures emerge from the political process rather than the courts. Legislative enactment requires the support of at least a majority of legislators (or voters, in the case of the initiative process) and is relatively easily reversed through a new vote of legislators (or voters). California voters, for example, recently approved a ballot measure (placed on the ballot by the California legislature) that overturned a stringent campaign finance initiative voters passed just a few years before and replaced it with less stringent rules. And legislators who pass unpopular or ineffective laws promoting contested equality claims may face the wrath of voters at reelection time.

The relative ease of change (at least compared to overturning constitutional decisions of the Supreme Court—I do not want to overstate the ease of passing legislation) and the large number of jurisdictions (not just states but also counties, cities, and other governmental bodies) that may pass laws promoting contested versions of equality allow for a great deal of experimentation that will be healthy for the democratic process. The experimentation may lead to the emergence of a new consensus about the meaning of political equality in a particular area. Perhaps, for example, if enough states enact laws providing for public financing of state campaigns, such financing will eventually become a core equality requirement. Sometimes the pursuit of equality may have negative consequences in other areas of political life, and jurisdictions can learn from one another about what works and does not work.

Court deference to value judgments about equality made by political branches is not a license for the political branches to trample other constitutional provisions. The Court still must maintain its role in protecting the core of those other provisions as well, as I explore in detail below.

Moreover, the Court must be especially careful of measures that legislatures enact in the name of political equality. The potential for self-interested legislation lurks behind all election laws and the courts must skeptically inquire whether the means of achieving equality closely fit the ends of the law. The skepticism serves as a substitute for a probe of legislative "motive" in passing these election laws.

This skepticism is not warranted in the case of initiatives, however, where legislative self-interest is absent. In that case, the Court should be even more deferential to the value judgments about political equality made by voters, without regard to the self-interest problem.[4] Thus far, however, the Court has refused to hold that laws passed through the initiative process should be subject to any different standard of review than those passed by a legislature.[5]

The remainder of this chapter pursues the appropriate form of balance in three important contexts: campaign finance regulation and its potential clash with the First Amendment; congressional action to further political equality consistent with Congress's enforcement powers under the Fourteenth and Fifteenth Amendments; and (federal, state, and local) legislation that seeks to redress one form of political equality only to run the risk of creating new inequalities.

Campaign Finance and the Clash between Equality and Liberty

Campaign finance regulation remains an arena full of clashes between those who argue that the role of money in politics must be reduced to assure political equality and those who argue that any limit on the use of money in political campaigns severely infringes on the freedoms of speech and association guaranteed by the First Amendment. As we shall see, the Supreme Court has sided, though inconsistently, against the equality rationale and in favor of a "free market" version of the First Amendment.

Cass Sunstein has eloquently made the equality argument for campaign finance regulation. Noting that political equality (but not economic equality) "is time-honored in the American constitutional tradition," Sunstein argues that "[e]fforts to redress economic inequalities, or to ensure that they are not turned to political inequalities, should not be seen as impermissible redistribution, or as the introduction of government regulation into a place where it did not exist before."[6]

L. A. Powe, Jr., has made a powerful argument against the equality rationale. Powe argues that

> [t]o surrender the interests of individual autonomy and to attempt to tone down a debate (or one side of it) in the interests of enhancing the [political] marketplace is to give up something that is directly traceable to the First Amendment in order to achieve a speculative gain. It is attempted on the speculative basis that a legislature knows at what points the problem of market failure is likely to surface and that enhancement is an effective means of avoiding them. . . . Furthermore, it rests on an assumption that less speech may well be better than more, an assumption that appears wildly at odds with the normal First Amendment belief that more speech is better.[7]

Finally, some commentators like Owen Fiss see *within* the First Amendment itself principles that support the equality rationale for campaign finance regulation. Fiss argues against the "autonomy" version of the First Amendment and instead asks whether the speech enriches public debate. "Speech is protected when (and only when) it does, and precisely because it does, not because it is an exercise of autonomy." Fiss adds that "[w]hat the phrase 'the freedom of speech' in the first amendment refers to is a social state of affairs, not the action of an individual or institution."[8]

This debate is important and complex, and I do not purport to make the case here that the equality rationale for campaign finance regulation should prevail over arguments like Powe's, representing what I will call the "First Amendment hawk" position. The question instead that I consider in this part is whether the Court or the political branches should determine how to strike the balance between these equality and liberty interests in campaign finance regulation.

I begin with a detailed history of the Court's inconsistent views on both the equality rationale and the proper amount of deference to legislative judgments in the campaign finance arena. I then consider how the Court properly should have handled these cases. In particular, I argue that the Court has shown not enough deference to the value judgments made by legislatures and the people about how to balance equality interests with the First Amendment, yet at times has given too much deference to bare legislative assertions that the means legislatures have advanced to promote equality actually can accomplish such a goal.

BUCKLEY v. VALEO: THE COURT'S REJECTION OF THE EQUALITY RATIONALE FOR CAMPAIGN FINANCE REGULATION

In 1976, the Supreme Court decided *Buckley v. Valeo*,[9] a case that set the ground rules for the constitutionality of campaign finance laws for a generation. The case concerned the 1974 Amendments to the Federal Election Campaign Act (or "FECA"). The FECA Amendments were complex, establishing (among other things) limits on the amounts that individuals or organizations could contribute to candidates (contribution limits), limits on the amounts that individuals or organizations could spend to support or oppose candidates for federal office independent of candidates (independent expenditure limits),[10] public financing for major presidential candidates, and the creation of the Federal Election Commission (FEC).

The Court, in probably its longest *per curiam* (unsigned) opinion in history, covering 138 pages in the *U.S. Reports* (along with an additional 83 pages of concurring and dissenting opinions), upheld the FECA's contribution limits, struck down the expenditure limits, upheld the public financing system, and struck down the means for the appointment of members of the FEC.

Most notable for our purposes here is the Court's decision to uphold the campaign contribution limits but to strike down the expenditure limits. Although recognizing that any law regulating campaign financing was subject to the "exacting scrutiny required by the First Amendment,"[11] the Court mandated divergent treatment of contributions and expenditures for two reasons. First, the Court held that campaign expenditures were core political speech, but a limit on the amount of campaign contributions only marginally restricted a contributor's ability to send a message of support for a candidate.[12] Thus, expenditures were entitled to greater constitutional protection than contributions. Second, the *Buckley* Court recognized only the interests in prevention of corruption and the appearance of corruption as justifying infringement on First Amendment rights.

The Court held that large contributions raise the problem of corruption "[t]o the extent that large contributions are given to secure a political *quid pro quo* from current and potential officeholders."[13] But truly independent expenditures do not raise the same danger of corruption because a *quid pro quo* is more difficult if politician and spender cannot communicate about the expenditure.[14]

With the corruption interest having failed to justify a limit upon independent expenditures, the Court considered the alternative argument that expenditure limits were justified by "the ancillary governmental interest in equalizing the relative ability of individuals and groups to influence the outcome of elections."[15] In one of the most famous (some would say notorious) sentences in *Buckley,* the Court rejected this equality rationale for campaign finance regulation, at least in the context of expenditure limits: "[T]he concept that government may restrict the speech of some elements of our society in order to enhance the relative voice of others is wholly foreign to the First Amendment."[16] The strong statement, in which seven of the eight justices deciding the case concurred (Justice Stevens, new to the Court, did not participate), appeared to leave no room for equality rationales for campaign finance regulation.

The drafting history, however, reveals much greater division on the equality question than the final draft shows.[17] Five justices—Chief Justice

Burger, and Justices Stewart, Powell, (then-Justice) Rehnquist, and Black-mun—could be characterized, like L. A. Powe, as First Amendment hawks who utterly rejected the equality rationale. In contrast, three justices—Brennan, Marshall, and White—were more deferential to a congressional determination that the FECA, by limiting the role of money in politics, furthered First Amendment values and could potentially promote political equality.

Before argument, Justice Powell had rejected the equality rationale. His clerk's bench memorandum noted that Congress enacted the FECA as "an attempt to lower barriers to political competition in order to increase the range of voter choice. But the attempt to open access for the many necessarily involves limiting the power of the few to exercise rights of speech and association protected by the Constitution." After the words "open access for the many," Justice Powell added these handwritten remarks: "Are the 'many' really denied access now? This has not been my experience in campaigns." Justice Powell also noted in a preconference memo that the media exception to the law (by which the media were exempt from limits on expenditures favoring or opposing candidates for federal office)[18] "tends to exacerbate the disadvantages this Act imposes on challengers and unpopular figures. This is not irrelevant in light of the vast concentration of media power in this country since the advent of electronics."

At the justices' conference following oral argument, Justice White voiced his "hesitat[ion] to differ with Congress." Justice Brennan remarked, along the lines later echoed by Owen Fiss, that the FECA promoted First Amendment values and that "self-gov[ernmen]t is arguably furthered" by the law. Justice Marshall expressed his agreement with Justice Brennan, although he took the position that the limits on a candidate's expenditures of personal or family money were unconstitutional. In contrast, the First Amendment hawks emphatically disagreed with Justice Brennan's position. Justice Rehnquist responded to Justice Brennan that people who argue that the FECA "*furthers* 1st A[mendment] values argue an absurdity."

Chief Justice Burger assigned to Justice Stewart the task of writing the portion of the opinion concerning the constitutionality of the contribution and expenditure limits. After the initial circulation of Justice Stewart's draft that included the language rejecting the equality rationale, Justice Brennan wrote a memorandum to the other justices expressing doubts about the invalidation of the limit on independent expenditures. Justice Brennan nonetheless stated his leaning toward agreeing with the draft that the independent expenditure limits were unconstitutional; his reason was a concern over vagueness of the statute, not a rejection of the equality rationale.[19]

Justice Brennan also indicated that he intended to adhere to his vote in conference to sustain limits on expenditures by candidates from personal or family funds, and nothing in the papers reveals why Justice Brennan ultimately reversed his decision on this point. Finally, Justice Brennan stated that Justice Stewart's draft "seems to me unnecessarily to downplay the invasion of First Amendment freedoms, rather than frankly to acknowledge the seriousness of the invasion but justify it by the compelling governmental interests supporting contribution limits."

Justices White and Marshall came even closer than Justice Brennan to embracing the equality rationale throughout the drafting process and in their separate opinions. In his partial dissent, Justice White noted that a limit on the spending of a candidate's personal funds "helps to assure that only individuals with a modicum of support from others will be viable candidates. This in turn would tend to discourage any notion that the outcome of elections is primarily a function of money."[20] Justice Marshall argued in his separate opinion for the constitutionality of the limit on the use of a candidate's personal and family funds,[21] noting "the interest [in promoting equality that has been derided by the Court] is more precisely the interest in promoting the reality and appearance of equal access to the political arena."[22] Justice Marshall did not explain why this rationale did not apply equally to the regulation of individual expenditures.

In the end, a vote on the equality question that appeared to be a 7-1 rejection in fact was a more closely divided 5-3 vote. The five First Amendment hawks appeared to give no deference to congressional determinations about how to balance liberty and equality concerns in the campaign finance arena. The three other justices were willing to give much more deference to the congressional determination as to the balancing of liberty and equality, although they divided on other issues.

THE EARLY POST-*BUCKLEY* CASES: REJECTING EQUALITY-LIKE RATIONALES AND DEFERENCE TO LEGISLATIVE BODIES

After *Buckley,* the Court decided a series of cases strongly hostile to campaign finance regulation. In the first, *First National Bank of Boston v. Bellotti,*[23] the Court rejected a Massachusetts law aimed at limiting the participation of corporations in ballot measure campaigns.

Bellotti's holding is not startling, given *Buckley*'s premises. *Bellotti* involved a ballot measure campaign, not candidate campaigns, where the possibility of *quid pro quo* corruption or the appearance of such corruption is absent. What is more interesting for purposes here is how the Court handled an equality-like argument. Defending the law, the state argued that corporate participation in the referendum process would exert an undue influence on the outcome of the vote "and—in the end—destroy the confidence of the people in the democratic process and the integrity of government. . . . According to [the state], corporations are wealthy and powerful and their views may drown out other points of view."[24]

The Court gave this equality-like rationale mere lip service. The Court first stated that if these arguments "were supported by record or legislative findings that corporate advocacy threatened imminently to undermine democratic processes, thereby denigrating rather than serving First Amendment interests, these arguments would merit our consideration."[25] But the Court in the following paragraph quoted *Buckley*'s rejection of the equality rationale after noting "the fact that advocacy may persuade the electorate is hardly a reason to suppress it."[26] The sentence undermined any relevance that such legislative findings might have on the constitutional inquiry.

The dissenters came closer to embracing the equality-like rationale. Justice White, writing for himself and Justices Brennan and Marshall, began his *Bellotti* dissent by noting that the values of self-expression protected by the First Amendment did not apply to business corporations. Then, turning to the rejection of the equality rationale in *Buckley*, Justice White wrote:

> Although *Buckley* provides support for the position that the desire to equalize the financial resources available to candidates does not justify the limitation upon the expression of support which a restriction upon individual contributions entails, the interest of Massachusetts and the many other States which have restricted corporate political activity is quite different. It is not one of equalizing the resources of opposing candidates or opposing positions, *but rather of preventing institutions which have been permitted to amass wealth as a result of special advantages extended by the State for certain economic purposes from using that wealth to acquire an unfair advantage in the political process,* especially where, as here, the issue involved has no material connection with the business of the corporation. . . . [Corporate] expenditures may be viewed as seriously threatening the

role of the First Amendment as a guarantor of a free marketplace of ideas. Ordinarily, the expenditure of funds to promote political causes may be assumed to bear some relation to the fervency with which they are held. Corporate political expression, however, is not only divorced from the convictions of individual corporate shareholders, but also, because of the ease with which corporations are permitted to accumulate capital, bears no relation to the conviction with which the ideas expressed are held by the communicator.[27]

Note in Justice White's dissent the shift in the equality rationale from a concern about *absolute spending* leading to large voices "drowning out" the voices of others to a more subtle equality rationale concerned with *relative spending*: Justice White suggested that the amount of expenditures on campaigns should bear some relation to public support for the positions that the expenditures funded. As we shall see, this "barometer" approach to equality has gained ground in more recent Supreme Court cases, in particular as applied to corporations.

The *Bellotti* majority held out the possibility of a state's presenting evidence to support its argument that the corporate role of money in politics threatened the health of democracy. In *Citizens Against Rent Control v. City of Berkeley,*[28] a similar issue appeared. That case concerned a city ordinance imposing contribution limits on committees formed to support or oppose ballot measures. The California Supreme Court had upheld the measure as a means of preserving "voters' confidence" in the ballot measure process, but the Supreme Court, in rejecting the ordinance, flatly stated that "the record in this case does not support" the lower court's conclusion that the ordinance was necessary to preserve such voter confidence.[29] It did not explain what evidence would be sufficient to make such a showing.

Justice White in dissent again was more supportive of such rationales: "Recognition that enormous contributions from a few institutional sources can overshadow the efforts of individuals may have discouraged participation in ballot measure campaigns and undermined public confidence in the referendum process."[30]

During this post-*Buckley* period of hostility to campaign finance regulation, the Court sometimes failed to defer to legislative determinations even about the need for such regulation to stem corruption or the appearance of corruption (the interests recognized as compelling in *Buckley*). In *Federal Election Commission v. National Conservative Political Action Com-*

mittee (NCPAC),[31] the Court rejected a provision of the federal law providing public financing for presidential candidates that limited to $1,000 independent expenditures supporting or opposing a presidential candidate who has accepted public financing. The law in effect prevented most individuals and organizations from engaging in collective action to spend money in support of or opposition to a presidential candidate.

NCPAC is a straightforward application of *Buckley*'s principle that expenditure limitations cannot be justified by mere *assertion* of anticorruption concerns. But the FEC tried to *prove* a connection between the independent spending by political action committees and corruption or its appearance. It pointed "to evidence of high-level appointments in the Reagan administration of persons connected with the PACs and newspaper articles and polls purportedly showing a public perception of corruption."[32] Without elaboration, the majority stated it would defer to the lower court's finding that the evidence of corruption or its appearance was "evanescent."[33]

Justice White predictably dissented, although he did not directly address the quantum of evidence necessary to prove corruption or its appearance. Significantly, Justice Marshall in *NCPAC* also dissented, abandoning his prior adherence to the distinction between contributions and expenditures. He stated his new position that expenditure limits "are justified by the congressional interests in promoting 'the reality and appearance of equal access to the political arena.'"[34]

NCPAC's requirement of a high degree of proof appeared to backpedal from the position the Court had taken in a case predating *NCPAC, Federal Election Commission v. National Right to Work Committee (NRWC)*.[35] In *NRWC*, the Court was deferential to a congressional anticorruption rationale for a law limiting whom corporations could solicit for contributions to their political action committees. It accepted the government's rationale that the law "ensur[ed] that substantial aggregations of wealth amassed by the special advantages which go with the corporate form of organization should not be converted into political 'war chests' which could be used to incur political debts from legislators who are aided by the contributions."[36]

AN EMBRACE OF THE "BAROMETER" EQUALITY RATIONALE:
MCFL AND *AUSTIN*

The Supreme Court's deference to legislative judgments about political equality appeared to take a turn beginning in the mid-1980s. Justice

Brennan transformed the anticorruption rationale of *NRWC*—preventing corporate war chests from being used to buy political favors—into the barometer version of the equality rationale in the 1986 case *Federal Election Commission v. Massachusetts Citizens for Life (MCFL)*.[37] *MCFL* concerned the constitutionality of a provision of the FECA barring corporations from using treasury funds to make expenditures in connection with any federal election except from a separate segregated fund (commonly known as a "political action committee," or "PAC"). The Court held that the FECA provision could not be applied to the Massachusetts Citizens for Life, a nonprofit, nonstock organization that was organized to pursue ideological goals, not to earn profits.

In dictum, Justice Brennan relied upon the *NRWC* language about the ability of corporations to amass "substantial aggregations of wealth" made in the context of corruption concerns to make the barometer equality argument:

> This concern over the corrosive influence of concentrated corporate wealth reflects the conviction that it is important to protect the integrity of the marketplace of political ideas. . . . Direct corporate spending on political activity raises the prospect that resources amassed in the economic marketplace may be used to provide an unfair advantage in the political marketplace. Political "free trade" does not necessarily require that all who participate in the political marketplace do so with exactly equal resources. Relative availability of funds is after all a rough barometer of public support. The resources in the treasury of a business corporation, however, are not an indication of popular support for the corporation's political ideas. They reflect instead the economically motivated decisions of investors and customers. The availability of these resources may make a corporation a formidable political presence, even though the power of the corporation may be no reflection of the power of its ideas.[38]

That dictum became a holding in a case decided four years later, *Austin v. Michigan Chamber of Commerce*.[39] At issue was a Michigan law that barred corporations, other than media corporations, from using general treasury funds for independent expenditures in state election campaigns. Under the reasoning of *Buckley,* the law regulating independent expenditures should have been struck down, at least absent proof that corporate independent expenditures in fact allowed for *quid pro quo* corruption. Instead, the Court accepted the barometer equality rationale for the regulation, while using the incorrect label of corruption:

> Regardless of whether [the] danger of "financial *quid pro quo*" corruption may be sufficient to justify a restriction on independent expenditures, Michigan's regulation aims at a different type of corruption in the political arena: the corrosive and distorting effects of immense aggregations of wealth that are accumulated with the help of the corporate form and that have little or no correlation to the public's support for the corporation's political ideas.[40]

Justice Marshall's opinion for the Court then "emphasize[d] that the mere fact that corporations may accumulate large amounts of wealth is not the justification for [the law]; rather, the unique state-conferred corporate structure that facilitates the amassing of large treasuries warrants the limit on independent expenditures."[41]

The Court curiously couched its holding in the language of "corruption" and limited the holding to corporations rather than explicitly recognizing an equality rationale for campaign finance regulation. Justice Scalia asked in dissent, why, under the majority's rationale, "is it perfectly all right if advocacy by an individual billionaire is out of proportion with 'actual public support' for his positions?"[42] The majority had no coherent response. Indeed, the Court's position was at odds with Justice Marshall's most recent statement from *NCPAC* endorsing the equality rationale for campaign finance regulation.

The drafting history of *Austin* provides some clues, suggesting that Justice Marshall wrote the opinion the way he did to maintain his majority. The majority opinion went through eight drafts. The first draft more forthrightly recognized that the "danger of 'financial *quid pro quo*' corruption may be insufficient to justify a restriction on independent expenditures."[43] And it did not include the sentence emphasizing the "unique state-conferred corporate structure."

After the circulation of Justice Marshall's initial draft, Chief Justice Rehnquist sent a memorandum to Justice Marshall and the other justices indicating his intent to concur in the opinion, provided that Justice Marshall add some language responding to the argument that by banning expenditures by corporations but not unions, the law violated the Equal Protection Clause of the Fourteenth Amendment.[44] Justice Marshall made the change and continued to circulate drafts with minor changes.

Justice Brennan then sent a memorandum to Justice Marshall (but apparently not to the other justices) requesting that the opinion "state more clearly that the special elements conferred by the corporate structure provide a unique basis for State regulation that is not immediately applicable to all types of aggregations of money (wealthy individuals and groups, for example)."[45] The next day, Justice Marshall circulated his fourth draft, which included the language about the "unique state-conferred corporate structure."[46]

Justice Stevens then indicated (in a memorandum sent only to Justice Marshall) his intent to concur, but he asked Justice Marshall to leave open the question whether the Michigan law could be justified by a concern with *quid pro quo* corruption.[47] Justice Marshall made this change as well.[48] Then, in response to Justice Kennedy's circulation of his draft dissenting opinion, Justice Brennan indicated that he would write a short concurrence "emphasizing my feeling that this case is controlled by" *MCFL*.[49]

By the final draft, Justice Marshall responded to the argument in Justice Kennedy's dissent (joined by Justices O'Connor and Scalia) that the Michigan law attempts "to equalize the relative influence of speakers on elections."[50] The majority argued that it was permissible for Michigan to pass a law that "ensure[d] that expenditures reflect actual public support for the political ideas espoused by corporations."[51] With this sentence, a Court majority had finally endorsed the barometer equality rationale, though cabined to apply only to corporations.

THE UNCERTAIN FUTURE OF THE EQUALITY RATIONALE IN THE CAMPAIGN FINANCE CASES

Austin marks something of a high water mark for the equality rationale on the Court. *Austin* represents the first and only case in which a majority of the Court accepted, in deed if not in word, the equality rationale as a permissible state interest. The personnel of the Supreme Court has changed much since 1990, and at the beginning of the new century the justices remained deeply divided on the equality rationale. Four of the six justices in the *Austin* majority had left the Court—Blackmun,[52] Brennan, Marshall and White—while the three *Austin* dissenters—Kennedy, O'Connor, and Scalia—remained.

The two justices in the *Austin* majority remaining on the Court by 2000, Chief Justice Rehnquist and Justice Stevens, divided on the equality question. Chief Justice Rehnquist has never accepted the equality rationale outside the context of corporations. Justice Stevens, in contrast, explicitly endorsed *an* equality rationale (though perhaps not the barometer equality rationale) in a 1996 case involving the constitutionality of limits on independent expenditures by political parties. He wrote: "I believe the Government has an important interest in leveling the electoral playing field by constraining the cost of federal campaigns."[53]

The replacements for the departed justices from the *Austin* majority—Breyer, Ginsburg, Souter, and Thomas—also have divided on the equality rationale. Justice Ginsburg concurred with Justice Stevens in the 1996 case, thereby endorsing an equality rationale. In a 2000 case involving the constitutionality of Missouri's low campaign contribution limits, Justice Breyer announced in a concurring opinion that *Buckley*'s statement about the equality rationale being wholly foreign to the First Amendment "cannot be taken literally."[54] Recognizing that "constitutionally protected interests lie on both sides of the legal equation," he explained:

> On the one hand, a decision to contribute money to a campaign is a matter of First Amendment concern—not because money *is* speech (it is not); but because it *enables* speech. . . . On the other hand, restrictions upon the amount any one individual can contribute to a particular candidate seek to protect the integrity of the electoral process—the means through which a free society democratically translates political speech into concrete governmental action. Moreover, by limiting the size of the largest contributions, such restrictions aim to democratize the influence that money itself may bring to bear on the electoral process. In doing so, they seek to build public confidence in that process and broaden the base of a candidate's meaningful financial support, encouraging the public participation and open discussion that the First Amendment itself presupposes.[55]

Justice Breyer, like Justice Stevens in the 1996 case,[56] further endorsed strong deference to legislative judgments on equality: "I agree that the legislature understands the problem—the threat to electoral integrity, the need for democratization—better than do we."[57]

In sharp contrast, Justice Thomas forcefully called for *Buckley* to be overruled so as to bar both contribution limits and expenditure limits. He argued against the constitutionality of even a limit on contributions in the name of fighting corruption,[58] the essence of *Buckley*'s holding supporting contribution limits. He certainly would reject the equality rationale for regulation.

Justice Souter's views on the equality rationale were less clear. However, he has shown remarkable deference to legislative judgments on the need for campaign finance regulation to fight corruption and the appearance of corruption. Writing for the majority in *Nixon v. Shrink Missouri Government PAC*,[59] Justice Souter held that Missouri could justify the need for its contribution limits to fight corruption or the appearance of corruption by some pretty flimsy evidence: the affidavit from the Missouri legislator who stated that "large contributions 'have the real potential to buy votes'"; newspaper accounts suggesting possible corruption in Missouri politics; and the passage of an earlier Missouri voter initiative establishing campaign contribution limits.

Going into the new century, the future of the equality rationale (even limited to corporations) remained very much in doubt, and, like so much of the jurisprudence discussed in this book, depended heavily on the composition of the Court.

THE CAREFUL BALANCING APPROACH TO CAMPAIGN FINANCE REGULATION IN THE NAME OF POLITICAL EQUALITY

Certainly some First Amendment hawks such as Justice Thomas or L. A. Powe would reject Justice Breyer's statement in *Shrink Missouri* that "constitutionally protected interests lie on both sides of the legal equation." But they would be hard pressed to deny the existence of a significant and thoughtful group of well-meaning judges and scholars who have taken that position. Nor could Justice Breyer deny the existence of a similar group of First Amendment hawks who find such arguments, in the words of Chief Justice Rehnquist, "absurd." The issue is one of enduring controversy that has only intensified in the generation since the Court decided *Buckley*.

In the face of such a longstanding conflict concerning the health of our democratic system—both in terms of elections and free speech—the Court should be more deferential to the *value judgments* made by political actors as to the appropriate balance between liberty and equality in the campaign finance context. Leaving such value judgments to the political process better serves the goals of the democratic system by assuring both experimentation and flexibility so as to strengthen democratic institutions.

Recall that Powe criticized the supposed egalitarian benefits of campaign finance regulation as "speculative." He correctly stated that the speculation was based on a legislative judgment that the political market is failing and that the legislature had come up with an "effective means" to solve the problem. But Powe's constitutionalization of a deregulatory campaign finance regime simply assures that claims that campaign finance regulation promotes political equality remain speculative. So long as states are prevented from experimenting with various means of promoting political equality, society is deprived of important information about various ways to properly balance liberty and equality interests and thereby to enhance democracy.[60] The accountability of public officials assures that failed experiments will eventually be corrected.

Court deference to legislative value judgments in this area would *not* be an abdication of the Court's role to protect the speech and association rights protected by the First Amendment. The Court would retain a crucial role in assuring that the *means* the legislature has put forward to promote political equality in fact are likely to achieve those ends. The purpose of this close scrutiny is to serve as a substitute for a test of legislative *motive*. Legislators may be tempted to regulate in the name of political equality but do so really to protect themselves from competition or to further their own agendas. But proof of such motive is often absent, suggesting the means-ends testing as a second-best solution. When the means and ends do not match well, the reason may be that the ends asserted are not the ends intended.

Of course, in the face of actual evidence of improper legislative motive, the Court should certainly disapprove campaign finance regulation enacted in the name of political equality. An actual example here is the *Bellotti* case. In *Bellotti*, there was strong evidence that the Massachusetts legislature acted specifically to ban corporate expenditures in ballot measure elections because corporations had been successful in the past in blocking an income tax initiative favored by a majority of legislators (but that required voter approval for enactment). The action smacked of silencing an opponent on a particular issue, not a broader attempt either to assure that all voices are heard (the initial equality rationale rejected in *Buckley*) or to assure that campaign spending was a rough barometer of public support for an issue.

Most cases will lack such compelling evidence of motive, leaving the Court instead to engage in a close means-end testing. In a preconference internal memorandum in *Buckley*, Justice Powell remarked that

> *[a]lthough I am convinced that the central thrust of the Act is to favor in-cumbents and seriously disadvantage challengers (both individuals and minor parties),* I agree that the federal government has a compelling inter-est in doing what it can to promote "purity" of elections—however illu-sory a goal this may be in fact. Therefore, unless we are to invalidate the entire Act, I am inclined to think that limitations on contributions are an essential element—and perhaps the key element—in legislation of this kind.[61]

This kind of deference is particularly inappropriate in the case of elec-tion-related legislation. Given Justice Powell's beliefs that the FECA's "cen-tral thrust" was incumbency protection, he should have insisted on a closer connection between the means the FECA devised (contribution limits) and the ends put forward by the government (preventing corrup-tion). The Court should have applied a similar means-ends analysis be-tween the FECA expenditure limits and the goal of promoting equality.

A lack of serious means-ends scrutiny pervades the campaign finance cases, with the Court being either too dismissive or too accepting of such rationales. In cases such as *Citizens Against Rent Control* or *NCPAC,* the Court refused to engage in a serious analysis of the evidence addressing the purported legislative purpose before *rejecting* it. That is not to say that these cases were wrongly decided; they raised serious collective action concerns. But the Court erred in failing to look more closely at the con-nection between means and ends.

In *Austin,* the Court refused to engage in serious analysis of the evi-dence before *accepting* it. The Court upheld the Michigan law barring cor-porate expenditures on grounds it "ensures that expenditures reflect actual public support for the political ideas espoused by corporations." Yet the majority failed to probe why the Michigan legislature legitimately would have chosen to limit such a barometer equality rationale only to corpora-tions.

Recall that at Justice Brennan's urging, Justice Marshall's opinion for the Court pointed to the unique state-conferred benefits that corporations receive. But that fact begged the question. No doubt, some very wealthy individuals (whose expenditures remained unlimited under Michigan law) would be making campaign expenditures in ways that did not reflect actual public support for the ideas these individuals funded. And what about the exclusion of unions from the expenditure limits, a strong politi-cal force in Michigan? Both of these exclusions suggest the Michigan legislature may have had something else in mind in singling out corporations for special campaign finance treatment.

It may well be that there were persuasive answers to these questions. The Michigan legislature, for example, may have determined that union political spending is more of a "rough barometer" of public support for ideas than is corporate political spending. Or the legislature might have relied upon some evidence that corporate political spending was a much greater threat to the barometer goal than spending by wealthy individuals or a legislative judgment that corporate funded speech (as Justice White argued in his *Bellotti* dissent) was less deserving of protection than individual speech. But the Court simply assumed (or at least stated) that corporations presented greater problems and deferred to the legislature's implied conclusion that the means were closely related to the ends.

Such deference has become even more enshrined in the contribution limit context as applied to the anticorruption rationale. The Court in *Shrink Missouri* markedly lowered the bar for approval of campaign contribution–limit laws, requiring virtually no proof beyond legislative supposition that low contribution limits are necessary to prevent corruption or its appearance.[62]

If the Court makes changes on these two fronts—greater deference to legislative value judgments and less deference on the means-ends testing—we may or may not end up with the Court upholding more campaign finance laws. In any event, the campaign finance laws that the Court would uphold would be laws that engage in experimentation and attempt to balance liberty and equality interests in a meaningful way.

If legislatures must assure a closer fit between the means and ends of legislative enactments, legislators will do a better job both articulating ends and crafting means. As for ends, we have seen that there is no single "equality rationale." Instead, the Court has considered equality rationales aimed at both absolute spending and relative spending. Indeed, there are other equality-oriented rationales as well that legislative bodies might target. For example, campaign finance regulation may be justified to assure that those with wealth cannot use campaign contributions or expenditures to buy access to elected officials.[63] The choice about which, if any, of the equality rationales to pursue through campaign finance legislation should be left to politically accountable bodies.

Legislatures also can begin experimentation that fits ends better with means. For example, if a legislature wishes to impose a barometer equality rationale, it might pursue more narrowly tailored means than a ban on corporate independent expenditures in candidate campaigns. For example, it might replace the current privately financed system for congressional campaigns with publicly financed campaign finance vouchers. Voters could allocate such vouchers to candidates, parties, or interest groups as voters see fit. This market-like mechanism will do a much better job than current public finance systems (that typically use a threshold test to receive the public financing benefit) in funding campaign-related speech in rough proportion to the intensity of support for the candidates, parties, and interest groups.[64]

The Power of Congress to Regulate Political Equality under the Fourteenth and Fifteenth Amendments

If the pattern in the campaign finance cases has been initial Court rejection of legislative attempts to foster political equality followed by at least partial acceptance, the pattern in the voting rights area may prove to be the opposite, at least when it comes to congressional mandates applicable to states and localities. In short, although the Court in the Warren era was mostly accepting of congressional action regulating state and local election practices through the Voting Rights Act, there is good reason to believe that the Court's recent cases in other areas portend a shift away from such acceptance.

The issue of congressional power in the voting rights area begins with the structure of the Constitution itself, which allows Congress to act pursuant only to "enumerated powers" set forth in the document. For example, Congress may regulate the campaign financing of federal elections because the Constitution grants Congress such power under Article I, Section 4 of the Constitution. This provision expressly allows Congress to make its own laws and override any state laws regulating the time, place, and manner of elections of federal officers.

THE EARLY VOTING RIGHTS CASES

When Congress passed the Voting Rights Act in 1965, some southern states immediately challenged it as exceeding congressional power. In the first of these cases, *South Carolina v. Katzenbach*,[65] South Carolina challenged the core provisions of the act. One provision used a formula to define certain jurisdictions (later known as "covered jurisdictions") that would be subject to rules set forth in the act; South Carolina was such a jurisdiction under the formula. A second provision prevented covered jurisdictions from imposing a test or device for voting for a limited period; South Carolina had a test for voting that included both a property qualification and a literacy test.[66] A third provision prevented a covered jurisdiction from denying the right to vote to any person for failure to comply with a voting qualification or procedure that had been put in place after November 1, 1964, and that had not been first approved (later known as "precleared") by the Justice Department or a special three-judge federal court panel in Washington, D.C.

The Court rejected South Carolina's argument that these three provisions "exceed[ed] the powers of Congress and encroach[ed] on an area reserved to the States by the Constitution."[67] The Court held that Congress had acted appropriately under its powers granted in Section 2 of the Fifteenth Amendment. Section 1 of that amendment prevented the United States or any state from denying or abridging the right of citizens of the United States to vote "on account of race, color, or previous condition of servitude." Section 2 declared "Congress shall have the power to enforce this article by appropriate legislation."

In so holding, the Court gave considerable deference to congressional determinations about the means necessary to "enforce" the Fifteenth Amendment. It explained that this enforcement power "is the same as in all cases concerning the express powers of Congress with relation to the reserved powers of the States." It quoted Chief Justice John Marshall in the seminal case of *McCulloch v. Maryland,* writing about the scope of that power: "Let the end be legitimate, let it be within the scope of the constitution, and all means which are appropriate, which are plainly adapted to that end, which are not prohibited, but consist[ent] with the letter and spirit of the constitution, are constitutional."[68]

Turning to the challenge to the act itself, the Court in *South Carolina v. Katzenbach* began by noting that

> Congress had found that case-by-case litigation was inadequate to combat widespread and persistent discrimination in voting, because of the inordinate amount of time and energy required to overcome the obstructionist tactics invariably encountered in these lawsuits. After enduring nearly a century of systematic resistance to the Fifteenth Amendment, Congress might well decide to shift the advantage of time and inertia from the perpetrators of the evil to its victims.[69]

Turning to the specific provisions, the Court quickly rejected a challenge to the coverage formula. It noted that Congress had used "reliable evidence of actual voting discrimination in a great majority of the States and political subdivisions affected by the new remedies of the Act" and created a formula that described these areas. "No more was required to justify the application to these areas of Congress' express power under the Fifteenth Amendment."[70]

South Carolina then argued that Congress did not have the power to ban South Carolina's literacy test for five years, given that the Court had held in the 1959 *Lassiter* case that fairly applied literacy tests were constitutional.[71] The Court held that *Lassiter* did not prevent Congress from acting under its power to enforce the Fifteenth Amendment. First, the Court noted that the record showed that South Carolina and most other states covered by the act had enacted various tests and devices "with the purpose of disenfranchising Negroes."[72] The Court then called a five-year suspension of literacy tests "a legitimate response to the problem. . . . Underlying the response was the feeling that States and political subdivisions which had been allowing white illiterates to vote for years could not sincerely complain about 'dilution' of their electorates through the registration of Negro illiterates."[73] The Court also noted that the continued use of the tests, even fairly administered, "would freeze the effect of past discrimination in favor of unqualified white registrants."[74]

Finally, the Court upheld the preclearance provisions. Calling the requirement that a covered jurisdiction obtain federal approval before changing its own laws "uncommon," the Court declared that "exceptional conditions can justify legislative measures not otherwise appropriate. Congress knew that some of the [covered states] had resorted to the extraordinary stratagem of contriving new rules of various kinds for the sole purpose of perpetuating voting discrimination in the face of adverse federal court decrees."[75] Justice Black dissented on the constitutionality of the preclearance provision. "It is inconceivable to me that such a radical degradation of state power was intended in any of the provisions of our Constitution or its Amendments."[76]

South Carolina v. Katzenbach showed a Court highly deferential to congressional determinations about how to expand political equality rights, and such deference for the most part continued in the three other cases in which the Court faced arguments over the scope of congressional power to enact various provisions of the Voting Rights Act. In *Katzenbach v. Morgan*,[77] the Court upheld a provision of the act that prevented denial of the right to vote on account of inability to read or write English to any person who had successfully completed the sixth grade in a public school in, or a private school accredited by, the Commonwealth of Puerto Rico in which the language of instruction was other than English. A group of New York City voters challenged the law, which prohibited enforcement of an English literacy test in New York. The United States defended the law as a legitimate exercise of Congress's enforcement powers under Section 5 of the Fourteenth Amendment. The language of Section 5 of the Fourteenth Amendment mirrors Section 2 of the Fifteenth Amendment; Section 5 gives Congress the power to "enforce," among other things, the Equal Protection Clause of the Fourteenth Amendment.

Viewing the enforcement powers of Section 5 of the Fourteenth Amendment as expansively as it viewed the enforcement powers of Section 2 of the Fifteenth Amendment in *South Carolina v. Katzenbach,* the Court in *Morgan* upheld the law. It noted congressional intent to secure the rights of the Fourteenth Amendment to persons who were educated in American-flag schools in which the predominant classroom language was other than English. It held that the challenged provision "may be viewed as a measure to secure for the Puerto Rican community residing in New York nondiscriminatory treatment by government—both in the imposition of voting qualifications and the provision or administration of governmental services, such as public schools, public housing and law enforcement."[78] The Court added:

> It was for Congress, as the branch that made this judgment, to assess and weigh the various conflicting considerations—the risk or pervasiveness of the discrimination in governmental services, the effectiveness of eliminating the state restriction on the right to vote as a means of dealing with the evil, the adequacy or availability of alternative remedies, and the nature and significance of the state interests that would be affected by the nullification of the English literacy requirement as applied to residents who have successfully completed the sixth grade in a Puerto Rican school.[79]

The Court did place one limitation on the expansive view of congressional enforcement power under Section 5 of the Fourteenth Amendment. In what has come to be known as the "ratchet theory," Justice Brennan wrote for the Court that Section 5 "does not grant Congress power to exercise discretion in the other direction and to enact 'statutes so as in effect to dilute equal protection and due process decisions of this Court.'"[80]

Congress could therefore overenforce the Equal Protection Clause, but it could not take away basic equal protection guarantees recognized by the Court.

In *Oregon v. Mitchell*,[81] Arizona challenged a 1970 amendment to the Voting Rights Act making a literacy test ban nationwide and extending it another five years. The Court unanimously upheld the nationwide ban as an exercise of congressional power under Section 2 of the Fifteenth Amendment.[82] The Justices in *Mitchell* divided on other questions, most notably Congressional power to lower the voting age in state and local elections from 21 to 18 years of age. Four justices—Brennan, Marshall, and White in one opinion and Douglas in another—took the position that Congress could lower the voting age pursuant to its power under Section 5 of the Fourteenth Amendment to bar discrimination against persons between the ages of 18 and 21.[83] That position, however, did not command a majority of the justices.

Finally, in *City of Rome v. United States*,[84] the Court rejected another challenge to the preclearance provisions of the Voting Rights Act. The City of Rome, Georgia, noted that under the act the U.S. Department of Justice could not grant preclearance to an election law change made by the city unless the department found that the plan had neither a discriminatory purpose nor a discriminatory effect. The city argued that Congress could not prohibit voting changes with only a discriminatory *effect* under its powers granted in Section 2 of the Fifteenth Amendment because the Fifteenth Amendment, properly interpreted, barred only *purposeful discrimination*.

Assuming *arguendo* that the Fifteenth Amendment barred only purposeful discrimination,[85] the Court held that Congress had the power to bar laws with a discriminatory effect under its Fifteenth Amendment enforcement powers. "Congress could rationally have concluded that, because electoral changes by jurisdictions with a demonstrable history of intentional racial discrimination in voting create the risk of purposeful discrimination, it was proper to prohibit changes that have a discriminatory impact."[86]

Then-Justice Rehnquist dissented, in language that reappeared in the next set of cases we consider. He argued that Congress could not properly command the U.S. Department of Justice to bar state and local changes with only a discriminatory *effect* under its enforcement powers of the Fourteenth or Fifteenth Amendments. Justice Rehnquist acknowledged that Congress could do more than simply prohibit unconstitutional conduct; it could "act *remedially* to enforce the judicially established substantive prohibitions of the Amendments."[87] Thus, he argued that Congress could properly impose a nationwide literacy test as a remedial measure, "effectively preventing purposeful discrimination in the application of the literacy tests as well as an appropriate means of remedying prior constitutional violations by state and local governments in the administration of education to minorities."[88] What Congress could *not* do, Justice Rehnquist wrote, was to "determine for itself that . . . conduct violates the Constitution."[89] Because he believed that the "effects" test was not remedial to prevent purposeful discrimination, he would have held that this element of the act's preclearance provision exceeded congressional powers.

Justice Rehnquist wrote his dissent in 1980, speaking only for himself and Justice Stewart. Times changed, however, and the Rehnquist theory has gained adherents in cases outside the Voting Rights Act. This recent history raises serious concerns about the constitutionality of the 1982 amendments to the Voting Rights Act and to any future preclearance provisions that Congress may enact.

THE FEDERALISM REVOLUTION

Justice Rehnquist's *City of Rome* dissent sided with states and localities opposing a broad view of federal government power to regulate state and local voting rules. Justice Powell's separate dissent in *City of Rome* focused even more directly on concerns that the federal government was intruding on state and local power.[90] But these "federalism" arguments in *City of Rome* failed to persuade a majority of justices in 1980.

In the past decade, however, we have witnessed a federalism revolution in the Supreme Court.[91] Among other things, the Court has limited congressional power under the Commerce Clause[92] (previously thought to be virtually limitless) and, through its Eleventh Amendment jurisprudence, it has increased the scope of the immunity of states from suits for damages or other retrospective relief for violation of federal law.[93]

The details of this fascinating and seismic shift in power from the federal government to the states are well beyond the scope of the analysis here. Instead, I focus on one aspect of the federalism cases that casts serious doubt on the constitutionality of recent (and proposed) congressional voting rights legislation.

The most relevant case in this regard is a 1997 federalism case, *City of Boerne v. Flores.*[94] *Boerne* involved the constitutionality of a congressional statute, the Religious Freedom Restoration Act of 1993 (RFRA). RFRA was a congressional reaction to the Supreme Court's controversial 1990 decision in *Employment Division Department of Human Resources v. Smith*,[95] a case holding that "neutral, generally applicable laws may be applied to religious practices even when not supported by a compelling governmental interest."[96] Thus, the *Smith* Court held that it did not violate the constitutional guarantee of the "free exercise" of religion[97] for the state of Oregon to deny unemployment benefits to Native Americans who lost their jobs for using the illegal drug peyote for sacramental purposes.

Congress enacted RFRA to restore the pre-*Smith* law by preventing government entities from substantially burdening a person's exercise of religion, even through a rule of general applicability, unless the government could demonstrate that the burden was in furtherance of a compelling governmental interest and was the least restrictive means of furthering that governmental interest.[98]

In *Boerne*, the Catholic archbishop of San Antonio, Texas, sought a building permit to enlarge a church in Boerne, Texas. Local zoning authorities denied the permit, relying upon an ordinance governing historic preservation in a district that, they argued, included the church. The archbishop brought suit, challenging the denial under RFRA. The Supreme Court held that RFRA, as applied to state and local governments, exceeded congressional power under Section 5 of the Fourteenth Amendment.

The Court's analysis began by citing the Voting Rights Act precedents described above as standing for the "broad" power of Section 5. But the Court then held that the Section 5 power was limited only to *enforcing* the provisions of the amendment. In explaining what the Court believed it meant to "enforce" the amendment, the Court drew a line between legislation that is "remedial," which is within Congress's power, and legislation that makes a "substantive change," which exceeds congressional power: "Congress does not enforce a constitutional right by changing what the right is. It has been given the power 'to enforce,' not the power to determine what constitutes a constitutional violation."[99] The Court further explained that "[t]here must be a congruence and proportionality between the injury to be prevented or remedied and the means adopted to that end. Lacking such a connection, legislation may become substantive in operation and effect."[100]

In so holding, the Court rejected the "ratchet theory" Justice Brennan advanced for the Court in *Morgan*. Although the *Boerne* Court agreed that there was language in *Morgan* "which could be interpreted as acknowledging a power in Congress to enact legislation that expands the rights contained in § 1 of the Fourteenth Amendment," the *Boerne* Court rejected the theory on grounds it would allow Congress to alter the Fourteenth Amendment's meaning without going through the "difficult and detailed amendment process contained in Article V" of the Constitution.[101]

The Court applied this new test for Section 5 power to RFRA and held that RFRA came up short. In so doing, the Court explicitly compared RFRA to the Voting Rights Act. The Court first looked at the evidence before Congress supporting the need for both laws. "In contrast to the record which confronted Congress and the Judiciary in the Voting Rights cases, RFRA's legislative record lacks examples of modern instances of generally applicable laws passed because of religious bigotry."[102]

Moreover, the Court held that while the voting rights laws approved in prior cases could be seen as remedial, "RFRA is so out of proportion to a supposed remedial or preventive object that it cannot be understood as a response to, or designed to prevent, unconstitutional behavior. . . . [Its sweeping] coverage ensures its intrusion at every level of government, displacing laws and prohibiting official actions of almost every description regardless of subject matter."[103]

The *Boerne* Court further noted with approval that the laws at issue in the Voting Rights Act cases contained termination dates and geographic restrictions and addressed themselves to remedy egregious unconstitutional practices in the states. "[L]imitations of this kind tend to ensure Congress' means are proportionate to ends legitimate under § 5."

Three more recent Supreme Court cases confirm *Boerne*'s substantial narrowing of congressional power under Section 5 of the Fourteenth Amendment. In *College Savings Bank v. Florida Prepaid Postsecondary Education Expense Board*,[104] the Court held that Congress could not use its Section 5 power to subject states to lawsuits for damages for violating a congressional statute governing patent infringement. The Court held that the statute failed to meet *Boerne*'s congruence and proportionality test because "Congress identified no pattern of patent infringement by the States, let alone a pattern of constitutional violations."[105]

In *Kimel v. Florida Board of Regents*,[106] the Court held that Congress could not use its Section 5 power to subject states to lawsuits for damages under the Age Discrimination in Employment Act (ADEA). As in *Florida Prepaid*, the Court in *Kimel* held that states could not be subject to federal age discrimination suits because of a lack of congruence and proportionality between the substantive requirements of the ADEA and the unconstitutional conduct that could conceivably be targeted by the act.

Finally, in *Board of Trustees v. Garrett*,[107] the Court confronted the same issue as applied to the Americans with Disabilities Act (ADA). As in *Kimel*, the Court in *Garrett* held that Congress failed to identify a pattern of irrational state discrimination in employment to justify the law's application to the states. Once again, the Court compared the challenged law to the Voting Rights Act, where the Court stated that Congress had documented a "marked pattern of unconstitutional action by the States" and passed a law providing a "detailed but limited remedial scheme."[108]

Four justices dissented in *Garrett*, focusing primarily on the Court's holding that Congress failed to provide sufficient legislative evidence of unconstitutional discrimination by the states against the disabled. The dissent detailed what it characterized as "powerful evidence" of discriminatory treatment that justified the law's application to the states. Furthermore, the dissent derided the majority for treating Congress as an "administrative agency" whose record it was reviewing, and it argued that there is

> simply no reason to require Congress, seeking to determine facts relevant to the exercise of its § 5 authority, to adopt rules or presumptions that reflect a court's institutional limitations.... Unlike courts, Congress directly reflects public attitudes and beliefs, enabling Congress better to understand where, and to what extent, refusals to accommodate a disability amount to behavior that is callous or unreasonable to the point of lacking constitutional justification.[109]

Finally, the dissent rejected the congruence and proportionality test, arguing that Section 5 gives Congress "the power to require more than the minimum that § 5 grants Congress."[110]

IMPLICATIONS FOR THE FUTURE CONSTITUTIONALITY OF THE VOTING RIGHTS ACT

If the Court considered the constitutionality of the revised section 2 of the Voting Rights Act today under these recent federalism precedents, would the Court uphold the act as constitutional? The section 5 preclearance provisions of the act expire in 2007. If Congress reenacts the preclearance provisions and they are challenged as going beyond congressional enforcement power under the Fourteenth or Fifteenth Amendments, would the preclearance provisions be upheld?

At first glance, there are good reasons (beyond avoiding controversy) for believing both provisions would be upheld as constitutional exercises of congressional enforcement power. In *Boerne* and *Garrett,* the Court pointed repeatedly to the old voting rights precedents as proper exercise of congressional power to enforce the Fourteenth or Fifteenth Amendments. In addition, these constitutional amendments were enacted to prevent race discrimination, and the Court has subjected race discrimination to strict scrutiny (unlike discrimination against the disabled or the aged in the two most recent cases). Such strict scrutiny suggests that Congress can impose stronger remedies to prevent state-imposed racial discrimination. If Congress has the power to apply its enforcement powers under these amendments to any subject matter, it likely has the power to remedy race discrimination in voting.

Another reason for believing the measures would pass constitutional muster is doctrinal. In 1984, the Supreme Court summarily affirmed (that is, affirmed without issuing a written opinion) a lower court case upholding the amended section 2 of the Voting Rights Act against charges that Congress, in enacting the statute, exceeded its enforcement powers under the Fifteenth Amendment.[111] The Court may view the issue as therefore settled, at least as to section 2 of the act.

A more recent and perhaps more significant case is *Lopez v. Monterey County.*[112] *Lopez* involved a challenge by Latino voters from a county in California covered under the Voting Rights Act to the state's failure to preclear changes in its laws governing judicial elections in that county. The Court rejected California's argument that it would exceed congressional enforcement power under the Fifteenth Amendment to require the state to preclear its voting changes in the absence of evidence that the state had been one of the "historical wrongdoers in the voting rights sphere." Although the Court cited *Boerne,*[113] it stated that its prior voting rights precedents of *South Carolina v. Katzenbach* and *City of Rome,* both of which had upheld preclearance provisions, governed the case. Noting that the act "by its nature, intrudes on state sovereignty," the Court upheld the intrusion because it "burden[ed] state law only to the extent that [the] law affects voting in jurisdictions properly designated for coverage."[114]

Justice Thomas dissented in *Lopez,* intimating that Congress did not have the authority to require preclearance by California. He distinguished

South Carolina v. Katzenbach and *City of Rome* as cases involving jurisdictions with a demonstrable history of actual voting discrimination on the basis of race. Justice Thomas suggested that under *Boerne*'s requirements of a match between the wrong and the remedy, preclearance would be unconstitutional absent evidence of similar discrimination by California.

Despite both this history and doctrine, the picture is not all that rosy when we dig deeper into the implications of the *Boerne* line of cases to congressional power to enact either section 2 of the Voting Rights Act or an extension of the preclearance provisions of the act in 2007.

Consider section 2 of the act first. As noted in chapter 1, Congress enacted the revised section 2 as a response to the Court's holding in *City of Mobile v. Bolden*[115] requiring proof of *intentional* discrimination in voting to make out a claim of unconstitutional vote dilution under the Equal Protection Clause. Section 2, as the Court later construed it in *Thornburg v. Gingles*,[116] required minority plaintiffs challenging a districting scheme to meet a threshold three-part test to prove vote dilution, followed by the "totality of the circumstances" test. The threshold test roughly required proof of racially polarized voting and proof that the minority group was sufficiently large and geographically compact to form a majority in a single-member district.[117] Intent was not required.

Douglas Laycock has observed a close parallel between Congress's enacting the amended section 2 of the Voting Rights Act as a response to *Bolden* and Congress's enacting RFRA as a response to *Smith*.[118] Both cases involved Congress disagreeing with a "new court-defined constitutional standard." More important, both RFRA and the amended section 2 did more than simply address violations of the Constitution as the Court had characterized them. Just as RFRA addressed state conduct that would not violate the Free Exercise Clause as the Court interpreted it in *Smith*, section 2 in particular aimed at minority voting power problems not caused by intentional state action.

This analysis suggests that section 2 could be attacked as not being "remedial" (that is, aimed at the constitutional violation in the way the Court has characterized it) but, rather, substantive. In other words, the Court could view congressional action in passing section 2 as seeking to enlarge the scope of the Equal Protection Clause to cover discriminatory effects, rather than to enforce unconstitutional intentional discrimination.[119]

In addition, those opposed to section 2's constitutionality could argue that the statute is not "congruent or proportional" to the scope of constitutional harms. Even if the congressional aim of section 2 was to target discriminatory purpose through prohibiting discriminatory effects, the effort here may be too broad, especially because it is limited neither in geographic proximity nor by time (section 2 has no sunset provision). As Laycock argues, "As with RFRA, the number of statutory violations appears disproportionately large in relation to the number of constitutional violations."[120]

This sort of reasoning would go counter to the Court's holding in *City of Rome*, essentially endorsing the view put forward by then-Justice Rehnquist in his *City of Rome* dissent. But *City of Rome* came before the Court's federalism revolution, and its reasoning perhaps would not command a majority today.

Furthermore, even assuming congruence and proportionality to state-initiated discrimination, given states' track record as it existed when Congress amended the Voting Rights Act in 1982, section 2 may no longer be constitutional today. As Mark Tushnet argues, "In 2002, a state says, 'No longer are there enough intentional exclusions for the broader ban on disparate impact to be proportional to the constitutional violations now occurring.' Whether a statute constitutional at the time it was enacted might become unconstitutional as time goes by is an interesting theoretical question."[121]

Finally, Congress may not have created an adequate legislative record of intentional discrimination under *Garrett* to justify the reach of section 2.[122] Of course, Congress did not know of the *Garrett* requirements in 1982, but the Court in *Garrett* did not indicate it would apply its legislative evidence rule prospectively only. Section 2's constitutionality therefore is now in serious doubt.

Most of these same arguments would apply if Congress reenacts the preclearance provisions of the Voting Rights Act when they expire in 2007. One advantage defenders of the new preclearance provisions would have over defenders of section 2 is the ability to create the strongest legislative record possible to support preclearance provisions. But with the decline in evidence of purposeful racial discrimination in the states since 1965 and even since 1982, Congress may have a difficult time coming up with an adequate record.

The Court will have to decide if Congress has provided enough evidence that denial of preclearance for plans with a retrogressive effect is "remedial" in preventing purposeful discrimination and not "substantive" in imposing the effects test. Moreover, given the admitted decline (though not elimination) of intentional racial discrimination in voting in the early twenty-first century, the Court must consider if the preclearance provision would be congruent and proportional to the permissible goal of preventing purposeful discrimination.

Pamela Karlan, writing after *Boerne* but before *Florida Prepaid, Kimel,* and *Garrett,* made a valiant effort to forestall such arguments against the amended section 2 and the current preclearance provisions. She argued that both provisions "are designed to address prior unconstitutional discrimination, both within and outside the electoral process, as well as to prevent future invidious conduct."[123] She further argued the provisions meet the congruence and proportionality test.

Karlan's evidence regarding state intentional discrimination comes primarily from the 1982 Senate Report of the Voting Rights Act amendments. The Court in its recent federalism cases has looked to such committee reports as important evidence of legislative intent,[124] but, given the scope of the evidence found insufficient in *Garrett,* it does not appear that the report contains *enough* evidence of *nationwide systemic problems with intentional state discrimination* to justify the dramatic remedy of section 2. Section 2 is not temporally limited, and it applies to all states and localities. Indeed, redistricting experts around the country will tell you that consideration of potential section 2 liability is an essential element of all redistricting processes in jurisdictions with sizeable minority populations.

The Court could well conclude that section 2 is not congruent or proportional to the alleged violations. This conclusion would be even stronger if the Court were to look to more recent evidence of intentional racial discrimination in voting, which appears to be diminishing.

Karlan further supported the case for congressional power to enact effects tests in the Voting Rights Act by noting the persistence of racial bloc voting, by which white voters refuse to vote for African-American preferred candidates. The prevalence of racial bloc voting is declining,[125] and in any case such private voting decisions, as Karlan admits, do not constitute state action evincing purposeful discrimination. Although Karlan is right that in the presence of such voting "the state [is] operating a forum that enable[s] white voters to engage in racial discrimination,"[126] that fact itself does not seem to be a constitutional violation.

Karlan further argued that some of this private discrimination in voting may be due to past discriminatory *state* action. "This action may play out either in different material interests or in a refusal to support candidates sponsored by voters of the other race simply because of racial tribalism."[127] The theory here is provocative, and mirrors somewhat the Court's debates over whether *de jure* discrimination or the end of such *de jure* discrimination in southern public schools caused white flight to the suburbs.[128] Karlan cites nothing to indicate Congress had this chain of causation in mind in enacting its amendments to the Voting Rights Act, or that any such evidence would satisfy the Court that past state discrimination has caused private discriminatory attitudes.

Finally, Karlan noted that the Supreme Court's own post-*Bolden* jurisprudence appears to meld the intent and effects tests by allowing proof of discriminatory effects to sometimes count as evidence of discriminatory purpose.[129] Even so, the Voting Rights Act's provisions target discriminatory effect directly, not as a means of proving discriminatory purpose. That much the Court made clear in *Gingles*. In any reenactment of the preclearance provisions, Congress would do well to set forth explicitly such links between discriminatory purpose and effect.

In sum, while I have much sympathy with the preemptive strike that Karlan has launched, I doubt it would be sufficient if the current Court made a close examination of these provisions of the Voting Rights Act in light of the federalism revolution.

The Court is even more likely to strike down provisions of the Voting Rights Act because of the *Shaw* line of cases discussed in earlier chapters establishing a cause of action for unconstitutional racial gerrymanders. These cases arose in the first place because jurisdictions were attempting to comply with section 2 and the preclearance provisions of the Voting Rights Act. They have been very controversial and, perhaps more important to the Court, they have taken up much of the Court's time and effort. A holding striking down the provisions of the Voting Rights Act would virtually eliminate any future *Shaw*-type claims because jurisdictions would be much less inclined to draw majority-minority districts (especially ones with bizarre shapes).

THE PROPER TEST FOR THE POWER OF CONGRESS TO REGULATE POLITICAL EQUALITY UNDER THE FOURTEENTH AND FIFTEENTH AMENDMENTS

Whether as a general matter the Court was correct beginning in *Boerne* to limit the scope of Congress's enforcement powers under the Fourteenth Amendment is an issue well beyond the scope of this book. I have a great deal of sympathy with arguments such as David Cole's that the Court and Congress should have "concurrent jurisdiction" to interpret the Fourteenth Amendment and that "[w]here Congress acts pursuant to one of its affirmative powers and does not contravene any affirmative constitutional prohibition, its actions should be upheld so long as they reflect a reasonable construction of the affirmative constitutional authority pursuant to which it has acted."[130] Along similar lines, Michael McConnell has set forth the constitutional history showing that the framers of the Fourteenth Amendment saw Congress, not the Court, as the primary federal branch ensuring that fundamental rights should not vary from state to state. McConnell argues that the Court should give "respectful attention—and probably the presumption of constitutionality—to the interpretive judgments of Congress."[131]

I also agree with Evan Caminker that assuming the Court was correct in *Boerne* in limiting Congress to remedial, rather than substantive, legislation, the Court should test the means and ends using a "rational relationship" test, rather than the "congruence and proportionality" test.[132] Such an interpretation of the means-ends relationship would give Congress almost as much leeway as Cole's test for the permissible scope of congressional power.

Whatever might be written about *Boerne* as a general matter, as applied to voting questions, there is no doubt that the Court's *Boerne* jurisprudence is misguided. To use the terminology earlier in this chapter, Congress should be allowed to use its powers to enact contested visions of political equality, without being able to take away core political rights. In other words, at least in the context of voting rights, it is time to readopt the ratchet theory.

Consider, for example, the question whether Congress could "decide tomorrow that promoting a well-informed electorate was an important national interest and require a literacy or an understanding test like the ones required for naturalization."[133] Congress could not do so because to do so would violate the core equality of the essential political rights principle by conditioning the vote on literacy. Under this theory, Congress could, however, pass a nationwide statute like section 2 of the Voting Rights Act, creating more opportunities for minorities to gain a more proportional share of political power, the "fair fight corollary" described in chapter 3. It is a reasonable extension by an elected body of the principles contained in the Equal Protection Clause.

Political safeguards prevent overreaching. Such legislation must pass both houses of Congress (including a supermajority in the Senate to avoid filibuster rules) and be signed by the president. Such legislation is also open to reversal if politically unpopular. This is an appropriate instance of congressional authority to assure greater political equality.

What remains to be considered about the *Boerne* line of cases is not the conflict between the Court and Congress but the conflict between Congress and the states. What should we make of the federalism argument in the context of voting rights? Beyond the historical evidence adduced by McConnell and others that the Fourteenth Amendment was designed to shift power from the states to Congress to protect political rights, there is a more contemporary response: Beginning in *Reynolds v. Sims, the Court itself* has nationalized equal protection jurisprudence. The Court, more than Congress, has intruded on state prerogatives beginning when it established the one person, one vote rule and ending most recently with the creation of the cause of action for a racial gerrymander and the decision in the 2000 presidential election.

Thus, a limit on *congressional* power in the equal protection realm is not a limit on *federal* power. It simply shifts all national power from Congress to the Court, and keeps the Court in control of state voting rights rules. Whatever may be said of state autonomy in this area today, it is impossible given the Court's own precedents.

This view does not mean that the Court should simply rubber-stamp any legislation in the voting rights area. Besides protecting core political equality rights, the Court should ensure, as in the campaign finance context, that congressional legislation purportedly aimed at promoting political equality is really aimed in that direction, rather than having a self-interested purpose.

Self-interest in the area of voting rights may seem a bit less apparent than in the campaign finance context, but it exists nonetheless. Indeed, throughout the 1990s an odd coalition of liberal African-American Democrats and the Republican Party pushed for the creation of more majority-minority districts under the Voting Rights Act. The gains for the African-American Democrats are more seats; the goal for the Republican Party has been to place as many Democrats into the smallest number of districts possible, thereby aiding Republican efforts overall.[134]

Policing conduct aimed at partisan advantage but passed in the guise of political equality requires a closer look at the connection between means and ends. Thus, if the Court were to follow my suggestion and give much broader powers to Congress to enact measures pursuing political equality, it should look (as in the campaign finance context) for a close fit between the means and ends. Caminker's arguments should carry less weight in a regime of strong congressional power, with the Court recognizing the possibility of self-interested legislation.

The Clash of Equalities

The final area to consider here arises when Congress (assuming it has the power) or a state or local legislative body enacts a law ostensibly to promote political equality that arguably creates political inequality at the same time. For example, in the 1972 New York state redistricting process, the New York legislature drew new state Senate and Assembly district lines that divided the tight-knit Hasidic Jewish community of Williamsburg, Brooklyn, into two Senate districts and two Assembly districts. The legislature defended the line-drawing as an effort to comply with a Justice Department preclearance request to increase the size of the nonwhite populations in these districts, although it appears that the legislature may have been able to meet the Justice Department's goals without slicing the Hasidic community in half by moving other white voters into the districts.[135]

In a case that made it to the Supreme Court, the Hasidim challenged the districting by raising a variety of statutory and constitutional claims. Significantly, they did "not press any legal claim to a group voice as Hasidim."[136] The Court rejected the argument that as members of the undifferentiated white majority, the Hasidim's voting strength was unconstitutionally diluted.[137]

But suppose the Hasidim had pressed such a claim. Should it have been successful? As argued earlier, a state (and Congress commanding the states through the Voting Rights Act) should be allowed to require more proportional representation of minority groups in the political process; legislatures may permissibly act to adopt contested views of political equality. But when faced with a claim that such action violates the political equality rights of other individuals or voters, the Court should consider whether the action interferes with the core political equality rights of others. If so, the legislative action is impermissible.

Thus, it would be impermissible for the New York legislature, in order to promote minority voting rights, to give two votes to every member of a minority group but only one vote to every member of the white majority (or one vote to every member of the Hasidic community in the affected districts). Such unequally weighted votes would violate the essential political rights of members of the white majority (or the Hasidim).

In the real case involving the Hasidim, however, the Hasidim likely should not be successful in challenging a districting plan that diluted the Hasidim's voting strength. There is no core political equality right to proportional interest representation. Given the history of racial discrimination in voting, the legislature could reasonably choose to guarantee something like proportional interest representation only to those groups most strongly affected by past discrimination.

This legislative power has an important limit, however. As the legislature makes it more difficult for a political cohesive group like the Hasidim to engage in collective action, the legislature faces the danger it is violating the core right of members of that group under the collective action principle to organize for effective political action. For this reason, legislatures would do well to avoid actions like splitting up cohesive political groups when political equality aims could be achieved by equally effective alternative means.

Conclusion

The common theme that emerges from these three disparate areas of election law is that the Supreme Court should give considerable leeway and deference to legislative value judgments about whether and how to promote peripheral political equality claims. Leaving such judgments to the political branches removes the danger of ossification and entrenchment that would accompany Court constitutionalization of peripheral equality claims. The political processes also can be counted on to constrain most legislative excesses.

Although Court deference is appropriate to legislative value judgments, the Court must take a closer look at the connection between means and ends. This scrutiny serves to police legislative self-interest in the guise of political equality. In addition, as protector of core political equality principles, the Court would continue to play an important role as a backstop and guarantor of essential political rights, without the dangers that accompany its acceptance or rejection of new political equality claims under the Constitution.

5

Equality, Not Structure
The End of Individual Rights?

The changes I have advocated in the three preceding chapters recognize that courts (and the law professors providing them with unsolicited advice!) do not have particular expertise in the design of political systems or government entities across the United States. But courts remain the government actors of last resort who must referee some high-stakes political battles and protect basic rights of political equality, and the Supreme Court by necessity sets these basic refereeing rules and defines the protective floor.

If the Supreme Court adopted the procedural and substantive changes to political equality jurisprudence of chapters 2, 3, and 4, American election law would change substantially. The Court would show much greater institutional modesty in defining the scope of new equal protection rights, following as much as leading society. In reviewing challenges to existing election laws, the Court would fulfill its primary purpose by protecting core equality principles from government intrusion. In appropriate cases, the Court would balance infringements on individual and group core political equality rights with other government interests, such as the interest in preventing voter confusion. In this careful balancing, the Court would police the problem of legislative self-interest through close means-ends scrutiny. It would not accept claims of voter confusion at face value. The Court also would defer to legislative value judgments about appropriate steps to expand political equality. Again, the Court would use close means-ends scrutiny to distinguish between measures aimed truly at expanding political equality and those measures masquerading as political equality measures enacted simply for legislative self-protection.

As novel as my program is, there are elements that are familiar, even conservative. Calls for judicial modesty or minimalism echo conservative calls for judicial restraint. And balancing remains a readily familiar tool when faced with competing claims between the government and individuals (or groups of individuals).

Just arriving over the horizon, however, is a much more radical approach to election law cases. The approach views balancing of rights and state interests as passé. Instead of balancing, constitutional adjudicators should examine the "structure" or "functioning" of the election process and make appropriate adjustments consistent with defined systemic goals for the political system. Election law becomes transformed into "political regulation."[1]

The trend, which Pamela Karlan has termed "structural equal protection" in its judicial manifestation,[2] has gained adherents both on the Supreme Court and among prominent members of the legal academy. It is about judicial hubris rather than judicial modesty or restraint. Because these structural theories require great intrusion by the judiciary into the political processes without sufficient justification, they are misguided and dangerous.

I begin by describing the rise of structural equal protection in the Supreme Court, which Karlan and others have chronicled well. I focus the bulk of this chapter on a critique of structural theories in the legal academy, particularly the "political markets" model of Samuel Issacharoff and Richard H. Pildes. The Issacharoff-Pildes model is becoming the new election law orthodoxy, and this chapter offers a dissenting view at least to its more revolutionary strand.

Structural Equal Protection in the Courts

According to Karlan, under structural equal protection, "[t]he Court deploys the Equal Protection Clause not to protect the rights of an identifiable group of individuals, particularly a group unable to protect itself through operation of the normal political processes, but rather to regulate the institutional arrangements within which politics is conducted."[3] Karlan's Exhibit "A" is *Shaw v. Reno.*[4]

Readers will recall that *Shaw* arose out of North Carolina's redistricting for the United States House of Representatives after the 1990 census. In order to satisfy Justice Department preclearance requirements under section 5 of the Voting Rights Act as the Justice Department then understood it, the North Carolina legislature created an extremely odd shaped second majority-minority district. The Court held that the creation of such a district could violate the Constitution's equal protection guarantees, even absent proof that such a district diluted anyone's voting rights.

As Karlan explains, *Shaw* cannot be understood as a traditional voting rights case. The North Carolina districting denied no one the right to vote nor minimized anyone's voting strength. "It was a claim that the very use of race in the process of redistricting was divisive and harmful."[5] The *Shaw* Court wrote that the use of race in redistricting "reinforces the perception that members of the same racial group—regardless of their age, education, economic status, or the community in which they live—think alike, share the same political interests, and will prefer the same candidates at the polls."[6] The Court suggested that such race-conscious districting exacerbates racial bloc voting and sends a message to an elected representative that she need represent only members of her group.

The *Shaw* Court emphasized the bizarre shape of the North Carolina district in question, declaring "reapportionment is one area in which appearances do matter."[7] But the Court, in an opinion written by Justice O'-Connor, failed to clearly define the nature of the injury, not even the elements necessary to prove it or who had standing to raise it. These matters have been fleshed out, more or less, as the consistent five-member majority (Chief Justice Rehnquist and Justices Kennedy, O'Connor, Scalia, and Thomas) worked through subsequent racial gerrymandering cases. The cases are particularly fact intensive—a big problem for the courts in this area, given the correlation between race and partisan identification (African-American voters, for example, overwhelmingly support Democratic candidates), is figuring out whether a legislature has engaged in impermissible districting based on race, or permissible districting based upon partisan affiliation. Indeed, in the most recent of the cases Justice O'Connor sided with the usual four dissenters in the *Shaw* cases in upholding the *fourth* Supreme Court challenge to a North Carolina legislative districting plan in eight years.[8] Partisanship, not race, explained the lines, the Court declared.

After the Court decided *Shaw*, Pildes and political scientist Richard Niemi wrote an important article discussing this new constitutional cause of action. They characterized a *Shaw* claim as an "expressive harm":

> One can only understand *Shaw*, we believe, in terms of a view that what we call expressive harms are constitutionally cognizable. An expressive

harm is one that results from the ideas or attitudes expressed through governmental action, rather than from the more tangible or material consequences the action brings about. On this view, the meaning of a governmental action is just as important as what that action does. Public policies can violate the Constitution not only because they bring about concrete costs, but because the very meaning they convey demonstrates inappropriate respect for relevant public values.[9]

Explaining that the harm in expressive harm cases is "social rather than individual,"[10] Pildes and Niemi wrote "*Shaw* . . . rests on the principle that, when government appears to use race in the redistricting context in a way that subordinates all other relevant values, the state has impermissibly endorsed too dominant a role for race."[11]

Pildes and Niemi did not opine on whether *Shaw* was correctly or incorrectly decided, calling the application of the expressive harms theory in constitutional law "intriguing and undoubtedly controversial."[12] But Pildes and Niemi's explanation of *Shaw* as an expressive harms case provided its supporters on the Court with a coherent (if controversial) argument in support of the cause of action. Justice O'Connor latched on to the post hoc explanation of the case, declaring in a 1996 racial gerrymandering case out of Texas that "[w]e are aware of the difficulties faced by the States, and by the district courts, in confronting new constitutional precedents, and we also know that *the nature of the expressive harms with which we are dealing,* and the complexity of the districting process, are such that bright-line rules are not available."[13]

Commentators have criticized the *Shaw* line of cases in a variety of ways beyond its lack of doctrinal clarity. Some have noted that although the cases are premised upon a notion of what Justice O'Connor in *Shaw* called "political apartheid," the districts in question are among the most integrated in the country.[14] Others, including Issacharoff, have noted that *Shaw* is based upon "casual empirical assumptions" that race-conscious districting exacerbates racial bloc voting or sends a message to an elected representative that she need represent only members of her group.[15] Still others fault the opinion for intruding on the values of federalism that the members of the *Shaw* majority have elsewhere espoused[16] or for undermining the political power of minorities.[17]

Many of these criticisms have merit, and I agree that they provide more than enough reason for the Court to overturn the *Shaw* line of cases.

Shaw, however, is more dangerous than might appear from the mere establishment of the new cause of action for an unconstitutional racial gerrymander. After all, recent Court interpretations of the Voting Rights Act likely will deter the Justice Department from pressuring states to create more majority-minority districts, thereby lessening the number of successful *Shaw* claims.[18] My concern with *Shaw* is more general: it is the danger of recognizing such "structural equal protection" claims.

Karlan has noted that *Shaw* does not involve disenfranchisement or vote dilution. But we can go even further than that using the terminology developed in earlier chapters. Taking race into account in districting violates *no core equality principle*. It denies no one essential political rights; it does not violate the antiplutocracy principle by taking wealth or property ownership into account; and it violates no collective action principle. It does not even violate any *contested* political equality principle that the Court might recognize. In short, although the *Shaw* Court used the label of equal protection, there does not appear to be any political equality problem at issue in these cases. Even when the government "sends a message with its conduct" in a political equality case, we should view that message as irrelevant if it has no bearing on real political power relationships.[19]

The case would be different if the empirical assumptions underlying the *Shaw* claim were proven. In other words, if the government-sent "message" created by race conscious districting had identifiable deleterious effects on core political equality rights of individuals or groups, the Court would have been correct in barring the practice. The available evidence, however, goes strongly against the *Shaw* thesis that race-conscious districting creates legislators responsive to only their own groups.[20] And in an era when jurisdictions created new majority-minority districts, the rate of racial bloc voting decreased, not increased.[21] Thus, there is no reason to believe the so-called expressive harms caused real harms.

I recognize that in extreme cases, the Court should *presume* the presence of real harms to political equality coming out of an expressive harm. Thus, if a state today created "separate but equal" polling places for whites and African-Americans, a court could reasonably conclude that the "message" such separation would send might in fact exacerbate racial tensions in voting. These tensions could lead to increased racial bloc voting, and enough racial bloc voting would undermine the collective action principle: separate polling booths would be an unreasonable impediment on individuals who wish to organize into groups to engage in collective action for political purposes.

That extreme case is a far cry from *Shaw,* in terms of both the factual issues (races were not really separated in *Shaw,* and the correlation of race and partisanship makes it likely that legislators sometimes used race as a proxy for party affiliation; there would be no factual dispute as to the rationale for separate voting areas) and the extent of the empirical assumptions necessary to make a plausible case that the practice will have real effect on political equality. In any event, *Shaw* does not require any such proof for a racial gerrymandering claim to be successful.[22]

Indeed, the real problem of *Shaw* is the "message" that the Court has sent about future political equality cases: an equal protection claim may be entirely unmoored from any real-world concerns about political equality. Karlan views *Bush v. Gore*[23] as another structural equal protection case: "Whatever interest the Supreme Court's decision [in *Bush v. Gore*] vindicated, it was not the interest of an identifiable individual voter. Rather it was a perceived systemic interest in having recounts conducted according to a uniform standard or not at all. It was structural equal protection, just as the *Shaw* cases have been."[24]

Structural Theory in the Academy: A Critique of the Political Markets Approach

As the *Shaw* cases worked their way up and down the federal courts in the late 1990s, a parallel structural theory gained a foothold in the legal academy, a theory that has come to be called the "political markets" approach.[25] Its leading proponents are Samuel Issacharoff and Richard Pildes. The theory is still a work-in-progress, making it somewhat of a moving target. And recent separate writings of Issacharoff and Pildes suggest they have different views on the contours and the extent of the political markets approach. For this reason, I carefully delineate the approach's history and evolution in my critique.

The approach originated in Issacharoff and Pildes's 1998 *Stanford Law Review* article, *Politics as Markets: Partisan Lockups of the Democratic Process.*[26] There, the authors rejected the current Supreme Court's approach to election law cases in which an individual claims that the government has infringed on her political rights, the government provides a reason or reasons justifying the law, and the Court balances rights and interests. To Issacharoff and Pildes, this framework is "stagnant discourse" that leads to "sterile balancing."[27]

The authors argued instead for a "process-based" or "functional" inquiry in which the Court would view "politics as akin . . . to a robustly competitive market—a market whose vitality depends on both clear rules of engagement and on the ritual cleansing born of competition." Politicians constitute "a managerial class, imperfectly accountable through periodic review to a diffuse body of equity holders known as the electorate." The judiciary's role is to take a hard look at political self-promotion, particularly the use of election laws to "lock up" the political process. The judiciary should "destabilize political lockups in order to protect the competitive vitality of the electoral process" and to preserve an "appropriately competitive political order."[28]

The authors analogized laws that legislators pass to protect one-party dominance or two-party duopoly in the electoral arena to corporate lockups. A lockup in corporate law occurs when a corporation faces, or is about to face, a takeover bid. Under the lockup, target management promises to confer a benefit on a bidder if that bidder ultimately loses a bidding contest. Management of the target corporation sometimes will agree to a lockup in exchange for personal benefits or a promise of future employment as managers after the acquisition. A lockup procured with such a "management deal" is inefficient because it lessens the possibility of a hostile takeover, which can discipline managers to run their companies efficiently.[29]

Many election law scholars began citing the initial political markets approach favorably. Daniel Ortiz, for example, celebrated the move in election law "from rights to arrangements."[30] But, as I will detail below, more recent writings on the political markets approach, at least as applied by Issacharoff, suggest the celebration is premature.

Initial criticisms of the political markets approach fell into three categories. First, the theory lacked any kind of precision about what it would mean for the Court to ensure "appropriate" political competition. Consider two examples in *Politics as Markets* where the authors applied their analysis to election law issues. In *Timmons v. Twin Cities Area New Party*,[31] as detailed in chapter 3, the Court upheld Minnesota's ban on fusion, which is the electoral support of a single set of candidates by two or more parties. Issacharoff and Pildes argued that antifusion laws dramatically raise barriers to entry by third parties by requiring a third party to displace one of the major parties rather than influencing one of them. The authors opposed the outcome of *Timmons* because of its "primary intent of shoring up two-party exclusivity."[32]

In contrast to that analysis, Issacharoff and Pildes questioned whether section 2 of the Voting Rights Act (VRA) continues to be necessary (at least under what they call an antidiscrimination model of the act). They note that "[n]either Congress nor the courts have explored whether the policies of the VRA, or the constitutional doctrine on vote dilution, should be modified in light of the robust political markets that have emerged" in areas covered by the act. What makes these markets "robust" is the transformation in the past few decades from a one-party South to "intensely partisan arenas" where Democrats and Republicans actively compete for votes and use the VRA for partisan advantage.[33]

How is it that two-party competition in Minnesota's electoral system is not "appropriately competitive," whereas the South's emerging two-party competition is "robust"? The authors provided no answer. Missing from the initial political markets model was a theory of *appropriate* political competition. Lockup theory in corporate law is unhelpful because in corporate law the normative goal is maximizing shareholder wealth or overall social wealth. In deciding whether to allow lockups in the corporate sphere, we compare the gains and losses of shareholders (or society) under a legal regime allowing lockups to the gains and losses under a legal regime banning lockups in the presence of management self-dealing.

We thankfully do not design our political system like our system of corporate governance to ensure social wealth creation to the exclusion of all other values. (The idea is somewhat controversial even in the realm of corporate governance.) Politics may be like a market in some senses, but it is not a literal market in which the government legalizes the sale of political influence to the highest bidder. And Issacharoff and Pildes do not call for such a literally economic approach to politics. The initial political markets approach provided no normative baseline against which to measure the competitiveness of a political environment.

The second major criticism of the initial political markets approach was that it appeared to offer very little hope of actually meeting its goal of increased political competition, at least if "competition" is understood as allowing for the emergence of a multiparty system in the United States. The political science literature strongly suggests that single-member districts, presidential elections, and the direct primary are the significant factors determining the strength of a two-party system in the United States.[34] But Issacharoff and Pildes spent little attention on these issues, focusing instead on cases such as *Burdick v. Takushi*[35] involving Hawaii's decision to ban write-in votes. As Lowenstein remarked, "Issacharoff and Pildes do not expect the Supreme Court to eliminate single-member districts, presidential elections, or direct primaries. It is not clear, therefore, what difference it would make if the Court were to subscribe to their theory of partisan lockups as the key to election law adjudication."[36]

The final major criticism of the political markets model advanced by political scientist Bruce Cain was that it "leads inevitably to intrusive judicial involvement in states' political arrangements" by "requiring them to lock in particular theories of representation that are not necessarily fundamental to a democratic form of government."[37] Far from seeing the approach as ineffective along the lines of the second criticism, Cain saw as the approach's "logical conclusion"

> the most extreme forms of proportional representation. If the goal is to lower entry costs for third parties wherever possible, the first institutional barriers to be torn down might be marginally important institutions such as antifusion provisions, the rules for televised debates, or discriminatory campaign finance laws. But ultimately, the only really important discrimination against minor parties is the single-member simple plurality rule itself.[38]

That the initial theory could be viewed simultaneously as momentous or inconsequential (or as Pildes himself put it later, "radical or banal")[39] pointed out its immaturity. That is no criticism of Issacharoff and Pildes; they were courageous to open discussion in a provocative way on structural approaches to election law even before they had worked out the details of their theory.

Fortunately, Pildes and Issacharoff have now separately responded to these criticisms, providing a much better sense of the scope of the political markets approach. Indeed, the separate responses show two poles of the approach. Pildes refined the political markets approach to be akin to a balancing approach (though he would certainly disclaim the label), in effect endorsing the core "collective action" political equality principle described in chapter 3. Issacharoff, on the other hand, sees the political markets approach as a road map for the courts to rework the political makeup of every legislative district in the country to increase voter choice and the accountability of public officials to voters.

Pildes and Court Challenges to Single-Member Districts

Pildes rightly takes issue with critics who argue that it would be inconsequential for the Court to strike down antifusion laws, write-in bans, and other laws that inhibit activity of third parties. In recasting his prior call with Issacharoff for court creation of an "appropriately competitive partisan political environment" as more accurately a call for an "assurance that 'artificial' barriers to robust partisan competition not be permitted,"[40] Pildes argues that Court removal of "artificial" barriers could create a more competitive political environment without causing the downfall of the two-party system. Pildes plausibly explains the success of third-party Minnesota gubernatorial candidate Jesse Ventura as partly driven by Minnesota's third party friendly election laws, particularly its same-day voter registration and public financing of elections.[41] He reasons that changes in other state laws to mirror Minnesota's laws may well allow for greater success of third parties and independent candidates.

Pildes's argument reads much like my substantive arguments under the collective action principle of political equality. Antifusion laws likely constitute an unreasonable barrier to effective collective action by third parties. ("Unreasonable" is a better word than "artificial" because "reasonableness" connotes judgment and "artificiality" incorrectly suggests there is some "natural" political order.) States should have a good reason for imposing barriers beyond stifling competition, especially because third-party candidates might run not only to win, as in the case of Ventura, but also to influence the debate between the major-party candidates and to leverage marginal votes to gain political concessions from major-party candidates standing to lose from the minor candidate's participation. The Court was wrong to accept an anticompetitive reason (protection of the two-party system) as an acceptable justification for the law.

Pildes further moderates the political markets approach in considering Cain's claim that the logical implication of the approach is to declare unconstitutional winner-take-all elections. Although recognizing that winner-take-all elections should not be immune from "intellectual scrutiny," Pildes declares that the political market approach "will inevitably be limited, as with *any* single legal principle or value, by the other values or principles that law and political culture make relevant."[42] He lists the following "countervailing values [that] could be marshaled against judicial imposition" of proportional representation:

1) an original intent that recognized the winner-take-all structure even if not requiring it; 2) the longstanding historical fact of this structure's existence, which might carry weight in law even if not in ideal theory; 3) the importance of public acceptability and legitimacy to the soundness of judicial decisions, which can make revolutionary changes in democratic structures suspect when they emanate from courts; 4) the lack of any anticompetitive original purpose behind the winner-take-all system; and 5) the fact that important affirmative values can be offered for this electoral structure other than anticompetitive ones, such as the stronger ties between legislators and constituents that territorial districts arguably promote.[43]

It is not important for us to consider here *how* Pildes would strike the balance between these factors and the anticompetitive nature of the political markets approach. What is important to note is Pildes's *requirement of balancing*.[44] True, it is not a balancing of individual or group rights against state interests per se; it is a balancing *among* structural concerns of anticompetitiveness, responsiveness, and other values (though Pildes does not explain why history and tradition should be relevant in the structural analysis).

This milder interpretation of the political markets approach easily could be recast in the more traditional balancing test used by the Court or using my framework as a third-party candidate challenging the winner-take-all system as violative of the collective action principle through the Equal Protection Clause. The results and essential consideration of trade-offs appear to be the same, despite the semantic differences.

Like Pildes, I believe there are very strong arguments to balance against a claim that winner-take-all elections are unconstitutional; indeed, I view the issue as one properly left to the political process, particularly in jurisdictions that have an initiative process to overcome legislative self-interest problems in making such fundamental election reforms. The alternative is to enshrine into permanent law across the United States a highly contested view of political equality.

The main point here is that Pildes must resort to a balancing approach to explain how the Court should actually reach results in some difficult cases. And in this balancing, Pildes has acknowledged that he is concerned with substantive values, no less than my own concern with substantive values in chapters 3 and 4. Pildes acknowledges that the political markets approach "ultimately requires defending the substantive values (such as democratic responsiveness) that this competition would realize, as well as giving more precise substantive content to the boundaries between permissible and impermissible structuring of political competition."[45] When Pildes moves to the stage in his argument to define the substantive values supporting the political markets approach more explicitly, his argument may end up looking very much like the collective action principle of chapter 3.

Issacharoff and Partisan Gerrymandering

If Pildes represents the moderate side of the political markets approach, Issacharoff is its true revolutionary. In his most recent work on the subject, Issacharoff has called upon the courts to strike down all legislative districting conducted by partisan officials as presumptively unconstitutional, leading to districting conducted solely by nonpartisan commissions or by computer. Issacharoff makes this argument in the name of political competition, and I have little doubt that, if he takes his own approach seriously, he would urge courts to strike down winner-take-all districts as well to promote such competition.

Issacharoff's boldness is of very recent vintage. In 2001, Issacharoff wrote an article applying the political markets approach to analyze *California Democratic Party v. Jones*,[46] the Supreme Court's case striking down California's "blanket primary." The Court in *Jones* held that the state of California violated the First Amendment "associational rights" of a political party by forcing it to hold primaries in which voters not registered with the party could decide to cross over on election day and vote for that party's candidates in any and all races on the ballot.[47]

Consistent with the political markets approach, Issacharoff rejected the Court's rights-based analysis (which asked whether political parties have rights of association that the government infringed through enacting the blanket primary) in favor of a structural analysis considering whether "alterations of the party candidate selection processes threaten to thwart the parties' ability to carry forth as the indispensable organizational vehicles for republican politics, and [] threaten as well the incentive to undertake voter education and mobilization in the political process."[48] He ultimately (and reluctantly) concluded that the structural argument against the blanket primary failed for lack of empirical support: states with such primaries did not have emasculated political parties.

In reaching the conclusion that his structural argument did not align with his personal policy preferences for striking down the blanket primary, Issacharoff stressed that he had resisted the urge to descend into "ad hoc constitutionalization."[49] He defended the "lockup metaphor" as necessary to prevent judges from "evaluat[ing] whether outcomes in the political process are proper." Responding to my earlier argument that the initial political markets approach failed to define "appropriate" political competition, Issacharoff explained that "absent an intent-based condemnation of the motives underlying the conduct of incumbent officials [through the lockup metaphor], broad-gauged constitutional principles turn out to be exceptionally difficult to apply to limit the potential range of institutional arrangements consistent with republican governance."[50]

But the political markets approach has proven to be similarly uncabined in Issacharoff's hands. In a recent *Harvard Law Review* article,[51] Issacharoff makes the case, under the political markets approach, for the unconstitutionality of all districting done by partisan officials.

Issacharoff's article is particularly valuable in setting forth a normative justification for his approach; as he had remarked in 2000, any approach to political regulation "requires . . . a normative structure that explains what the goals of regulation of the political process should be."[52] Like Pildes's suggestion that the normative justification for the political markets approach may well be "democratic responsiveness," Issacharoff argues that the approach protects "a core tenet of democratic legitimacy: accountability to shifting voter preferences." To Issacharoff, the risk of gerrymandering is that it "constrict[s] the competitive processes by which voters can express choice."[53]

I will return shortly to the question whether the normative values of "responsiveness" or "voter choice" should be considered paramount values (or even on par with the equality rationale) in regulating politics. But even taking Issacharoff's normative value judgments as a given, Issacharoff's argument offers no real limits on judicial intervention. If the main goal of political regulation is "accountability to shifting voter preferences," or "responsiveness," why not lawsuits to (1) increase the frequency of elections; (2) require the use of the initiative process, or at least to require legislators to honor instructions given to legislators; (3) and eliminate winner-take-all elections, which constrain voter choice? Might term limits now be constitutionally required, or at least (extra) public financing of third-party and independent candidates for office?[54] The normative justification put forward by Issacharoff thus far provides no limiting principle to separate permissible from impermissible state regulation of elections.

Like Pildes, Issacharoff responds to this concern about the imprecision of the political markets approach by echoing Martin Shapiro's call for policing of illegal gerrymandering even absent a theory of proper legislative districting: "[A]ll those called upon to make ethical decisions . . . are often in a position to identify *a wrong* without being able to define *the right*."[55] Issacharoff argues that "[i]t is possible to distinguish between enabling rules that define the engagement and restraining rules that are designed to frustrate challenge."[56] Returning to the analogy of the economic market, he further argues that even if the precise number of competitors necessary for a competitive economic market is unclear, it is "possible to identify anticompetitive behavior that artificially restricts the ability of new entrants to emerge or improperly entrenches the privileged position of the dominant actors."[57]

Issacharoff is far more sanguine than I am that one may distinguish between "enabling rules that define the engagement" and "restraining rules that are designed to frustrate challenge." More important, he does not explain why enabling rules (which I presume would include winner-take-all elections) should be insulated from the "intellectual scrutiny" that Pildes has demanded. Indeed, a serious approach to political competition would subject electoral enabling rules to the *greatest* challenge because it is there that the empirical evidence shows the strongest link between partisan competition and election law. This is a point that Issacharoff must recognize eventually if he continues to advocate the political markets approach.

In addition, although it may not be literally impossible to identify "artificial" restrictions on political competition compared to real or natural ones, Issacharoff has not provided the tools to do so. We have no theory of natural political competition. I suggest that drawing this line will inevitably require a balancing, and a look at the reasons behind the government action as well as its reasonableness. Reasonableness and strict means-ends scrutiny should separate permissible election laws that inhibit political competition from impermissible ones.

In calling for courts to outlaw most legislative districting in the United States, Issacharoff at the very least should require strong evidence that the practice in fact has prevented accountability to shifting voter preferences. After all, it was Issacharoff who criticized the *Shaw* Court for failing to examine empirical evidence to support its assertion that dividing voters according to race in districts in fact increased racially polarized voting or caused legislators to be less responsive to constituents not of their race. And it was Issacharoff who a year before his *Harvard Law Review* article wrote that the Court erred in striking down California's blanket primary because there was inadequate empirical evidence that the form of primary had in fact weakened political parties.

But Issacharoff now claims that evidence of a link between districting and political competition is unnecessary:

> Ultimately . . . this Article does not rise or fall on the narrow empirical question whether gerrymandering is the predominant cause of the increase in uncontested or uncompetitive elections. . . . Even if the extent of the effect . . . remains a matter of debate, the question is whether deliberate use of powers over redistricting to attempt to insulate incumbent officeholders from meaningful challenge is normatively proper and constitutionally tolerable.[58]

As with the expressive harms in *Shaw*, I see nothing normatively improper (much less constitutionally intolerable) about a practice that causes no harm to individuals or groups of individuals. Even Issacharoff at bottom is concerned about individuals—not on grounds of equality but to preserve voter choice and government responsiveness. If there is no link between gerrymandering and these individual concerns, there is no harm to be remedied. How he can argue that his policy recommendation does not rise or fall on the empirical question is puzzling.

On the empirical question itself, Nathaniel Persily has ably and exhaustively refuted Issacharoff's argument that purposeful districting removes voter choice and responsiveness.[59] Persily builds upon a vast political science literature, including the important work of Stephen Ansolabehere and James Snyder, who found that incumbents have been returned to office in high numbers in recent decades whether coming from gerrymandered districts or no districts at all (as in the case of state executives).[60] Given that fact, it is hard to see that districting is making much difference to the incumbency advantage. Persily also points out that Issacharoff ignores evidence of both intense competition for the control of legislatures and remarkable levels of legislative turnover, the latter due in large part on the state level to term limits. Persily also considers how Issacharoff could rightly be measuring governmental responsiveness, questioning whether a districting system that produces many competitive races over one that produces generally proportional representation of party interests in the legislature better serves the needs of government responsiveness.

The empirical case alone is reason to be wary of Issacharoff's proposal. But the concern is much greater, the same concern I expressed earlier in relation to the *Shaw* cause of action: it is a concern about judicial hubris, about the belief that the Court not only can and should make deeply contested normative judgments about the appropriate functioning of the political process but also come down on one side of an empirical debate without really taking a serious look at the evidence.

Why Equality and Not "Structure"?

I return now to a question flagged a bit earlier but deferred, whether the Court in addressing election law questions should consider the goal of "political competition" (in support of the normative value of governmental responsiveness) paramount to, or on par with, the political equality concerns I have addressed throughout out this book. I am tempted to provide a textual answer. The Constitution specifically provides for equal protection of the laws and for nondiscrimination in voting on the basis of race, gender, and age (for those at least age 18). Persily notes in his critique of Issacharoff that Issacharoff does not even bother advancing a "textual hook" upon which to hang his rule against partisan districting.[61] So it could be said that my equality arguments are properly based in the Constitution and that political competition arguments are not—after all, a major goal of the initial Issacharoff and Pildes article was to demonstrate that our rather old Constitution, compared to post–World War II European constitutions, does not deal adequately with matters of political competition.[62]

The textual argument proves too much, however. There seems little doubt that the drafters of the Equal Protection Clause of the Fourteenth Amendment did not intend it to apply to issues of voting, but that has not stopped the Court from often applying it there, nor does it stop me from relying on those cases in crafting my argument for Court protection of core equality principles. My argument is premised upon social consensus about the core concerns of equality and as such it is anti-originalist. And I have little doubt that if he bothered, Issacharoff could find the requisite textual hook. He suggested that a Court ruling striking down California's blanket primary could have been based upon the Guaranty clause[63] and perhaps the antipartisan districting rule could find a home there too.

Instead, this issue comes down to a straight-out value judgment about what it is that the Court should (and can effectively) do. I no longer trust the Court to make contested value judgments in political cases. And I have become skeptical that the justices are committed to doing a good job examining the social science evidence regarding the effects of court-mandated regulation of the political process. *Timmons*'s blind acceptance of the two-party stability rationale and *Shaw*'s sheer speculation about the effects of assumed expressive harms prove that point.

Having said that, I continue to believe that there are certain core rights that the Court must continue to protect. I want the Court to police the equality outliers, those jurisdictions that would deny the right to vote on account of race, or allow a party to impose a fee to vote in a party primary, or make it all but impossible for a third-party challenger to gain a place on the electoral ballot.

I do not believe that Issacharoff or Pildes have made the case that we need a Court to ensure an appropriate level of legislative responsiveness.[64] At least some jurisdictions (the largest being California) have a vibrant initiative process that allows for somewhat of a legislative bypass to create conditions for greater governmental responsiveness if desired by the majority.[65] The Court in the blanket primary case got it exactly wrong in deferring to the parties over the electoral process—this was a case all about government responsiveness, where California voters wanted parties to nominate candidates closer to the position of the average (or median) voter. Even on the congressional level, where we do not have the option of a legislative bypass, partisan competition is at its highest levels in a generation. Issacharoff is trying to solve a problem that likely does not exist.

I will begin to be concerned with a lack of legislative responsiveness when we see jurisdictions with a legislative bypass enacting election laws that are substantially different from those enacted in states without a legislative bypass, or where a single party dominates politics on the federal level. And elevating political competition unmoored to equality values will simply embolden the Court to engage in further political regulation depending upon the particular value judgments of the Court's members.

This minimalist argument against judicial intervention in the political process applies more broadly than just to Issacharoff and Pildes's calls for promotion of political competition. It applies as well to the Court's quixotic attempt to prevent "expressive harms" from the ostensible separation of races in jurisdictions that are among the most integrated in the country. It applies to the Court's unwarranted ending of the 2000 presidential election by failing to remand for a recount conducted along the lines of a uniform standard. Pildes is correct that *Bush v. Gore* should be seen as the latest in a line of cases in which a Court majority has protected another structural concern: an interest in political stability *Über alles.*[66] All of these case are symptomatic of a belief in unlimited judicial wisdom.

Conclusion

No doubt, there is an allure to structural theories. Even Persily, who has rightly criticized Issacharoff's antipartisan districting proposal, argues for a "functional" theory to justify the rights of political parties over the people to determine the appropriate form of party primary.[67] Such calls may be in line with the latest intellectual fad, but they may soon run their course.

Even the labeling of a theory as "structural" has its costs. In a thoughtful article, Heather Gerken criticized the Supreme Court's voting rights jurisprudence for the Court's embrace of an atheoretical, individually oriented approach to voting rights. She suggested that such claims instead should be considered hybrid individual-group rights claims (or "aggregate harms") because the harms depend upon how other members of a voters' group are treated in the political process.[68]

Gerken is right to criticize the Court for failing to consider (at least explicitly) the group-oriented nature of some harms. The core equality principles I have defined in earlier chapters would force explicit consideration of harms to groups, whether by requiring a relatively equally weighted vote, limiting the role of wealth in the electoral process, or, most directly, preventing the government from placing unreasonable barriers in front of groups of individuals who wish to engage in collective action.

Where Gerken errs is in classifying her aggregate harms approach as a structural one.[69] She is concerned about the allocation of political power among groups of voters, not the proper functioning of the political process in some abstract sense, like a call to promote "political competition." Labeling her theory as "structural" just obscures the real power relationships at issue in the voting rights cases she describes.

In examining structural theories in law, I am reminded of the rise and fall of such theories in political science more than a generation ago. At one point, Talcott Parsons's theories of "structural functionalism" dominated debate about the proper workings of political systems. Parsonian theory has now become viewed as tautological,[70] giving rise to an excess of methodological individualism in political science that goes under the name "rational choice theory."

Perhaps I am drawing a bigger distinction than necessary. At bottom, I suspect that structural theories are all about individual and group rights after all. Justice O'Connor does not really care about expressive harms per se but, rather, cares about the effects that government messages may have on individual voters. Issacharoff and Pildes do not value competition for its own sake (although many view politics as a sport) but value it as a means to promote government responsiveness to particular voter preferences.

Recognizing the underlying normative values that structural theories are intended to promote will provide the great benefit of allowing apples-to-apples comparisons among normative theories of judicial intervention in politics. And in those apples-to-apples comparisons, taking into account the limits of judicial competence and the evidence supporting empirical claims about political problems, a minimalist theory that protects core equality rights stacks up well against the competition.

Conclusion
Political Equality and a Minimalist Court

Political Equality and Legal Realism

Back in March 1965, Justice Black got burned. Seeing six votes to affirm a lower court ruling upholding the power of the states to impose a poll tax in state elections (absent congressional legislation or constitutional amendment), the justice probably concluded quite reasonably that there was little risk in calling for a full hearing in *Harper v. Virginia Board of Elections*. Justice Goldberg's proposed dissent from the anticipated summary affirmance enunciated an expansive view of the Court's nascent political equality jurisprudence begun in *Baker, Reynolds, Gray,* and *Wesberry,* and Justice Black likely wanted the Court to positively state that issues like voter qualifications were not on the table. After all, it was as recently as 1959 that the Court upheld literacy tests in the *Lassiter* case.

As detailed in chapter 1, Black's plan backfired. Justice Fortas replaced Justice Goldberg on the Court. Fortas too opposed the poll tax, and three other justices—Brennan, Clark, and White—switched their votes to a reversal after *Harper* was set for a full hearing. *Harper* has since been canonized as one of the landmark Warren era cases establishing the right to vote as a fundamental right.

The Constitution was not amended in 1965; three justices simply changed their minds about its meaning. Justice Black in his *Harper* dissent protested that the Court had overruled prior precedent "not by using its limited power to interpret the original meaning of the Equal Protection Clause, but by giving that clause a new meaning which it believes represents a better governmental policy."[1] Two days before the opinion issued, Justice Douglas added a sentence to the *Harper* majority opinion responding to Justice Black's point: "Our conclusion, like that in *Reynolds v. Sims,* is founded not on what we think governmental policy should be, but on what the Equal Protection Clause requires."[2]

If the history of the Court's political equality jurisprudence that I have chronicled shows anything, it shows that there has been no distinction between the justices' views of the meaning of the Equal Protection Clause and what the Constitution requires. As has often been remarked, the Supreme Court is not final because it is right; it is right because it is final. At least in the area of political equality, there is little question the justices of the Warren Court (like the justices of the Burger and Rehnquist Courts that followed) have "made it up" as they went along, even if the justices, like Justice Douglas, have perceived a need to profess Blacksonean notions of "discovering the law" to preserve their legitimacy.

Harper is not by far the only example, and significant changes have come in other political equality cases without changes in Court personnel. For example, Justices Blackmun, Marshall, Powell, and Scalia each reversed positions over time on key constitutional questions in the campaign finance area.

Harper itself was correctly decided in my view because the Court followed emerging social consensus, though it does not appear the *Harper* majority thought itself bound to follow social consensus. But *Harper* in following social consensus is the exception in the political equality cases rather than the rule.

David Strauss, who is involved in a project to show that landmark Warren Court cases such as *Brown v. Board of Education*[3] and *Miranda v. Arizona*[4] followed emerging trends in the common law and were not just examples of the justices making up the law as they went along, cannot make a convincing argument along these lines for the reapportionment cases.[5] He contends that cases such as *Reynolds* and its one person, one vote rule "carried out a development that extended back to the earliest days of the Republic—the inexorable (although not uninterrupted) expansion of the franchise."[6] But Strauss paints too rosy of a picture of this expansion: although the pre-Warren court upheld literacy tests in 1959 in the *Lassiter* case, remember that Arizona was still pushing for the right to impose a literacy test as late as 1970. Universal suffrage was hardly the norm in 1964, the year of *Reynolds*. More important, universal suffrage does not mandate the one person, one vote rule.

Social consensus has done little to rein in conservative justices any more than liberal justices. *Shaw v. Reno* and *Bush v. Gore* are as indefensible as *Reynolds* or *Wesberry* in this regard. Frankly, neither liberals nor conservatives have shown any affection for a limiting principle in political equality cases in the past forty years.

Getting to a Minimalist Court on Political Equality Cases

One of the criticisms of process theory that I have advanced is that it has not constrained the Court. *Bush v. Gore* is the most recent and important example of the Court's hearing a political equality case where the political process arguably was working. Why should my call for justices to protect a limited core of equality rights and to defer to political branches on contested equality claims fare any better?

I begin with the premise that arguments on the left to recognize proportional interest representation in cases such as *City of Mobile v. Bolden* beget arguments on the right to prevent race-based districting in cases such as *Shaw v. Reno*. Ironically, this point that judicial activism on one side of the political spectrum breeds judicial activism on the other opens up a small possibility for a mutually advantageous agreement among the justices: If you do not want the constitutionalization of a new right in *City of Mobile* (or *Shaw*), then agree not to interpret the Constitution to include a *Shaw* (or *City of Mobile*) claim. The question becomes one of Pareto superiority—is an agreement here possible among liberal and conservative justices that makes both groups of justices better off?[7]

If enough justices believe that in a reasonable time frame it is possible for the Court's balance of power to shift against the ideological direction that a particular justice favors, the deal looks like a good one: I'll give up my liberal activism on political equality issues if you'll give up your conservative activism. The argument supposes that both liberals and conservatives are more satisfied with a minimal Court that does less damage when in the "wrong" ideological position than with the benefits that come from being able to legislate political equality when the "right" ideological position holds a Court majority.

My argument certainly will cause some squirming by constitutional law scholars who believe that judicial deal making is indefensible as a jurisprudential matter. I believe the practice is not only defensible but laudatory. My argument does not require justices to vote against ideological self-interest. That is, a justice who believes that the Court should reach out and create a new equal protection cause of action in *City of Mobile* or *Shaw* does not vote against those values in rejecting the claim. The justice instead seeks to maximize an ideologically appealing basket of political equality cases over time.[8] The negative value of one of those cases in that basket may well exceed the positive value of the others.

In contrast to the constitutional law scholars, legal realists and political scientists may see my argument as too Pollyannaish. If a strong ideologue on the Court expects a Court majority in her favor for the foreseeable future, there is little incentive to engage in such a mutual nonaggression pact. Then, it is politically advantageous to build as much activist precedent as possible, leaving it for the Court way down the road to face the task of undoing firmly established precedent. My argument thus necessarily requires some uncertainty about the future ideological direction of the Court.

Even assuming enough uncertainty about the future ideological makeup of the Court, there is also the question of getting there from here. After all, justices in the past, like a lame duck legislature, have pushed through their ideological agendas in advance of an anticipated ideological shift in the Court. One unconfirmed story in this regard appears in the case history of the October 1968 Supreme Court term written by Justice Brennan's law clerks. According to the clerks (and I stress I cannot confirm this story), Justice Marshall was reluctant to join in Justice Brennan's opinion striking down a New York congressional districting plan with a 13.1 percent deviation in district populations.[9] When Marshall did not appear to want to cast the deciding vote in favor of striking down the plan, Brennan went to Chief Justice Warren, who then talked to Marshall. Warren "reputedly argued to Marshall the importance of defining the scope of the reapportionment decisions . . . before new appointments to the Court are made which may well change the balance on reapportionment issues. Justice Marshall joined Justice Brennan's opinions immediately after that conversation."[10]

Given this possibility, why should a justice like Justice Scalia temper himself in the political equality cases even if he received an assurance from a justice like Justice Ginsburg that she would do the same if her views ever command a majority on the Court? There is no enforceable contract. The key is to build mutual trust on the Court in the form of signaling. Justices could signal more moderate positions on issues, particularly in the form of dicta in majority opinions or through concurring and dissenting opinions. The cost of such signals is low: dicta and statements in concurring or dissenting opinions do not necessarily bind the justices to a position, but there is a reputational cost associated with changing one's position after publicly announcing it. Dicta are just the right instruments for building trust.

The issue of deference to political branches' interpretations of various means to expand political equality creates a more difficult situation for the emergence of a Pareto-superior agreement. Such deference likely favors liberals; for example, when a jurisdiction declines to enact campaign finance regulation to promote political equality, the Court need not do anything (because there is no core political equality right to public financing of political campaigns). It is only when the jurisdiction *enacts* such regulation to promote political equality that the Court is called upon to defer. In other words, liberals benefit more than conservatives by a rule that says that courts should defer to decisions by the political branches to embrace contested political equality arguments.

Thus, the emergence of such deference appears to require one of two conditions: either (1) liberal justices control the Court for the foreseeable future and therefore see no need to compromise (meaning the possibility of an activist Court on core equality issues); or (2) liberal justices make a convincing argument to the conservatives that deference on political equality questions should be thrown into the basket of compromise as well, and that it would benefit conservatives to agree on deference in exchange for liberal Court justices refraining from constitutionalizing more equality rights. To give an example, the liberal justice could in effect offer not to constitutionalize a right to public financing of electoral campaigns in exchange for the conservative justice's agreeing not to block campaign finance regulation enacted in the name of political equality.

Lessons for the Court's Constitutional Jurisprudence outside the Context of Political Equality

Readers convinced by my arguments in the context of the political equality cases may wonder whether the Court strategies I advocate should be cabined to political equality or extended more broadly to constitutional jurisprudence. I do not have a firm answer to this question but, rather, some tentative intuitions.

Although I have not done any serious archival or other research on major areas of constitutional law—such as the right to privacy or general views of the First Amendment or substantive due process—to rival what I have done with the political equality cases, I feel comfortable drawing three tentative conclusions.

First, whatever differences there may be between political equality cases and other constitutional cases, the benefit of moving slowly as cases grow in increasing novelty cuts across constitutional domains. Thus, even though I cannot accurately assess the consequences of the Court's getting it "wrong" in a case like *Romer v. Evans*,[11] proscribing certain forms of discrimination against gays and lesbians under the Equal Protection Clause, there are bound to be some costs—if only from upsetting some settled expectations in the at least partial overruling of the *Bowers v. Hardwick*[12] case. *Bowers* upheld some forms of discrimination against gays and lesbians. Those who condemn the murkiness of the *Romer* opinion may not appreciate that there are benefits to the Court's allowing lower courts to play with potential readings of *Romer* and work out the contours of the new equal protection right recognized there.

Murkiness and tentativeness appear in other areas of constitutional law as well. The often-derided "I know it when I see it" obscenity standard[13] fits this bill well, as does the Court's slow approach to remedying racial segregation in schools.[14]

Second, social consensus seems relevant across constitutional domains. It is explicitly built into the Eighth Amendment's ban on "cruel and unusual punishment," and it extends to social consensus created by Court decisions themselves. The fact that the Court can create social consensus through its rulings no doubt serves as a temptation to justices to create a constitutional order in line with their own worldviews.

Third, the possibility of a Pareto-superior exchange among justices toward greater judicial restraint is not limited to political equality cases. Indeed, one can imagine (likely tacit) trades among justices across different kinds of cases as well. This is especially possible because, although I have been using the shorthand labels "liberals" and "conservatives," issues do not always break down neatly across such lines. In a multimember body deciding a range of issues, there are likely to be at least some shifting alliances among Court members. This possibility raises the potential benefits (and therefore the possibility) of mutual agreements toward judicial restraint. Restraint by one set of justices on a political equality case might be paid back with restraint by another set of justices on issues of substantive due process.

On (Not) Defining Political Equality

An astute (or even not so astute) reader will notice that I have managed to write a book about political equality without ever providing a single definition of the term. The choice is deliberate. My argument is that most political equality claims remain highly contested, and the central question about political equality is not what it is but who gets to craft it. There is a very small set of political equality principles deep in the core that the Court should protect regardless of public consensus, such as no discrimination in who gets to vote on the basis of race or gender. But beyond the small universe of rights for the Court to protect regardless of social consensus, political equality questions should be left to the political process.

Should jurisdictions draw majority-minority districts when redistricting? Is it appropriate to regulate campaign spending consistent with the barometer equality rationale? Should we eliminate direct primaries, first-past-the-post elections, and our presidential system in favor of one of the myriad forms of proportional representation used in other democracies?

These are interesting and important questions that should be debated in the universities, in the legislatures, in the workplace, in the home, and in the streets. But the Court as a matter of constitutional interpretation should not decide them. We should not want the Court to bind future generations (or bind us at least until a [new] Court majority changes its mind) to its views of these devices of democracy.

Providing a uniform (and by necessity, abstract) definition of political equality begins lawyers down the slippery slope of analogies. Whatever benefit a litigant might realize in pushing an abstract equality argument to the next stage, the harm inures to all of us. Democracy should be vibrant and contentious; it should be debated and it should be the subject of experimentation. Constitutionalization stops all of that, and the Court should resort to constitutionalization of political equality issues only when there is a very good reason to do so.

The Final Scorecard: Assessing the Mighty Platonic Guardians in Their Foray into the Political Thicket

This book opened with some startling statistics on the extent of the Supreme Court's involvement in the political process beginning in the 1960s. It would be interesting, though impractical, to evaluate whether each of the political equality cases since 1960 was correctly or incorrectly decided under the standards set forth in the book. Actually, it would be more complicated than a simple "yes" or "no" question in the cases raising multiple issues: for example, *Buckley* correctly upheld the right of the government to impose campaign contribution limits, but it may have erred on the expenditure limit question (depending upon the close means-ends scrutiny that the Court should have applied). In addition, in evaluating how well the Court has done, cases that established new equal protection rights such as *Shaw v. Reno* should be weighed heavier than cases such as *Miller v. Johnson* that further refined the new right.

But when we think of the most important constitutional political equality cases of the past forty years, the Court's record is mixed at best. The major cases I would count as probably correctly decided (though not necessarily on correct reasoning) include *Austin, Baker, Carrington v. Rash, City of Mobile, Davis v. Bandemer, Harper, Richardson v. Ramirez,* and *Williams v. Rhodes.* I count as incorrectly decided *Avery, Bush v. Gore, California Democratic Party v. Jones, Lubin, Karcher, Munro, Salyer Land, Shaw v. Reno,* and *Timmons.* I am unsure or conflicted on aspects of *Buckley, Kramer,* and *Reynolds v. Sims.*

My intuition suggests that, applying my normative standards, the Court has been wrong in deciding important political equality cases more than half the time. And the differences persist whether we consider more liberal Warren Court cases or more conservative Burger or Rehnquist Court cases.

I stated in the introduction that this book is not an exit manual. The Court has shown no inclination to leave the political thicket, and given the need for the Court to protect certain core equality issues it should not. But the Court could do much better than it already does by acting with some humility.

There is a key difference between members of the Supreme Court and the cave dweller who had seen the light and then returned to the cave in Plato's Allegory of the Cave. The returning cave dweller possessed better *factual information* than those who had never been out of the cave from which to make *factual judgments* about what the shadows on the cave wall represented. Thus, there was a clear link between the superior feature of the cave dweller who had seen the light and the nature of the judgment he was called upon to make.

Supreme Court justices in the political equality cases are asked to make *normative judgments* about the proper means of assuring political equality, judgments that depend upon often contested *empirical assumptions.* Supreme Court justices are well trained in legal analysis, but that does not necessarily qualify them to make such normative judgments or to assess the strength of empirical evidence.

We may well need to cast these nine lawyers in the role of mighty Platonic guardians when necessary to preserve core political equality principles, but it hardly seems the best way to engage in general political regulation for 250 million people. Our democracy deserves better.

Appendix 1

Twentieth-Century Election Law Cases Decided by the Supreme Court in a Written Opinion

1901–1910

Swafford v. Templeton, 185 U.S. 487 (1902)
Giles v. Harris, 189 U.S. 475 (1903)
James v. Bowman, 190 U.S. 127 (1903)
Giles v. Teasley, 193 U.S. 146 (1904)
Pope v. Williams, 193 U.S. 621 (1904)
Jones v. Montague, 194 U.S. 147 (1904)
Selden v. Montague, 194 U.S. 153 (1904)
Albright v. Territory of New Mexico ex rel. Sandoval, 200 U.S. 9 (1906)
Burton v. United States, 202 U.S. 344 (1906)
Elder v. Colorado, 204 U.S. 85 (1907)
United States v. Thayer, 209 U.S. 39 (1908)
Richardson v. McChesney , 218 U.S. 487 (1910)
Franklin v. State of South Carolina, 218 U.S. 161 (1910)

1911–1920

Pacific States Telephone and Telegraph Company v. Oregon, 223 U.S. 118 (1912)
Marshall v. Dye, 231 U.S. 250 (1913)
Guinn v. United States, 238 U.S. 347 (1915)
Newman v. United States ex rel. Frizzell, 238 U.S. 537 (1915)
Myers v. Anderson, 238 U.S. 377 (1915)
United States v. Mosley , 238 U.S. 383 (1915)
State of Ohio ex rel. Davis v. Hilderbrant, 241 U.S. 565 (1916)

United States v. Gradwell, 243 U.S. 476 (1917)
United States v. Bathgate, 246 U.S. 220 (1918)

1921–1930

Newberry v. United States, 256 U.S. 232 (1921)
Fairchild v. Hughes, 258 U.S. 126 (1922)
Leser v. Garnett, 258 U.S. 130 (1922)
Love v. Griffith, 266 U.S. 32 (1924)
Nixon v. Herndon, 273 U.S. 536 (1927)
Reed v. County Commissioners of Delaware County, Pennsylvania, 277 U.S. 376 (1928)
Barry v. United States ex rel. Cunningham, 279 U.S. 597 (1929)
United States v. Wurzbach, 280 U.S. 396 (1930)

1931–1940

Smiley v. Holm, 285 U.S. 355 (1932)
Koenig v. Flynn, 285 U.S. 375 (1932)
Carroll v. Becker, 285 U.S. 380 (1932)
Nixon v. Condon, 286 U.S. 73 (1932)
Wood v. Broom, 287 U.S. 1 (1932)
Burroughs v. United States, 290 U.S. 534 (1934)
Grovey v. Townsend, 295 U.S. 45 (1935)
United States v. Norris, 300 U.S. 564 (1937)
Breedlove v. Suttles, 302 U.S. 277 (1937)
Lane v. Wilson, 307 U.S. 268 (1939)

1941–1950

United States v. Classic, 313 U.S. 299 (1941)
Snowden v. Hughes, 321 U.S. 1 (1944)
McDonald v. Commissioner of Internal Revenue, 323 U.S. 57 (1944)
Smith v. Allwright, 321 U.S. 649 (1944)
U.S. v. Saylor, 322 U.S. 385 (1944)
Colegrove v. Green, 328 U.S. 549 (1946)
United States v. C.I.O., 335 U.S. 106 (1948)
MacDougall v. Green, 335 U.S. 281 (1948)
South v. Peters, 339 U.S. 276 (1950)

1951–1960

Gerende v. Election Board, 341 U.S. 56 (1951)

Day-Brite Lighting, Inc. v. Missouri, 342 U.S. 421 (1952)

United States v. Hood, 343 U.S. 148 (1952)

Ray v. Blair, 343 U.S. 214 (1952)

Terry v. Adams, 345 U.S. 461 (1953)

United States v. UAW-CIO, 352 U.S. 567, (1957)

Farmers Educational & Cooperative Union of America v. WDAY, 360 U.S. 525 (1959)

Lassiter v. Northhampton Election Board, 360 U.S. 45 (1959)

United States v. Raines, 362 U.S. 17 (1960)

United States v. Thomas, 362 U.S. 58 (1960)

United States v. Alabama, 362 U.S. 602 (1960)

Hannah v. Larche, 363 U.S. 420 (1960)

Gomillion v. Lightfoot, 364 U.S. 339 (1960)

1961–1970

Baker v. Carr, 369 U.S. 186 (1962)

Scholle v. Hare, 369 U.S. 429 (1962)

Wood v. Georgia, 370 U.S. 375 (1962)

Gray v. Sanders, 372 U.S. 368 (1963)

Anderson v. Martin, 375 U.S. 399 (1964)

Wesberry v. Sanders, 376 U.S. 1 (1964)

Wright v. Rockefeller, 376 U.S. 52 (1964)

Reynolds v. Sims, 377 U.S. 533 (1964)

WMCA, Inc. v. Lomenzo, 377 U.S. 633 (1964)

Maryland Committee for Fair Representation v. Tawes, 377 U.S. 656 (1964)

Davis v. Mann, 377 U.S. 678 (1964)

Roman v. Sincock, 377 U.S. 695 (1964)

Lucas v. Forty-Fourth General Assembly of Colorado, 377 U.S. 713 (1964)

Fortson v. Dorsey, 379 U.S. 433 (1965)

Fortson v. Toombs, 379 U.S. 621 (1965)

Carrington v. Rash, 380 U.S. 89 (1965)

United States v. Mississippi, 380 U.S. 128 (1965)

Louisiana v. United States, 380 U.S. 145 (1965)

Harman v. Forssenius, 380 U.S. 528 (1965)
Parsons v. Buckley, 379 U.S. 359 (1965)
Scott v. Germano, 381 U.S. 407 (1965)
WMCA, Inc. v. Lomenzo, 382 U.S. 4 (1965)
Swann v. Adams, 383 U.S. 210 (1966)
South Carolina v. Katzenbach, 383 U.S. 301 (1966)
Harper v. Virginia Board of Elections, 383 U.S. 663 (1966)
Burns v. Richardson, 384 U.S. 73 (1966)
Mills v. Alabama, 384 U.S. 214 (1966)
Katzenbach v. Morgan, 384 U.S. 641 (1966)
United States v. Johnson, 383 U.S. 169 (1966)
Cardona v. Power, 384 U.S. 672 (1966)
Bond v. Floyd, 385 U.S. 116 (1966)
Fortson v. Morris, 385 U.S. 231 (1966)
Swann v. Adams, 385 U.S. 440 (1967)
Kilgarlin v. Hill, 386 U.S. 120 (1967)
Moody v. Flowers, 387 U.S. 97 (1967)
Zwicker v. Koota, 389 U.S. 241 (1967)
Sailors v. Board of Education of the County of Kent, 387 U.S. 105
    (1967)
Lucas v. Rhodes, 389 U.S. 212 (1967)
Rockefeller v. Wells, 389 U.S. 421 (1967)
Avery v. Midland County, 390 U.S. 474 (1968)
Williams v. Rhodes, 393 U.S. 23 (1968)
Allen v. State Board of Elections, 393 U.S. 544 (1969)
Hadnott v. Amos, 394 U.S. 358 (1969)
Kirkpatrick v. Preisler, 394 U.S. 526 (1969)
Wells v. Rockefeller, 394 U.S. 542 (1969)
McDonald v. Board of Election Commissioners, 394 U.S. 802
    (1969)
Moore v. Ogilvie, 394 U.S. 814 (1969)
Gaston County v. United States, 395 U.S. 285 (1969)
Powell v. McCormack, 395 U.S. 486 (1969)
Kramer v. Union Free School District No. 15, 395 U.S. 621 (1969)
Cipriano v. City of Houma, 395 U.S. 701 (1969)
Brockington v. Rhodes, 396 U.S. 41 (1969)
Golden v. Zwickler, 394 U.S. 103 (1969)
In re Herndon, 394 U.S. 399 (1969)
Hall v. Beals, 396 U.S. 45 (1969)

Hadley v. Junior College District of Metropolitan Kansas City, 397
U.S. 50 (1970)
Mitchell v. Donovan, 398 U.S. 427 (1970)
City of Phoenix v. Kolodziejski, 399 U.S. 204 (1970)
Turner v. Fouche, 396 U.S. 346 (1970)
Evans v. Cornman, 398 U.S. 419 (1970)
Oregon v. Mitchell, 400 U.S. 112 (1970)

1971–1980

Perkins v. Matthews, 400 U.S. 379 (1971)
Connor v. Johnson, 402 U.S. 690 (1971)
Whitcomb v. Chavis, 403 U.S. 124 (1971)
Jenness v. Fortson, 403 U.S. 431 (1971)
Ely v. Klahr, 403 U.S. 108 (1971)
Abate v. Mundt, 403 U.S. 182 (1971)
Connor v. Williams, 404 U.S. 549 (1972)
Roudebush v. Hartke, 405 U.S. 15 (1972)
Bullock v. Carter, 405 U.S. 134 (1972)
Socialist Labor Party v. Gilligan, 406 U.S. 583 (1972)
O'Brien v. Brown, 409 U.S. 1 (1972)
United States v. Brewster, 408 U.S. 501 (1972)
Dunn v. Blumstein, 405 U.S 330 (1972)
Sixty-Seventh Minnesota State Senate v. Beens, 406 U.S. 187 (1972)
O'Brien v. Brown, 409 U.S. 1 (1972)
Taylor v. McKeithen, 407 U.S. 191 (1972)
Pipefitters Local Union No. 562 v. United States, 407 U.S. 385
(1972)
Goosby v. Osser, 409 U.S. 512 (1973)
Mahan v. Howell, 410 U.S. 315 (1973)
Marston v. Lewis, 410 U.S. 679 (1973)
Burns v. Fortson, 410 U.S. 686 (1973)
Rosario v. Rockefeller, 410 U.S. 752 (1973)
Columbia Broadcasting System, Inc. v. Democratic National Com-
mittee, 412 U.S. 94 (1973)
Brown v. Chote, 411 U.S. 452 (1973)
Georgia v. United States, 411 U.S. 526 (1973)
Gaffney v. Cummings, 412 U.S. 735 (1973)
White v. Regester, 412 U.S. 755 (1973)

White v. Weiser, 412 U.S. 783 (1973)

National Association for the Advancement of Colored People v. New York, 413 U.S. 345 (1973)

O'Brien v. Skinner, 414 U.S. 524 (1974)

Broadrick v. Oklahoma, 413 U.S. 601 (1973)

Salyer Land Co. v. Tulare Lake Basin Water Storage District, 410 U.S. 719 (1973)

Kusper v. Pontikes, 414 U.S. 51 (1973)

CSC v. Letter Carriers, 413 U.S. 548 (1973)

Richardson v. Ramirez, 418 U.S. 24 (1974)

Communist Party of Indiana v. Whitcomb, 414 U.S. 441 (1974)

Lubin v. Panish, 415 U.S. 709 (1974)

Storer v. Brown, 415 U.S. 724 (1974)

American Party of Texas v. White, 415 U.S. 767 (1974)

Lehman v. City of Shaker Heights, 418 U.S. 298 (1974)

Anderson v. United States, 417 U.S. 211 (1974)

Cousins v. Wigoda, 419 U.S. 477 (1975)

Harris County Commissioners v. Moore, 420 U.S. 77 (1975)

Chapman v. Meier, 420 U.S. 1 (1975)

Hill v. Stone, 421 U.S. 289 (1975)

Dallas County v. Reese, 421 U.S. 477 (1975)

Connor v. Waller, 421 U.S. 656 (1975)

City of Richmond v. United States, 422 U.S. 358 (1975)

White v. Regester, 422 U.S. 935 (1975)

Hill v. Printing Industries of Gulf Coast, 422 U.S. 937 (1975)

Buckley v. Valeo, 424 U.S. 1 (1976)

East Carroll Parish School Board v. Marshall, 424 U.S. 636 (1976)

Beer v. United States, 425 U.S. 130 (1976)

Hynes v. Mayor of Oradell, 425 U.S. 610 (1976)

Elrod v. Burns, 427 U.S. 347 (1976)

Greer v. Spock, 424 U.S. 828 (1976)

Connor v. Coleman, 425 U.S. 675 (1976)

United States v. Board of Supervisors of Warren County, Mississippi, 429 U.S. 642 (1977)

United Jewish Organizations v. Carey, 430 U.S. 145 (1977)

Town of Lockport v. Citizens for Community Action, 430 U.S. 259 (1977)

Connor v. Finch, 431 U.S. 407 (1977)

Mandel v. Bradley, 432 U.S. 173 (1977)

Briscoe v. Bell, 432 U.S. 404 (1977)

Abood v. Detroit Board of Education, 431 U.S. 209 (1977)

Morris v. Gressette, 432 U.S. 491 (1977)

United States v. Board of Commissioners of Sheffield, Alabama, 435 U.S. 110 (1978)

McDaniel v. Paty, 435 U.S. 618 (1978)

Wise v. Lipscomb, 437 U.S. 535 (1978)

Berry v. Doles, 438 U.S. 190 (1978)

First National Bank of Boston v. Bellotti, 435 U.S. 765 (1978)

Dougherty County Board of Education v. White, 439 U.S. 32 (1978)

Holt Civic Club v. City of Tuscaloosa, 439 U.S. 60 (1978)

Marchioro v. Chaney, 442 U.S. 191 (1979)

Helstoski v. Meanor, 442 U.S. 500 (1979)

Illinois State Board of Elections v. Socialist Workers Party, 440 U.S. 173 (1979)

Connor v. Coleman, 440 U.S. 612 (1979)

Crowell v. Mader, 444 U.S. 505 (1980)

City of Mobile v. Bolden, 446 U.S. 55 (1980)

City of Rome v. United States, 446 U.S 156 (1980)

Branti v. Finkel, 445 U.S. 507 (1980)

United States v. Gillock, 445 U.S. 360 (1980)

1981–1990

Democratic Party v. Wisconsin ex rel. La Follette, 450 U.S. 107 (1981)

Ball v. James, 451 U.S. 355 (1981)

McDaniel v. Sanchez, 452 U.S. 130 (1981)

California Medical Association. v. Federal Election Commission, 453 U.S. 182 (1981)

CBS v. FCC, 453 U.S. 367 (1981)

Federal Election Commission v. Democratic Senatorial Campaign Committee, 454 U.S. 27 (1981)

Citizens Against Rent Control/Coalition for Fair Housing v. City of Berkeley, 454 U.S. 290 (1981)

Blanding v. DuBose, 454 U.S. 393 (1982)

Bread Political Action Committee v. Federal Election Commission, 455 U.S. 577 (1982)

Upham v. Seamon, 456 U.S. 37 (1982)

Common Cause v. Schmitt, 455 U.S. 129 (1982)

Brown v. Hartlage, 456 U.S. 45 (1982)

Rodriguez v. Popular Democratic Party, 457 U.S. 1 (1982)

Hathorn v. Lovorn, 457 U.S. 255 (1982)

Clements v. Fashing, 457 U.S. 957 (1982)

Rogers v. Lodge, 458 U.S. 613 (1982)

Brown v. Socialist Workers '74 Campaign Committee, 459 U.S. 87 (1982)

City of Port Arthur v. United States, 459 U.S. 159 (1982)

Federal Election Commission v. National Right to Work Committee, 459 U.S. 197 (1982)

City of Lockhart v. United States, 460 U.S. 125 (1983)

Anderson v. Celebrezze, 460 U.S. 780 (1983)

Karcher v. Daggett, 462 U.S. 725 (1983)

Brown v. Thomson, 462 U.S. 835 (1983)

McCain v. Lybrand, 465 U.S. 236 (1984)

Members of the City Council of the City of Los Angeles v. Taxpayers for Vincent, 466 U.S. 789 (1984)

Escambia County v. McMillan, 466 U.S. 48 (1984)

National Association for the Advancement of Colored People v. Hampton County Election Commission, 470 U.S. 166 (1985)

Hunter v. Underwood, 471 U.S. 222 (1985)

Federal Election Commission v. National Conservative PAC, 470 U.S. 480 (1985)

Thornburg v. Gingles, 478 U.S. 30 (1986)

Davis v. Bandemer, 478 U.S. 109 (1986)

Munro v. Socialist Workers Party, 479 U.S. 189 (1986)

Pacific Gas & Electric Co. v. Public Utilities Commission of California, 475 U.S. 1 (1986)

Tashjian v. Republican Party of Connecticut, 479 U.S. 208 (1986)

Federal Election Commission v. Massachussetts Citizens for Life, Inc., 479 U.S. 238 (1986)

McNally v. United States, 483 U.S. 350 (1987)

City of Pleasant Grove v. United States, 479 U.S. 462 (1987)

Communications Workers of America v. Beck, 487 U.S. 735 (1988)

Meyer v. Grant, 486 U.S. 414 (1988)

Eu v. San Francisco Democratic Central Committee, 489 U.S. 214 (1989)

Board of Estimate of City of New York v. Morris, 489 U.S. 688
(1989)
Quinn v. Millsap, 491 U.S. 95 (1989)
Austin v. Michigan Chamber of Commerce, 494 U.S. 652 (1990)
Rutan v. Republican Party of Illinois, 497 U.S. 62 (1990)

1991–2000

Kay v. Ehrler, 499 U.S. 432 (1991)
Clark v. Roemer, 500 U.S. 646 (1991)
Houston Lawyers' Association v. Attorney General of Texas, 501 U.S.
419 (1991)
Chisom v. Roemer, 501 U.S. 380 (1991)
McCormick v. United States, 500 U.S. 257 (1991)
Renne v. Geary, 501 U.S. 312 (1991)
Norman v. Reed, 502 U.S. 279 (1992)
Presley v. Etowah County Commission, 502 U.S. 491 (1992)
United State Department of Commerce v. Montana, 503 U.S. 442
(1992)
Burson v. Freeman, 504 U.S. 191 (1992)
Evans v. United States, 504 U.S. 255 (1992)
Burdick v. Takushi, 504 U.S. 428 (1992)
Franklin v. Massachusetts, 505 U.S. 788 (1992)
Growe v. Emison, 507 U.S. 25 (1993)
Voinovich v. Quitter, 507 U.S. 146 (1993)
Shaw v. Reno, 509 U.S. 630 (1993)
Holder v. Hall, 512 U.S. 874 (1994)
Federal Election Commission v. NRA Political Victory Fund, 513
U.S. 88 (1994)
Johnson v. De Grandy, 512 U.S. 997 (1994)
U.S. Term Limits, Inc. v. Thornton, 514 U.S. 779 (1995)
U.S. v. Hays, 515 U.S. 737 (1995)
McIntyre v. Ohio Election Commission, 514 U.S. 334 (1995)
Miller v. Johnson, 515 U.S. 900 (1995)
Wisconsin v. City of New York, 517 U.S. 1 (1996)
Morse v. Republican Party of Virginia, 517 U.S. 186 (1996)
Shaw v. Hunt, 517 U.S. 899 (1996)
O'Hare Truck Service, Inc. v. City of Northlake, 518 U.S. 712 (1996)
Bush v. Vera, 517 U.S. 952 (1996)

Colorado Republican Federal Campaign Committee v. FEC, 518
    U.S. 604 (1996)
Board of County Commissioners v. Umbehr, 518 U.S. 668 (1996)
Lopez v. Monterey County, 519 U.S. 9 (1996)
Young v. Fordice, 520 U.S. 273 (1997)
Timmons v. Twin Cities Area New Party, 520 U.S. 351 (1997)
Reno v. Bossier Parish School Board, 520 U.S. 471 (1997)
Abrams v. Johnson, 521 U.S. 74 (1997)
Lawyer v. Department of Justice, 521 U.S. 567 (1997)
Chandler v. Miller, 520 U.S. 305 (1997)
Foreman v. Dallas County, 521 U.S. 979 (1997)
City of Monroe v. United States, 522 U.S. 34 (1997)
Foster v. Love, 522 U.S. 67 (1997)
Arkansas Education Television Commission v. Forbes, 523 U.S. 666
    (1998)
Federal Election Commission v. Atkins, 524 U.S. 11 (1998)
Lopez v. Monterey County, 525 U.S. 266 (1999)
United States v. Sun-Diamond Growers of California, 526 U.S. 398
    (1999)
Buckley v. American Constitutional Law Foundation, 525 U.S. 182
    (1999)
Department of Commerce v. House of Representative, 525 U.S. 316
    (1999)
Hunt v. Cromartie, 526 U.S. 541 (1999)
Gutierrez v. Ada, 528 U.S. 250 (2000)
Sinkfield v. Kelley, 531 U.S. 28 (2000)
Reno v. Bossier Parish School Board, 528 U.S. 320 (2000)
Nixon v. Shrink Missouri Government PAC, 528 U.S. 377 (2000)
Rice v. Cayetano, 528 U.S. 495 (2000)
California Democratic Party v. Jones, 530 U.S. 567 (2000)
Bush v. Gore, 531 U.S. 98 (2000)

Appendix 2

Justice Goldberg's Proposed Dissent to a
Per Curiam *Summary Affirmance in*
Harper v. Virginia State Board of Elections

SUPREME COURT OF THE UNITED STATES

HARPER ET AL. v. VIRGINIA STATE BOARD OF ELECTIONS ET AL.

APPEAL FROM THE UNITED STATES DISTRICT COURT FOR THE EASTERN DISTRICT OF VIRGINIA.

No. 835. Decided March —, 1965.

PER CURIAM.

The motion to affirm is granted and the judgment is affirmed.

MR. JUSTICE GOLDBERG, with whom THE CHIEF JUSTICE and MR. JUSTICE DOUGLAS join, dissenting.

The Court today affirms the judgment of a three-judge District Court, —— F. Supp. ——, holding constitutional the provisions of Virginia law (Va. Const., § 18; Va. Code, 1952, §§ 24–17, 24–22, 24–67, 24–120), which require the payment of poll taxes as a prerequisite to voting in state and local elections. This affirmance, although summary, constitutes a holding by this Court that such poll taxes imposed upon citizens too poor to pay them are constitutional.[1] With all deference, I dissent from this holding.

---

[1] If this were a petition for certiorari, the granting of which "is not a matter of right, but of sound judicial discretion, and will be granted only where there are special and important reasons therefor," Supreme Court Rules, 38, and the denial of which would "not remotely imply approval or disapproval" of the decision below, *Maryland* v. *Baltimore Radio Show*, 338 U. S. 912, 919 (opinion of Mr. Justice Frankfurter), the facts that there are now only four states which employ a poll tax as a prerequisite for voting, that, it might appear that the use of a poll tax in this fashion is dying out, and that the Twenty-Fourth Amendment has eliminated the use of the poll tax as a requirement for federal elections, would be appropriately considered in determining whether or not certiorari should be granted. However, this is an appeal, which by statute (28 U. S. C. §§ 1253, 2101 (b), we must and do determine on the merits. Whatever, may

2 HARPER *v.* VIRGINIA ELECTION BOARD.

It is undisputed that appellants, and other persons similarly impecunious, possess all of the other state qualifications for voting including residence requirements and that they desire to vote. They are precluded from voting solely because they do not have the means to pay the poll tax.

In *Reynolds* v. *Sims*, 377 U. S. 533, 554–555, we stated, "Undeniably the Constitution of the United States protects the right of all qualified citizens to vote, in state as well as federal elections. . . . The right to vote freely for the candidate of one's choice is the essence of a democratic society, and any restrictions on that right strike at the heart of representative government."

In *Baker* v. *Carr*, 369 U. S. 186; *Gray* v. *Sanders*, 372 U. S. 368; *Reynolds* v. *Sims, supra,* and our recent decision of *Carrington* v. *Rash,* —— U. S. ——, we held that the Equal Protection Clause of the Fourteenth Amendment prohibits a State from invidiously discriminating against a class of citizens in denying or diluting this constitutional right.

Gray v. *Sanders, supra,* at 379, plainly stated that discrimination between otherwise eligible voters based upon income is invidious. "Once the geographical unit for which a representative is to be chosen is designated, all who participate in the election are to have an equal vote— whatever their race, whatever their sex, whatever their occupation, whatever their *income* and wherever their home may be in that geographical unit. This is required by the Equal Protection Clause of the Fourteenth Amendment." (Emphasis added.)

In *Carrington* v. *Rash, supra,* decided this Term, we held unconstitutional a provision of the Texas Constitution which prohibited from voting in state and federal elections servicemen who had acquired bona fide residences. Such a provision, we declared imposed "an in-

---

have been my decision as to whether or not certiorari should be granted on this issue, since this case is an appeal, I am compelled to face up to the substantial constitutional issue presented.

HARPER *v.* VIRGINIA ELECTION BOARD. 3

vidious discrimination in violation of the Fourteenth Amendment," *id.*, at ——, because the provision was not reasonably related to a legitimate state purpose.

The State does not seek to justify the poll tax in this case on the ground that it is a revenue-producing measure. Indeed, the Virginia Supreme Court of Appeals has recognized that "the imposition [of the poll tax] was not intended primarily for the production of revenue." *Campbell* v. *Goode,* 172 Va. 463, 466, 25 S. E. 456, 457. The Attorney General of Virginia has stated in testimony before a Committee of Congress that, although in form a head tax on all citizens, it has never been enforced that way, no attempt is made to collect the tax from those who do not vote, and it is used solely as a requirement for voting.[2] Hearings before the Subcommittee No. 5 of the House Committee on the Judiciary on Amendments to Abolish Tax and Property Qualifications for Electors in Federal Elections, 87th Cong., 2d Sess., 98 (hereinafter cited as Hearings). Moreover, as the House Committee on the Judiciary recognized, there are available to the State alternative methods of producing revenue which do not operate to deprive poor people of their basic and fundamental right to vote.

Nor does the State seek to dispute the unassailable fact that the purpose of adoption of the poll tax as a prerequisite for voting was solely and exclusively to restrict voting. The Debates of the Virginia Constitutionl Convention of 1902, 2947–3080, make this absolutely clear and do not contain even a hint of any other State purpose. The Debates also make it clear that the principle aim of this limitation was the disenfranchisement of the Negroes. See Debates, *supra,* at 2978–2981, 2989–2998, 2999–3011,

---

[2] By law assessments cannot even be made until the annual tax is three years in arrears. See *Campbell* v. *Goode, supra.* The nonenforcement of the poll tax except as a means of restricting voting is apparently the general practice in the poll tax states. See Ogden, The Poll Tax in the South, 59–76 (1958).

4 HARPER *v.* VIRGINIA ELECTION BOARD.

3047, 3070–3080.[3] This was clearly and frankly expressed in the Debates by the sponsor of the suffrage provisions, the Honorable Carter Glass:

> "Discrimination! Why that is exactly what we propose; that, exactly, was what this Convention was elected for—to discriminate to the very extremity of permissible action under the limitations of the Federal Constitution." Debates, *supra,* at 3076.

In addition to the primary desire to disenfranchise the Negro, the debates indicate that a motivating force in the adoption of the poll tax was the desire to disenfranchise poor white persons as well as Negroes.[4] An exhaustive study by one commentator has explained this desire in Virginia, as well as the other States which adopted the poll tax in the period from 1890 to 1910, as a reaction to the rise of the Populist movement. See Ogden, *supra,* at 20–29.

In practice the poll tax in Virginia and other States has resulted in making it burdensome and difficult for poor white people, as well as Negroes, to vote. See Hearings, *supra,* at 14–22, 49–53; Ogden, *supra,* at 111–177.

---

[3] The only real debate on this point was whether the provisions adopted were sufficient to accomplish the disenfranchisement of the Negro or whether an additional provision requiring the interpretation of the Constitution was necessary. See Debates, *supra,* at 2978–2981, 2989–2998, 2999–3011, 3070–3080. Cf. *Louisiana* v. *United States,* — U. S. —; *United States* v. *Mississippi,* — U. S. —.

[4] As one delegate to the Virginia Convention stated:

"The need [to restrict suffrage through a poll tax] is universal, not only in the country, but in the cities and towns; not only among the blacks but among the whites, in order to deliver the State from the burden of illiteracy and poverty and crime, which rests on it as a deadening pall. . . . It is not the negro vote which works the harm, for the negroes are generally Republicans, but it is the depraved and incompetent men of our own race, who have nothing at stake in government, and who are used by designing politicians to accomplish their purpose, irrespective of the welfare of the community." Debates, *supra,* at 2998.

HARPER *v.* VIRGINIA ELECTION BOARD. 5

The legitimate State purpose served by the poll tax, Virginia argues, is "to limit the right of suffrage to those who took sufficient interest in the affairs of the State to qualify themselves to vote," *Campbell* v. *Goode, supra,* at 466, 25 S. E., at 457, by paying what the State considers to be the small amount required.[5] See Hearings, at 76. With respect to the identical contention, the Committee on the Judiciary of the House of Representatives, in reporting out the Twenty-Fourth Amendment, said, "While the amount of poll tax now required to be paid in the several State is small and imposes only a slight economical obstacle for any citizen who desires to qualify in order to vote, nevertheless, it is significant that the voting in poll tax states is relatively low as compared to the overall population which would be eligible. . . . [T]he historical analysis . . . indicates that where the poll tax

---

[5] While the State argues that the amount of the tax is small, neither the lower court in this case, nor the decision of this Court in *Breedlove* v. *Suttles,* 302 U. S. 277, on which the lower court relied, rested on this ground. The principle asserted by the lower court would seem to apply even if the amount were greater. Moreover, it is undisputed that appellants here were financially incapable of paying the tax. Finally, I cannot agree that the amount is small. The $1.50 annual poll tax is cumulative with the right to register and vote expressly conditioned upon payment of all poll taxes for the past three years, with a 5% penalty for late payment. As with one appellant here, where there are two otherwise qualified voters in the household, the poll tax payments would amount to $9.48. This Virginia pattern would appear to be typical of the States that have poll taxes. Alabama's poll tax is $1.50 annually, Ala. Code, Tit. 15, § 237 (1958), cumulative for two years, Ala. Const., Amend. 96; Mississippi's varies from $2 to $3 annually, Miss. Code Ann. § 9751 (1943), and is cumulative for two years, *id.*, at § 3235; and Texas' poll tax is $1.50 annually, Vernon's Tex. Rev. Civ. Stat. Art. 2.01 (1964 Cum. Supp.), and is apparently not cumulative, *id.*, at Art. 5102. Moreover, Virginia law provides that it is unlawful for one to pay the poll tax of another unless the beneficiary is a member of the payor's household or closely related to him. Va. Code § 24–129.

6   HARPER *v.* VIRGINIA ELECTION BOARD.

has been abandoned . . . voter participation increased."
H. R. Rep. No. 182, 87th Cong., 2d Sess., p. 3.[6]

Testimony before a Committee of Congress by Virginia's own witnesses tends to show that there is no substantial connection between payment of the poll tax and interest in the affairs of the State.   Lieutenant Governor Mills E. Godwin, Jr., of Virginia, testified that of those who had paid their poll tax and were otherwise qualified to vote approximately 500,000 or 40% did not vote in the 1960 election.   Hearings, at 77.

Conversely, as this very case demonstrates, appellants and others similarly situated ardently desire to vote but are precluded by their economic circumstances from paying the poll tax.   The sole income of one of appellants is derived from federal social security benefits.   Another appellant has not regular income, is not gainfully employed, and is dependent upon her children for support.   A third appellant has a wife and nine children and his entire income is consumed in providing for their necessities of life. The District Court gave express recognition to "[t]he plaintiffs' impoverishment and eligibility to vote" except for their poverty.   —— F. Supp. ——.

It was established in the various hearings on this subject before Committees of Congress that in Virginia and other States which impose poll taxes as a prerequisite for voting there are many persons like appellants who are otherwise qualified to vote, but like them are ineligible solely because they are poor.   See Hearings, at 14–22, 49–53; Christensen, the Constitutionality of Anti-Poll Tax Bills, 33 Minn. L. Rev. 212, 228, and n. 60 (1949).   This class of persons includes those without any economic

---

[6] The Committee also expressly noted that the then "five States which still require payment of a poll tax were among the seven States with the lowest voter participation in the 1960 Presidential election." *Ibid.* At the time of this report Alabama, Arkansas, Mississippi, Texas and Virginia had poll taxes. Since that date Arkansas has repealed the poll tax as a prerequisite for voting. See Ark. Const., Amend. 51; note 2, *infra.*

HARPER *v.* VIRGINIA ELECTION BOARD. 7

means whatsoever and who are dependent for subsistence on relatives, friends, and in many instances public welfare or private charity. It likewise includes many employed in low-paying jobs, others who may be unemployed, and still others who have minimal incomes in the form of social security benefits, retirement pensions, unemployment compensation, medical disability payments, and the like.[7] Yet it cannot be assumed that all these people who cannot afford to pay the poll tax lack political capacity nor are they exempt from the obligations and burdens of citizenship such as military service.[8] The evidence before Congress as well as other statistical and polling studies (see Ogden, *supra*, at 111–177) points to the conclusion that precisely this class of persons substantially accounts for the increase in voting, noted by the House Committee, when poll tax barriers are removed and that the poll tax requirements prevent large groups of such persons—white and Negro—from voting. In view of the facts that substantial numbers of those who pay the poll tax do not vote and that substantial numbers of those who cannot afford to pay the poll tax qualify and

---

[7] The Federal Census for 1960 revealed that 27.9% of all families in Virginia have annual incomes below $3,000, the amount which is generally recognized as the boundary of poverty for a family of four. Annual Report of the Council of Economic Advisors to the President 58 (1964). Furthermore 17.4% of all Virginia families have an income even below $2,000. United States Department of Commerce, Bureau of the Census, 1960 Census of Population, Supplementary Report, P. C. (S 1)–43.

It can easily be seen that as to a family of four with an income of $2,000 or less, the $3 annual poll tax for two voters is at least one-half the family's entire daily allowance for subsistence, and the accumulated tax and penalties which for the three years amounts to almost $10 is at least almost twice the family's daily allowance. See also Hearings, *supra*, at 49–50.

[8] Although it is not so argued, if the theory of the poll tax is that only taxpayers should vote, there is little reason to limit the vote to those who pay the poll tax, for every consumer today pays at least hiddent taxes when he buys goods.

8 HARPER *v.* VIRGINIA ELECTION BOARD.

vote when poll tax barriers are removed, this justification advanced by Virginia cannot be accepted.[9]

The only other contention advanced is that administrative convenience is served by the poll tax in that the tax constitutes a method of identification and proof of residence. However, the 46 States which do not have poll taxes find no administrative difficulty in administering their electoral processes and enforcing valid residence, identification and similar requirements by other legally nondiscriminatory means. In dealing with an analogous contention concerning administrative convenience to the State as a justification for discrimination against a class of voters, we said in *Carrington*, "States may not casually deprive a class of citizens of the vote because of some remote administrative benefit to the State," *supra,* at ——. As we held in *Carrington*, even purported residence qualifications must be reasonable and must be finely tailored so as to test residence and not exclude persons who are legitimate residents.

Furthermore it is clear that the poll tax does not purport to nor does it serve as a trustworthy test of continuing residence. The tax is accompanied by no declaration of prior residence or intent to remain. The Virginia Constitution (§§ 18, 20, 21) and statutes (Va. Code § 24–17) provide for residence and the payment of poll tax as separate and distinct qualifications for voting. Virginia, like the 46 States that do not employ poll taxes to restrict voting, provides that election officials may challenge electors as to their residency and require an oath as well as proof of residency. See Va. Code §§ 24–253, 24–254 (1950). Payment of the tax must be made six months before an election; yet the date of the election

---

[9] It is obvious that the modern trend, by eliminating cumbersome paper ballots, increasing the number of polling places and extending the hours they are open, adopting permanent registration, etc., as well as by the elimination of the poll tax, is designed to encourage interest in public affairs precisely by removing barriers and impediments to voting.

HARPER *v.* VIRGINIA ELECTION BOARD. 9•

is the determinative date for residence under Virginia law. Va. Code § 24–17 (1950). Obviously paying a poll tax, which can even be mailed in, see Hearings, *supra*, at 81, six months before the date in question does not show residence on the date in question. For these reasons it must be concluded that no reasonable state interest is served by barring from voting those citizens who desire to vote but who lack the requisite funds.

In applying the Equal Protection Clause to the administration of criminal justice, this Court said, "Providing equal justice for poor and rich, weak and powerful alike . . . is the central aim of our entire judicial system." *Griffin* v. *Illinois*, 351 U. S. 12, 16–17. Providing an equal vote for poor and rich, weak and powerful alike, should be the "central aim" of our voting system. Cf. *Carrington* v. *Rash, supra*, at ——, where we stated that the right to vote is a matter "close to the core of our constitutional system." Just as "there can be no equal justice where the kind of trial a man gets depends on the amount of money he has," *Griffin* v. *Illinois, supra*, at 16–17, so in voting cases, there can be no equal protection of the laws where a man's vote "depends on the amount of money he has."

The application of these principles obviously does not mean that Government—State or Federal—must equalize all economic inequalities among citizens. Nor does it mean that the Government cannot impose burdens or exactions which by reason of economic circumstances fall more heavily upon some than others. Nor however desirable it may be as a matter of social and legislative policy, does it require the State affirmatively to provide relief for all the incidents of poverty. The Constitution does not command absolute equality in all areas. It does mean, however, that a State may not frustrate or burden the exercise of the basic and precious right to vote by imposing substantial obstacles upon that exercise by a class of citizens not justified by any legitimate state interest. In particular it means that with respect to the fundamen-

10 HARPER *v.* VIRGINIA ELECTION BOARD.

tal right to vote, a reverse means test cannot be applied. A classification based upon financial means embodied in a voting statute is inherently not "reasonable in light of . . . [the statute's] purpose." *McLaughlin* v. *Florida,* —— U. S. ——.

Nor does my view of this case mean that the States do not have "unquestioned power to impose reasonable residence restrictions" and "to establish, on a nondiscriminatory basis, and in accordance with the Constitution, other qualifications for the exercise of the franchise. *Carrington* v. *Rash, supra,* at ——. It does mean, however, that qualifications for voting, which the State establishes, and which they are authorized to establish under Art. I, § 2 of the United States Constitution are, as our cases hold, limited by other provisions of the Constitution, such as the Equal Protection Clause. *Carrington* v. *Rash, supra.*

The fact that historically property qualifications and poll taxes were imposed in some of the States does not immunize these statutes from constitutional condemnation. Much of this history is before the Fourteenth Amendment, and in any event we must consider voting rights in light of their full development, their "present place in American life throughout the nation," cf. *Brown* v. *Board of Education,* 347 U. S. 483, 492–493, and our present conception of the meaning and application of the Equal Protection Clause. See *Baker* v. *Carr, supra; Reynolds* v. *Sims, supra; Gray* v. *Sanders, supra; Carrington* v. *Rash, supra.* See also Christensen, *op. cit. supra,* at 232.

Breedlove v. *Suttles,* 302 U. S. 277, relied upon by the District Court, is in my view not controlling. The *Breedlove* case did not deal with the question of whether persons may be discriminated against on economic grounds in their voting rights; in fact they did not claim that they could not afford to pay the tax. The challenge to the poll tax statute in *Breedlove* under the Equal Protection Clause was solely on the ground that its exemptions in

HARPER *v.* VIRGINIA ELECTION BOARD. 11

favor of women, older persons, and minors resulted in an unreasonable classification to the disadvantage of those persons not exempt. The Court in *Breedlove* therefore did not rule directly on the question facing us.[10] Moreover, *Breedlove* was decided long before our recent decisions applying the Equal Protection Clause of the Fourteenth Amendment in the voting area so as to make it clear that the effect of the Fourteenth Amendment is to nullify invidious discrimination in the polling booth.

Finally, nothing in the language or history of the Twenty-Fourth Amendment, which was an affirmative effort to eliminate the poll tax in federal elections, even suggests that in so doing, Congress and the state legislatures attempted impliedly to repeal the operation of the Fourteenth Amendment in this fundamental area. In fact the long history of the Twenty-Fourth Amendment leads to just the opposite conclusion. The Hearings before a Committee of Congress, Hearings, *supra*, at 29–43, contain a long history of bills that had been introduced to abolish the poll tax in both state and federal elections by legislation based upon effectuation of the Fourteenth and Fifteenth Amendments. The fact that the measure was finally passed as a constitutional amendment applicable to federal elections shows, at best, that the passage of this Amendment in this manner was a compromise necessary at this time to get some progress in this area. Finally, the history of the inter-relationship of the Fourteenth and Fifteenth Amendments in the area of voting rights, shows that these constitutional Amendments are to be read together and not as implied repudiations of each other. See *Nixon* v. *Herndon,* 273 U. S. 536; *Louisiana* v. *United States,* —— U. S. ——; *United States* v. *Mississippi,* —— U. S. ——; *Davis* v. *Schnell,* 336 U. S. 933, affirming, 51 F. Supp. 872 (D. C. S. D. Ala.).

---

[10] *Butler* v. *Thompson,* 341 U. S. 937, was a summary affirmance without argument, presumably on the supposed authority of *Breedlove* v. *Suttles, supra.*

12 HARPER *v.* VIRGINIA ELECTION BOARD.

In *Wesberry* v. *Sanders*, 376 U. S. 1, 17–18, the Court said, "No right is more precious in a free country than that of having a voice in the election of those who make the laws under which, as good citizens, we must live. Other rights even the most basic, are illusory if the right to vote is undermined. Our Constitution leaves no room for classification of people in a way that unnecessarily abridges this right."

Our cases have recognized that the fundamental right of voting is the cornerstone of a citizen's rights. It is through the ballot box that the citizen can exert his power to make his representatives responsive to his needs and desires. A government is far less likely to mistreat any group of citizens and far more likely to respond to their needs when it is ultimately responsible to them through the ballot box. A government "of the people" and "by the people" is likely to be "for the people."

Benjamin Franklin deemed it necessary that the Government should fairly and equally represent the entire electorate, since "the *all* of one man is as dear to him as the *all* of another . . . the poor man has an *equal* right but the *more* need to have representatives in the legislature than the rich one." [11]

If the poor man is to be accorded his equal right to vote, which the Constitution guarantees, Virginia's poll tax cannot stand.

---

[11] Harris, The Quest For Equality, 14 (1960), quoting 10 The Writings of Benjamin Franklin 59–60, 130–131 (Smythe ed. 1910).

Notes

NOTES TO THE INTRODUCTION

1. 512 U.S. 874, 913 (1994).

2. Reynolds v. Sims, 377 U.S. 533 (1964) (mandating reapportionment on state level); Avery v. Midland County, 390 U.S. 474 (1968) (mandating reapportionment of local body); *but see* Salyer Land Co. v. Tulare Lake Basin Water Storage Dist., 410 U.S. 719 (1973) (carving out exception to one person, one vote rule for special purpose government districts). *See* Elrod v. Burns, 427 U.S. 347 (1976) (banning patronage firing); Rutan v. Republican Party of Illinois, 497 U.S. 62 (1990) (banning patronage hiring, transfers, and promotions); Buckley v. Valeo, 424 U.S. 1 (1976) (rejecting political equality as a compelling interest justifying campaign spending limits); Shaw v. Reno, 509 U.S. 630 (1993) (creating cause of action for an "unconstitutional racial gerrymander"); Bush v. Gore, 531 U.S. 98 (2000) (striking down recount rules created by the Florida Supreme Court in the 2000 presidential recount controversy).

3. Appendix 1 lists in chronological order the cases I categorized for figure I-1, Twentieth-Century Election Law Cases Decided by the Supreme Court in a Written Opinion.

4. 369 U.S. 186 (1962).

5. 446 U.S. 55 (1980).

6. 478 U.S. 30 (1986).

7. Robert J. Pushaw, Jr., Bush v. Gore: *Looking at* Baker v. Carr *in a Conservative Mirror,* 18 Const. Comment. 359 (2001).

8. *Baker,* 369 U.S. at 253 (Clark, J., concurring); *see also id.* at 259 (noting that the Tennessee Supreme Court held it could give no remedy for malapportionment).

9. *See* Robert G. Dixon, Jr., Democratic Representation: Reapportionment in Law and Politics 592 (1968).

10. John Hart Ely, Democracy and Distrust 117 (1980).

11. The part that has been criticized much more severely is Ely's argument for more searching judicial review of laws discriminating on the basis of race or other minority status. *See* Daniel R. Ortiz, *Pursuing a Perfect Politics: The Allure and Failure of Process Theory,* 77 Va. L. Rev. 721, 728–30 (1991).

12. 304 U.S. 144, 152 n.4 (1938).

13. The first paragraph called for stricter review when legislative actions contravened a "specific prohibition of the Constitution." *Id.* The third paragraph endorsed more searching review of statutes aimed "against discrete and insular minorities." *Id.*

14. Samuel Issacharoff and Richard H. Pildes, *Politics as Markets: Partisan Lockups of the Democratic Process,* 50 Stan. L. Rev. 643 (1998).

15. Pamela S. Karlan, *The Court Casts Its Vote,* N.Y. Times, Dec. 11, 2000, at A31; Elizabeth Garrett, *Leaving the Decision to Congress, in* The Vote: Bush, Gore, and the Supreme Court 38 (Cass R. Sunstein and Richard A. Epstein eds., 2001).

16. For an argument that legal scholars can serve this "checking function," see Michael C. Dorf and Samuel Issacharoff, *Can Process Theory Constrain the Courts?,* 72 U. Colo. L. Rev. 923 (2001).

17. *See* Laurence H. Tribe, *The Puzzling Persistence of Process-Based Constitutional Theories,* 89 Yale L.J. 1063, 1071 (1980) ("Who votes, it turns out, is a profoundly substantive question. For *who* participates—who counts—in the electoral process is a question that must precede any inquiry into the fairness of the process itself."); *see also id.* at 1077–78 ("Why *should* politics be open to equal participation by all? Doesn't that norm itself presuppose some substantive vision of human rights?"); Mark Tushnet, *Darkness on the Edge of Town: The Contributions of John Hart Ely to Constitutional Theory,* 89 Yale L.J. 1037, 1045 (1980) ("The fundamental difficulty with Ely's theory is that its basic premise, that obstacles to political participation should be removed, is hardly value-free.").

18. *See* Daniel H. Lowenstein, *Political Reform Is Political, in* U.S. House of Representatives: Reform or Rebuild? 194, 196–97 (Joseph F. Zimmerman and Wilma Rule eds., 2000) (noting that most electoral reforms in the United States were adopted by political means, not through judicial intervention).

19. *See* Christopher L. Eisgruber, Constitutional Self-Government 180 (2001) ("[E]ven though there are multiple ways to define the 'majority' in any representative system, and even though there are multiple legitimate ways for a democratic government to give minorities a share of power, it is impermissible for a minority to enjoy entrenched control of the legislature. That principle is sufficient justification for decisions like *Reynolds*.").

20. 198 U.S. 45 (1905).

21. *See* Lowenstein, *supra* note 18, at 196.

22. *Id.* at 196–97.

23. *Id.* at 206 n.9.

24. Personal communication from Daniel Lowenstein to author (Feb. 5, 2002) (on file with author). One of Lowenstein's reasons for liking the one person, one vote rule of *Reynolds* is that "it is important that there was a mechanical solution to the malapportionment problem, which meant that judicial oversight of redistricting could be minimal." *Id.* I will disagree with this point in chapter 2.

25. *See* Ortiz, *supra* note 11, at 728 ("The proper degree of influence to give an individual or a group relative to others . . . does not fall from the heavens."); Tribe, *supra* note 17, at 1072 (noting that process theorists can defend the one person, one vote rule "only hesitantly, claiming, for example, that it is merely a matter of administrative convenience.").

26. Ely, *supra* note 10, at 120–21; *see also* Michael J. Klarman, *The Puzzling Resistance to Political Process Theory,* 77 Va. L. Rev. 747, 758 n.53 (1991).

27. I defend this position in Richard L. Hasen, *"High Court Wrongly Elected": A Public Choice Model of Judging and Its Implications for the Voting Rights Act,* 75 N.C. L. Rev. 1305 (1997).

28. For a critique of Ely's process theory using the analogy to "Platonic guardians," see Samuel Estreicher, *Platonic Guardians of Democracy: John Hart Ely's Role for the Supreme Court in the Constitution's Open Texture,* 56 N.Y.U. L. Rev. 547 (1981). An oft-cited use of the term is Judge Learned Hand's, who remarked: "For myself it would be most irksome to be ruled by a bevy of Platonic Guardians, even if I knew how to choose them, which I assuredly do not." Learned Hand, The Bill of Rights 73 (1958).

29. Plato's Republic 123–42 (I. A. Richards ed. & trans., Cambridge University Press 1966).

30. *Id.* at 128.

31. 531 U.S. at 111.

32. *See* Pamela S. Karlan, *Exit Strategies in Constitutional Law: Lessons for Getting the Least Dangerous Branch Out of the Political Thicket,* 82 B.U. L. Rev. 667 (2002).

33. 478 U.S. 109, 144 (1986) (Burger, C.J., concurring). Serious resistance seems to have ended when Justice Harlan left the Court. *See* Avery v. Midland County, 390 U.S. 474, 488 (1968) (Harlan, J., dissenting) ("I continue to reject [the process theory] thesis as furnishing an excuse for the federal judiciary's straying outside its proper constitutional role.").

34. *See, e.g.,* Michael W. McConnell, *The Redistricting Cases: Original Mistakes and Current Consequences,* 24 Harv. J.L. & Pub. Pol'y 103 (2000). For a rare conservative voice questioning *Baker,* see Pushaw, *supra* note 7.

35. Judge Posner, for example, defended the Court's intervention in the political process to prevent a "crisis." *See* Richard A. Posner, Breaking the Deadlock: The 2000 Election, the Constitution and the Courts 4 (2001). For a critique of the crisis rationale, see Richard L. Hasen, *Book Review—A "Tincture of Justice": Judge Posner's Failed Rehabilitation of* Bush v. Gore, 80 Tex. L. Rev. 137, 146–49 (2001).

36. See Jesse H. Choper, *Why the Supreme Court Should Not Have Decided the Presidential Election of 2000,* 18 Const. Comment. 335, 357 n.92 (2001).

37. It is not just coincidence that liberals faced with more than twenty years of the Rehnquist Court are now calling for "judicial minimalism" and for "taking the Constitution away from the courts." *See* Cass R. Sunstein, One Case at a Time:

Judicial Minimalism and the Supreme Court (1999); Mark Tushnet, Taking the Constitution Away from the Courts (1999).

1. For a discussion of the phenomenon, see Daniel Hays Lowenstein and Richard L. Hasen, Election Law—Cases and Materials 252–81 (2d ed. 2001).

2. *See* Lani Guinier, The Tyranny of the Majority 14–16 (1994).

3. 446 U.S. 55 (1980).

4. Some commentators describe the debate between individual and group orientations as a choice between "pluralist" and "progressive" theories of representation. *See, e.g.,* Daniel H. Lowenstein, *The Supreme Court Has No Theory of Politics—And Be Thankful for Small Favors, in* The U.S. Supreme Court and the Electoral Process 283 (David K. Ryden ed., 2d ed. 2002).

5. Larry Alexander, *Still Lost in the Political Thicket (or Why I Don't Understand the Concept of Vote Dilution),* 50 Vand. L. Rev. 327 (1997).

6. *See, e.g.,* Guinier, *supra* note 2; Abigail M. Thernstrom, Whose Votes Count? (1987); Carol M. Swain, Black Faces, Black Interests (1993).

7. For a recent book exploring these issues empirically, see David T. Canon, Race, Redistricting and Representation: The Unintended Consequences of Black Majority Districts 171–72 (1999).

8. Holder v. Hall, 512 U.S. 874 (1994).

9. Douglas Rae et al., Equalities 133 (1981).

10. Veith v. Pennsylvania, 195 F. Supp. 2d 672 (M.D. Pa. 2002).

11. 42 U.S.C. § 1973 *et seq.* (2000).

12. The most comprehensive looks of which I am aware, though even these are not comprehensive, appear in the two election law casebooks, one of which I co-author. *See* Lowenstein and Hasen, *supra* note 1; Samuel Issacharoff, Pamela S. Karlan, and Richard H. Pildes, The Law of Democracy (2d ed. 2001). For a look at political representation cases in the Warren Court, see Howard Ball, The Warren Court's Conceptions of Democracy: An Evaluation of the Supreme Court's Apportionment Decisions (1971). For a look at these cases in the Burger Court, see Nancy Maveety, Representation Rights and the Burger Years (1991). For a look at these cases in the Rehnquist Court, see Jamin Raskin, Overruling Democracy: The Supreme Court v. the People (2003).

13. 497 U.S. 62 (1990).

14. *Rutan,* 497 U.S. at 108 (Scalia, J., dissenting). *See* Cynthia Grant Bowman, *"We Don't Want Anybody Anybody Sent": The Death of Patronage Hiring in Chicago,* 86 Nw. U. L. Rev. 57 (1991) (disputing Justice Scalia's characterization).

15. 410 U.S. 113 (1973).

16. 189 U.S. 475 (1903). Another example is the Court's failure to hold that the denial of the right to vote to women violated the Fourteenth Amendment's Privileges or Immunities Clause. Minor v. Happersett, 88 U.S. (21 Wall.) 162 (1875).

17. *See* Richard H. Pildes, *Democracy, Anti-Democracy, and the Canon,* 17 Const. Comment. 295 (2000).

18. See Daniel Hays Lowenstein, *Associational Rights of Major Political Parties: A Skeptical Inquiry,* 71 Tex. L. Rev. 1741, 1748–54 (1993).

19. 313 U.S. 299 (1941).

20. *Classic* reversed a contrary six-year-old holding in *Grovey v. Townsend,* 295 U.S. 45 (1935).

21. 360 U.S. 45 (1959).

22. The Court in *Lassiter* explained that a literacy test designed to discriminate against African-Americans would be unconstitutional. *Id.* at 53.

23. *Id.* at 51. Congress subsequently banned literacy tests in the Voting Rights Act. *See* 42 U.S.C. § 1973.

24. 372 U.S. 368 (1963).

25. *Id.* at 370.

26. *Id.* at 379–80 (citation omitted).

27. *Id.* at 381.

28. *Id.* at 384 (Harlan, J., dissenting).

29. 376 U.S. 1 (1964).

30. *Id.* at 8.

31. *Id.* at 26–27 (Harlan, J. dissenting).

32. *Id.* at 18 (Clark, J., concurring in part and dissenting in part).

33. *Reynolds,* 377 U.S. at 568.

34. *Id.*

35. *Id.*

36. *Id.* at 577.

37. Swann v. Adams, 385 U.S. 440 (1967).

38. 390 U.S. 474 (1968).

39. Abate v. Mundt, 403 U.S. 182 (1971).

40. Mahan v. Howell, 410 U.S. 315, 329 (1973). The Court noted that "[n]either courts nor legislatures are furnished any specialized calipers that enable them to extract from the general language of the Equal Protection Clause of the Fourteenth Amendment the mathematical formula that establishes what range of percentage deviations is permissible and what is not." *Id.*

41. Gaffney v. Cummings, 412 U.S. 735, 745 (1973).

42. Brown v. Thomson, 462 U.S. 835, 842 (1983).

43. *Id.* at 846–48

44. *Id.* at 847.

45. 394 U.S. 526 (1969).

46. *Id.* at 530–31.
47. Wells v. Rockefeller, 394 U.S. 542 (1969).
48. White v. Weiser, 412 U.S. 783 (1973).
49. 462 U.S. 725 (1983).
50. *Mahan,* 410 U.S. at 323. For an argument along similar lines, see Charles L. Black, Jr., *Representation in Law and Equity,* in 10 Nomos 131 (1968).
51. *See, e.g., Brown,* 462 U.S. at 851 (Brennan, J., dissenting) ("Under certain conditions the Constitution permits small deviations from absolute equality in state legislative districts, but we have carefully circumscribed the range of permissible deviations as to both degree and kind." [Footnote omitted]).
52. *Karcher,* 462 U.S. at 766 (White, J., dissenting).
53. *Brown,* 462 U.S. at 850 (O'Connor, J., concurring).
54. 360 U.S. at 51.
55. For an early case, see *Ex parte* Yarbrough, 110 U.S. 651 (1884).
56. *See* Carrington v. Rash, 380 U.S. 89, 97 (1965) (Harlan, J., dissenting) (noting the connection of this case on voter qualifications to the Court's new reapportionment jurisprudence).
57. *Id.*
58. *Id.* at 93.
59. *Id.*
60. *Id.* at 94.
61. *Id.* at 96.
62. The Court made the statement in *McDonald v. Bd. of Election Comm'rs,* 394 U.S. 802, 807 (1969). *McDonald* itself was somewhat out of line with the trend in these post-*Baker* cases. In *McDonald,* the Court unanimously rejected an equal protection argument brought by inmates of a county jail who challenged Illinois's failure to provide them with absentee ballots. It appeared significant to the Court that there was "nothing in the record to support [the] assumption[] that Illinois has in fact precluded [the inmates] from voting" through special polling booths or facilities on Election Day. *Id.* at 808 and n.6.
63. 395 U.S. 621 (1969).
64. *See, e.g.,* Evans v. Cornman, 398 U.S. 419 (1970) (holding Maryland could not deny the right to vote to individuals living on the grounds of the National Institutes of Health, a federal enclave located within the geographical boundaries of Maryland).
65. 405 U.S. 330 (1972).
66. *Id.* at 348.
67. Marston v. Lewis, 410 U.S. 679 (1973); *see also* Burns v. Fortson, 410 U.S. 686 (1973)(upholding Georgia's fifty-day period before an election to register to vote).
68. Holt Civic Club v. City of Tuscaloosa, 439 U.S. 60 (1978).
69. 418 U.S. 24 (1974).

70. *But see* Hunter v. Underwood, 471 U.S. 222 (1985) (striking down section of Alabama constitution disenfranchising individuals convicted of "moral turpitude" crimes; the evidence showed the state had enacted the provision with a racially discriminatory purpose).

71. Oregon v. Mitchell, 400 U.S. 112 (1970).

72. *See* Cabell v. Chavez-Salido, 454 U.S. 432 (1982).

73. 397 U.S. 50 (1970).

74. Id. at 56. *Board of Estimate v. Morris,* 489 U.S. 688 (1989), is the Court's most recent application of the one person, one vote principle to such regional arrangements.

75. 397 U.S. at 56. A similar statement appears in *Avery:* "Were the [county's governing body] a special-purpose unit of government assigned the performance of functions affecting definable groups of constituents more than other constituents, we would have to confront the question whether such a body may be apportioned in ways which give greater influence to the citizens most affected by the organization's functions." *Avery,* 390 U.S. at 483–84.

76. 410 U.S. 719 (1973).

77. *Id.* at 728, 729.

78. *Id.* at 737–38, 741 (Douglas, J., dissenting).

79. Ball v. James, 451 U.S. 355 (1981).

80. *See* Richard Briffault, *Who Rules at Home? One Person/One Vote and Local Governments,* 60 U. Chi. L. Rev. 339, 361–62 (1993).

81. "BIDs are state- or locally-authorized entities established to promote business activity within a specific geographic sub-area of a city." Issacharoff, Karlan, and Pildes, *supra* note 12, at 201 n.5. The Second Circuit has upheld over a dissent a challenge to the election procedures for a BID in New York City. *See* Kessler v. Grand Cent. Dist. Mgmt. Ass'n, Inc. 158 F.3d 92 (2d Cir. 1998). For a further discussion of the issue, see Richard Briffault, *A Government for Our Time? Business Improvement Districts and Urban Governance,* 99 Colum. L. Rev. 365 (1999).

82. 528 U.S. 495 (2000).

83. *Ex parte* Yarbrough, 110 U.S. 651 (1884).

84. For more of this history, see Alexander Keyssar, The Right to Vote: The Contested History of Democracy in the United States (2000).

85. 321 U.S. 649 (1944).

86. 345 U.S. 461 (1953).

87. The case was especially notable because ordinarily only state actors may be held to violate constitutional rights, and the association was private. *See* Lowenstein, *supra* note 18.

88. 364 U.S. 339 (1960).

89. *See* Lowenstein and Hasen, *supra* note 1, at 35.

90. 379 U.S. 433 (1965).

91. Voting in multimember districts works like at-large voting within a single district.

92. *Fortson,* 379 U.S. at 439.

93. Burns v. Richardson, 384 U.S. 73, 88 (1966); Whitcomb v. Chavis, 403 U.S. 124, 142–43 (1971).

94. 412 U.S. 755 (1973).

95. *Id.* at 769.

96. 446 U.S. 55 (1980).

97. 446 U.S. at 112 (Marshall, J., dissenting).

98. 458 U.S. 613 (1982).

99. 509 U.S. 630 (1993).

100. 383 U.S. 301 (1966).

101. 393 U.S. 544 (1969).

102. *Id.* at 586 (Harlan, J., concurring in part and dissenting in part).

103. Beer v. United States, 425 U.S. 130 (1976) (emphasis added).

104. *Id.* at 141.

105. *Id.*

106. Reno v. Bossier Parish School Bd., 520 U.S. 471 (1997).

107. Reno v. Bossier Parish School Bd., 528 U.S. 320 (2000).

108. 478 U.S. 30 (1986).

109. In addition to *White v. Regester,* the leading case on the "totality of the circumstances" test that Congressional Reports cited was a Fifth Circuit case, *Zimmer v. McKeithen,* 485 F.2d 1297 (5th Cir. 1973), *aff'd sub nom. East Carroll Parish School Board v. Marshall,* 424 U.S. 636 (1976) (*per curiam*).

110. *Gingles,* 478 U.S. at 50–51.

111. Some of the more important cases include Holder v. Hall, 512 U.S. 874 (1994) (holding section 2 does not require jurisdiction to increase the number of members of elected body so as to create a majority-minority district); Johnson v. De Grandy, 512 U.S. 997 (1994) (affirming that plaintiffs still must satisfy the totality of the circumstances test even if meeting the *Gingles* threshold test); Growe v. Emison, 507 U.S. 25 (1993) (discussing whether different minority groups may raise a claim that they constitute a single political bloc for purposes of the *Gingles* criteria and holding that *Gingles* applies to claims involving single-member districts); Presley v. Etowah County Comm'n, 502 U.S. 491 (1992) (holding section 2 does not apply to changes in voting procedures of local governing bodies); Chisom v. Roemer, 501 U.S. 380 (1991) (section 2 claims apply to judicial elections).

112. 376 U.S. 52 (1964).

113. *Id.* at 56.

114. 430 U.S. 144 (1977).

115. For a more detailed explanation on this point, see Lowenstein and Hasen, *supra* note 1, at 284–86.

116. *Shaw,* 509 U.S. at 647–48 (citations omitted).

117. Richard H. Pildes and Richard G. Niemi, *Expressive Harms, "Bizarre Districts," and Voting Rights: Evaluating Election-District Appearances After* Shaw v. Reno, 92 Mich. L. Rev. 483 (1993).

118. 515 U.S. 900 (1995).

119. *Id.* at 916 (emphasis added).

120. U.S. v. Hays, 515 U.S. 737 (1995).

121. *See, e.g.,* Bush v. Vera, 517 U.S. 952 (1996).

122. *See* Lowenstein and Hasen, *supra* note 1, at 271 n.z (noting the exception to this rule for Cuban-Americans).

123. 532 U.S. 234 (2001).

124. *Id.* at 258.

125. Daniel H. Lowenstein and Richard L. Hasen, Election Law 2nd Edition Teacher's Manual 65 (2001).

126. 383 U.S. 663 (1966).

127. *Id.*

128. *Id.* at 666.

129. Draft Dissent, Justice Goldberg, Harper v. Va. Bd. of Elections 9 (Mar. 3, 1965) (William J. Brennan, Jr., Papers, Manuscript Division, Library of Congress, Washington, D.C., Container I:128, Folder 6).

130. Justice Black wrote in a March 4, 1965, memorandum to the conference: "Brother Goldberg's circulation persuades me that our line of decisions since *Breedlove v. Suttles* presents new arguments against the Breedlove poll tax that call for consideration by the Court after full hearings. For that reason I shall vote against summary decision by a *per curiam* opinion." Memorandum from Justice Black to the Conference (Mar. 4, 1965)(William J. Brennan, Jr., Papers, Manuscript Division, Library of Congress, Washington, D.C., Container I:128, Folder 6).

131. Cipriano v. City of Houma, 395 U.S. 701 (1969) (revenue bonds); City of Phoenix v. Kolodziejski, 399 U.S. 204 (1970) (general obligation bonds). In *Turner v. Fouche,* 396 U.S. 346 (1970), the Court struck down a requirement that appointed school board members be freeholders.

132. 405 U.S. 134 (1972).

133. *Id.* at 149.

134. 415 U.S. 709 (1974).

135. 424 U.S. 1 (1976).

136. 494 U.S. 652 (1990).

137. 415 U.S. 724 (1974).

138. 478 U.S. 109 (1986).

139. 412 U.S. 755 (1973).

140. 530 U.S. 567 (2000).

141. 393 U.S. 23 (1968).

142. *Id.* at 31–32.

143. *Id.* at 32.

144. 460 U.S. 780 (1983). Before that, in *Buckley v. Valeo*, 424 U.S. 1 (1976), the Court rejected a challenge to the system for the public financing of presidential campaigns on grounds it discriminated against third parties and independent candidates.

145. 479 U.S. 189 (1986).

146. *Id.* at 200 (Marshall, J., dissenting).

147. 520 U.S. 351 (1997).

148. *Id.* at 367.

149. 523 U.S. 666 (1998).

150. *Id.* at 683.

151. *See, e.g.,* Alan M. Dershowitz, Supreme Injustice: How the High Court Hijacked Election 2000 (2001).

152. For a detailed chronology, see Lowenstein and Hasen, *supra* note 1, ch. 3.

153. The trial court opinion is unpublished. The trial judge determined that there was "no credible statistical evidence and no other competent substantial evidence to establish by a preponderance a reasonable probability that the results of the statewide election in the State of Florida would be different from the result which has been certified by the State Elections Canvassing Commission." *See* Bush v. Gore: The Court Cases and the Commentary 55 (E. J. Dionne, Jr., and William Kristol eds., 2001). Although the judge recognized that there was "voter error and/or less than total accuracy in regard to the punch-card voting devices utilized in Dade and Palm Beach Counties, which these counties have been aware of for many years," *id.,* he concluded that there was not enough evidence that a difference statewide would result from a recount. In addition, the judge concluded that the county canvassing boards that had failed to recount votes did not abuse their discretion.

154. Gore v. Harris, 772 So. 2d 1243, 1252 (Fla. 2000).

155. *Id.* at 1261–62.

156. *Id.*

157. *Id.* at 1264 n.26 (Wells, C.J., dissenting). It is not clear that all overvotes recounted by hand would necessarily be classified as invalid votes. For example, a voter who both wrote in Al Gore's name in the write-in portion of a ballot and punched out the chad for Al Gore clearly intended to vote for Al Gore, but the vote counting machine would record that vote as an overvote.

158. *Id.* at 1262.

159. *Id.*

160. Bush v. Gore, 531 U.S. 1046 (2000).

161. Bush v. Gore, 531 U.S. 98 (2000).

162. *Id.* at 112 (Rehnquist, C.J., concurring).

163. *Id.* at 123 (Stevens, J., dissenting); *id.* at 129 (Souter, J., dissenting); *id.* at 135 (Ginsburg, J., dissenting); *id.* at 144 (Breyer, J., dissenting).

164. *Id.* at 104–05 (full citations and parenthetical information omitted).

165. *Id.* at 105.
166. *Id.* at 107–10.
167. *See id.* at 129 (Souter, J., dissenting); *id.* at 144 (Breyer, J., dissenting).
168. 3 U.S.C. § 5 (2000).
169. Bush v. Gore, 531 U.S. at 110.
170. *See* Lowenstein and Hasen, *supra* note 1, at 161.

171. Pamela S. Karlan, *Nothing Personal: The Evolution of the Newest Equal Protection from* Shaw v. Reno *to* Bush v. Gore, 79 N.C. L. Rev. 1345, 1364 (2001); *see also* Heather K. Gerken, *New Wine in Old Bottles: A Comment on Richard Hasen's and Richard Briffault's Essays on* Bush v. Gore, 29 Fla. St. U. L. Rev. 407, 410 (2001) (under the structural view, *Bush* contains "a claim about how to order a well-functioning democracy, not a suit about individual rights.").

NOTES TO CHAPTER 2

1. An earlier version of this chapter appeared as *The Benefits of "Judicially Unmanageable" Standards in Election Cases under the Equal Protection Clause,* 80 N.C. L. Rev. 1469 (2002), as part of a symposium on *Baker v. Carr.*

2. 369 U.S. 186 (1962).

3. *See, e.g.,* John Hart Ely, Democracy and Distrust 117 (1980) ("[U]nblocking stoppages in the democratic process is what judicial review ought preeminently to be about, and denial of the vote seems the quintessential stoppage."); *id.* at 121 (noting that elected representatives have an incentive "toward maintaining whatever apportionment, good or bad, it is that got and keeps them where they are").

4. *Baker,* 369 U.S. at 289 (Frankfurter, J., dissenting).

5. Lucas v. Forty-Fourth Gen. Assembly, 377 U.S. 713, 750 (1964) (Stewart, J., dissenting); *see also* Ely, *supra* note 3, at 121 (calling administrability the one person, one vote standard's "long suit").

6. Cass R. Sunstein, One Case at a Time: Judicial Minimalism on the Supreme Court 4, 26 (1999).

7. Michael C. Dorf and Charles F. Sabel, *A Constitution of Democratic Experimentalism,* 98 Colum. L. Rev. 267 (1998). For a helpful discussion of the argument, see Mark Tushnet, *State Action, Social Welfare Rights and the Judicial Role: Some Comparative Observations,* 3 Chi. J. Int'l L. 435, 449–50 (2002).

8. *See, e.g.,* Abner J. Mikva, *Justice Brennan and the Political Process: Assessing the Legacy of* Baker v. Carr, 1995 U. Ill. L. Rev. 683, 688, 690, 694; Jeffrey G. Hamilton, Comment, *Deeper into the Political Thicket: Racial and Political Gerrymandering and the Supreme Court,* 43 Emory L.J. 1519, 1571 (1994); Jeremy M. Taylor, Comment, *The Ghost of Harlan: The Unfulfilled Search for Judicially Manageable Standards in Voting Rights Litigation,* 65 Miss. L.J. 431, 435 (1995). *But see* Paul S. Edwards and Nelson W. Polsby, *Introduction: The Judicial Regulation of Political*

Processes—In Praise of Multiple Criteria, 9 Yale L. & Pol'y Rev. 190 (1991) (arguing in favor of multiple criteria).

9. 446 U.S. 55 (1980).

10. 478 U.S. 109 (1986).

11. 328 U.S. 549, 556 (1946)(plurality opinion).

12. *Id.* at 552 (plurality opinion).

13. 369 U.S. at 217. The six categories are

a textually demonstrable constitutional commitment of the issue to a coordinate political department; or a lack of judicially discoverable and manageable standards for resolving it; or the impossibility of deciding without an initial policy determination of a kind clearly for nonjudicial discretion; or the impossibility of a court's undertaking independent resolution without expressing lack of respect due coordinate branches of government; or an unusual need for unquestioning adherence to a political decision already made; or the potentiality of embarrassment from multifarious pronouncements by various departments on one question.

Id. See generally Martin Shapiro, Law and Politics in the Supreme Court 207–09 (1964)(disputing the link between the political question doctrine and the need for judicially manageable standards).

14. *Baker,* 369 U.S. at 289 (Frankfurter, J., dissenting).

15. *Id.* at 226.

16. *Id.* at 223.

17. Michael W. McConnell, *The Redistricting Cases: Original Mistakes and Current Consequences,* 24 Harv. J.L. & Pub. Pol'y 103, 106–07 (2000).

18. *See id.* at 107–08.

19. Roy A. Schotland, *The Limits of Being "Present at the Creation,"* 80 N.C. L. Rev. 1505, 1508–09 (2002).

20. Memorandum from Justice Douglas, to Justice Brennan (Jan. 29, 1962) (William J. Brennan, Jr., Papers, Manuscript Division, Library of Congress, Washington, D.C., Container I:63, Folder 20).

21. The Supreme Court in Conference (1940–1985), at 846 (Del Dickson ed., 2001) [hereafter Conference] (quoting Justice Harlan). For additional historical accounts, see Bernard Schwartz, Super Chief: Earl Warren and His Supreme Court: A Judicial Biography 411–28 (1983); Anthony Lewis, *In Memoriam: William J. Brennan, Jr.,* 111 Harv. L. Rev. 29, *passim* (1997). An extended description of the drafting of *Baker,* written by Justice Brennan's clerks, appears in Opinions of William J. Brennan, Jr., October Term, 1961 (William J. Brennan, Jr., Papers, Manuscript Division, Library of Congress, Washington, D.C., Container II:6, Folder 4).

22. Conference, *supra* note 21, at 846 (quoting Justice Brennan).

23. *Id.* at 847 n.58.

24. *Id.* at 850 (quoting Justice Stewart).

25. Justice Brennan's Conference Notes on *Baker v. Carr* (William J. Brennan, Jr., Papers, Manuscript Division, Library of Congress, Washington, D.C., Container I:60, Folder 6)[hereafter *Baker* Conference Notes].

26. Conference, *supra* note 21, at 849.

27. *Id.* (quoting Justice Brennan).

28. *Baker* Conference Notes, *supra* note 25.

29. Conference, *supra* note 21, at 851 n.71.

30. 377 U.S. 533 (1964).

31. 372 U.S. 368 (1963).

32. 376 U.S. 1 (1964).

33. Conference, *supra* note 21, at 852 (quoting Justice Brennan).

34. *Wesberry,* 376 U.S. at 7–8.

35. Reynolds v. Sims, 377 U.S. 533, 568 (1964).

36. *Id.*

37. *Id.*

38. *Id.* at 579–80 (footnote omitted).

39. *Id.* at 580.

40. *Id.* at 581.

41. *See* Robert G. Dixon, Jr., Democratic Representation: Reapportionment in Law and Politics 4 (1968); *see also* Harold W. Stanley and Richard G. Niemi, Vital Statistics on American Politics 1999–2000, at 74–75, table 1-30 (2000) (showing deviations from equality in congressional and state legislative districts in the 1960s, 1980s, and 1990s).

42. *See* Robert B. McKay, *Reapportionment: Success Story of the Warren Court,* 67 Mich. L. Rev. 223, 228–29 (1968).

43. Ely, *supra* note 3, at 121.

44. 390 U.S. 474 (1968); *see also* Hadley v. Junior Coll. Dist., 397 U.S. 50, 56 (1970) (applying the one person, one vote rule to an election for a junior college district).

45. Justice Fortas made this point in his dissent. 390 U.S. at 509 (Fortas, J., dissenting).

46. 390 U.S. at 476.

47. Ball v. James, 451 U.S. 355, 370 (1981); Salyer Land Co. v. Tulare Lake Basin Water Storage Dist., 410 U.S. 719, 728 (1973).

48. Justice Harlan suggested the possibility of partisan gerrymandering in his *Reynolds* dissent. 377 U.S. 533, 622 (1964) (Harlan, J., dissenting).

49. McConnell, *supra* note 17, at 112.

50. See Dixon, *supra* note 41, app. A (contrasting state by state the malapportionment of state legislative districts before and after *Reynolds*).

51. Bruce E. Cain, *Election Law as a Field: A Political Scientist's Perspective,* 32 Loy. L.A. L. Rev. 1105, 1110 (1999) (footnote omitted); *see also* Edwards and

Polsby, *supra* note 8, at 201 (discussing the problem of the Bay Area regional government).

52. 489 U.S. 688, 690 (1989).

53. Richard Briffault, *Who Rules at Home? One Person/One Vote and Local Governments*, 60 U. Chi. L. Rev. 339, 404 (1993); *see also id.* at 344 (stating that "citizen understanding of and participation in government decisionmaking may be enhanced where regional government districts are coterminous with community or neighborhood lines, even where neighborhoods differ in population").

54. Baker v. Carr, 369 U.S. 186, 226 (1962).

55. 377 U.S. 713 (1964).

56. *See id.* at 751 (Stewart, J., dissenting).

57. *Id.* at 745 (Stewart, J., dissenting).

58. *Id.* at 746 (Stewart, J., dissenting).

59. *Id.* at 751 (Stewart, J., dissenting).

60. *Id.* at 753–54 (Stewart, J., dissenting).

61. *Id.* at 765 (Stewart, J., dissenting). He took various positions in the other cases decided concurrently. *See* Carl A. Auerbach, *The Reapportionment Cases: One Person, One Vote—One Vote, One Value,* 1964 Sup. Ct. Rev. 1, 58.

62. Reynolds v. Sims, 377 U.S. 533, 588 (1964) (Stewart, J., concurring).

63. *See, e.g.,* Auerbach, *supra* note 61, at 58–59 ("Mr. Justice Stewart justifies disproportionate representation as necessary to check the concentrated power of the most populous areas, but he does not indicate, satisfactorily, how much disproportionateness he would tolerate."); *see also id.* at 61 ("The difficulty with Mr. Justice Stewart's test of effective majority rule [and any other such test designed to sanction minority veto power] is that it is unable, logically, to specify any percentage short of 100 [or unanimity] which should empower the taking of affirmative action."); Note, *Reapportionment,* 79 Harv. L. Rev. 1228, 1246 (1966) ("The difficulty confronting all proposals [like Justice Stewart's] to overrepresent certain interests is that there are no standards for deciding which interests should be favored.").

64. *See* Richard H. Pildes, *Democracy and Disorder,* 68 U. Chi. L. Rev. 695, 714 (2001).

65. Briffault, *supra* note 53, at 415.

66. Jan G. Deutsch, *Neutrality, Legitimacy, and the Supreme Court: Some Intersections Between Law and Political Science,* 20 Stan. L. Rev. 169, 247 (1968); *see also* Ely, *supra* note 3, at 124 (endorsing Deutsch's view and explaining that the Court adopted the one person, one vote standard rather than Stewart's "in-between" standard "precisely because of considerations of administrability"); Auerbach, *supra* note 61, at 61 ("[A]ny effort to apply [Justice Stewart's] test practically calls for such a detailed evaluation of the politics of a state—which are always subject to change—that its application would hurl the Court back into the thicket of non-justiciable issues.").

67. See in chapter 1 the discussion of the Voting Rights Act cases and cases predating *City of Mobile v. Bolden* that considered issues of minority vote dilution.

68. *Cf.* Spencer A. Overton, *Rules, Standards, and* Bush v. Gore: *Form and the Law of Democracy,* 37 Harv. C.R.–C.L. L. Rev. 65, 95 (2002) ("[S]tandards allow judges to introduce arbitrary and subjective political biases into their deliberations and thus do not clearly confine the decision-making power of judges."). My point is simply that a bright-line rule like the one person, one vote standard similarly allows judges to introduce subjective political biases into the rule, though it is done in one fell swoop.

A separate criticism of Stewart's rule, raised by Lowenstein, is that the standard would have threatened the pluralist system of districting by requiring that the content (that is, outcome) of a districting process be rational. *See* Daniel H. Lowenstein, *The Supreme Court Has No Theory of Politics—And Be Thankful for Small Favors, in* The U.S. Supreme Court and the Electoral Process 283, 289 (David K. Ryden ed., 2d. ed. 2002).

69. Jerry R. Parkinson, Note, *Reapportionment: A Call for a Consistent Quantitative Standard,* 70 Iowa L. Rev. 663, 680–81 (1985).

70. 383 U.S. 663 (1966).

71. 395 U.S. 621 (1969).

72. 531 U.S. 98 (2000).

73. The tax was collected along with personal property taxes. Those who did not pay a personal property tax were not assessed for the poll tax, "it being their responsibility to take the initiative and request to be assessed." Harper v. Va. Bd. of Elections, 383 U.S. 663, 664 n.1 (1966).

74. *See id.* at 666 n.3. The dissenting justices agreed that a poll tax intended as a device to discriminate on the basis of race would be unconstitutional. *See id.* at 672 (Black, J., dissenting); *id. at* 683 n.5 (Harlan, J., dissenting).

75. *Id.* at 665.

76. *Id.* at 666.

77. *Id.*

78. Draft Dissent, Justice Goldberg, *Harper v. Va. Bd. of Elections* 9 (Mar. 3, 1965) (William J. Brennan, Jr., Papers, Manuscript Division, Library of Congress, Washington, D.C., Container I:128, Folder 6).

79. Ely, *supra* note 3, at 120; *see also* Richard A. Epstein, *"In Such Manner as the Legislature Thereof May Direct": The Outcome in* Bush v. Gore *Defended, in* The Vote: Bush, Gore, & the Supreme Court 13, 15 (Cass R. Sunstein and Richard A. Epstein eds., 2001) (characterizing *Harper* as a "free-form decision" that was "something of a stretch under classical equal protection law given that a poll tax is facially neutral and, unlike literacy tests, can be applied in a mechanical way that eliminates the dangers of political discretion").

80. Harlan raised the point to show that Congress or the constitutional amendment process could take care of the problem, and that it was not the Court's place to hold the poll tax unconstitutional.

81. *Harper,* 383 U.S. at 680, 685 (Harlan, J., dissenting).

82. *Id.* at 680 (Harlan, J., dissenting).

83. *Id.* at 685–86 (Harlan, J., dissenting).

84. *See* Cass R. Sunstein, Democracy and the Problem of Free Speech 93–101 (1993).

85. Kramer v. Union Free Sch. Dist. No. 15, 395 U.S. 621, 622 (1969).

86. *Id.* at 630–31.

87. *Id.*

88. *Id.* at 631.

89. *Id.* at 632.

90. *Id.* at 632 n.15 (emphases added).

91. Briffault, *supra* note 53, at 354–56.

92. Briffault writes:

[T]he Court's use of the term "interest," and its contrast between [plaintiff] and his fictional unemployed counterpart, suggests that the relevant interests were subjective states of mind, rather than objective ties to school board operations. Kramer was attentive to and concerned about local school affairs. He was, therefore, "interested." His fictional unemployed counterpart was indifferent when the subject of education came up and therefore, not "interested." Thus, the state statute had failed to discriminate with sufficient precision when it sought to vest the school board franchise only in those "interested."

Id. at 355–56.

93. *Id.* at 355.

94. 360 U.S. 45 (1959).

95. *Id.* at 51.

96. *Kramer* 395 U.S. at 634 (Stewart, J., dissenting).

97. Briffault, *supra* note 53, at 356.

98. 531 U.S. 98, 104–05 (2000) (full citations omitted).

99. *Id.* at 105.

100. *Id.*

101. Michael C. Dorf and Samuel Issacharoff, *Can Process Theory Constrain Courts?*, 72 U. Colo. L. Rev. 923, 932 (2001).

102. Overton, *supra* note 68, at 93.

103. 531 U.S. at 109.

104. *See* Richard L. Hasen, Bush v. Gore *and the Future of Equal Protection Law in Elections,* 29 Fla. St. U. L. Rev. 377 (2001).

105. Overton, *supra* note 68, at 93.

106. 509 U.S. 630 (1993).

107. Sanford Levinson, *Gerrymandering and the Brooding Omnipresence of Proportional Representation: Why Won't It Go Away?* 33 UCLA L. Rev. 257, 257 (1985).

108. *Id.* at 259.

109. Lucas v. Forty-Fourth General Assembly, 377 U.S. 713, 750 n.12 (1964).

110. *See* Levinson, *supra* note 107, at 259.

111. 446 U.S. 55 (1980).

112. *Id.* at 65–70 (plurality opinion).

113. *Id.* at 80 (Blackmun, J., concurring).

114. *Id.* at 93 (Stevens, J., concurring)("A contrary view 'would spawn endless litigation concerning the multi-member district systems now widely employed in this country,' and would entangle the judiciary in a voracious political thicket.")(citation omitted).

115. Justice White dissented on grounds that the plaintiffs had proved purposeful discrimination. *Id.* at 103 (White, J., dissenting).

116. *Id.* at 116–17 (Marshall, J., dissenting)(citations and footnotes omitted).

117. *Id.* at 75–76 (plurality opinion).

118. 42 U.S.C. § 1973(b) (2000).

119. 512 U.S. 997 (1994).

120. *See. e.g.,* Barnett v. City of Chicago, 141 F.3d 699, 702–05 (7th Cir. 1998). Heather Gerken chronicles the role that *De Grandy* has played here in Heather K. Gerken, *New Wine in Old Bottles: A Comment on Richard Hasen's and Richard Briffault's Essays on* Bush v. Gore, 29 Fla. St. U. L. Rev. 407, 418–19 (2001).

121. 478 U.S. 109 (1986).

122. *Id.* at 125.

123. *Id.* at 127–28 (plurality opinion).

124. *Id.* at 130 (plurality opinion).

125. *Id.* at 132 (plurality opinion).

126. Bernard Grofman, *Toward a Coherent Theory of Gerrymandering:* Bandemer *and* Thornburg, *in* Political Gerrymandering and the Courts 29, 30–32 (Bernard Grofman ed., 1990).

127. Daniel Hays Lowenstein, Bandemer's *Gap: Gerrymandering and Equal Protection, in* Political Gerrymandering and the Courts, *supra* note 126, at 64, 96.

128. Memorandum from Justice Brennan to Justice White, *Davis v. Bandemer* 2–3 (Dec. 17, 1985)(William J. Brennan, Jr., Papers, Manuscript Division, Library of Congress, Washington, D.C., Container I:702, Folder 10).

129. Laurence H. Tribe, American Constitutional Law 1083 (2d ed. 1988).

130. Daniel Hays Lowenstein and Richard L. Hasen, Election Law—Cases and Materials 197 n.8 (2d ed. 2001).

131. McConnell, *supra* note 17, at 114.

132. *Bandemer,* 478 U.S. at 155 (1986)(O'Connor, J., concurring).

133. Peter H. Schuck, *The Thickest Thicket: Partisan Gerrymandering and Judicial Regulation of Politics*, 87 Colum. L. Rev. 1325, 1361 (1987).

NOTES TO CHAPTER 3

1. 383 U.S. 663 (1966).
2. 415 U.S. 709 (1974).
3. 405 U.S. 134 (1972).
4. On the term "constitutionalization," see the important article Richard H. Pildes, *Constitutionalizing Democratic Politics, in* A Badly Flawed Election: Debating *Bush v. Gore*, The Supreme Court, and American Democracy 155 (Ronald Dworkin ed., 2002).
5. Colegrove v. Green, 328 U.S. 549 (1946).
6. Reynolds v. Sims, 377 U.S. 533, 565 (1964).
7. Harold J. Krent, *Should* Bouie *Be Buoyed? Judicial Retroactive Lawmaking and the* Ex Post Facto *Clause*, 3 Roger Williams U. L. Rev. 35 (1997).
8. Robert J. Pushaw, Jr., Bush v. Gore: *Looking at* Baker v. Carr *in a Conservative Mirror*, 18 Const. Comment. 359 (2001).
9. *Harper*, 383 U.S. at 686 (Harlan, J., dissenting).
10. *Compare* Atkins v. Virginia, 122 S. Ct. 2242 (2002) (holding it is cruel and unusual punishment to execute the mentally retarded) *with In re* Stanford, 123 S. Ct. 472 (2002) (Justice Stevens, dissenting from Court's decision not to reconsider whether it is cruel and unusual punishment to execute a person under age 18). *See* Akhil Reed Amar, *Shouldn't We, the People, Be Heard More Often by This High Court?* Wash. Post, June 30, 2002, at B3 (describing cruel and unusual punishment clause as a "built-in escalator clause" through which "the founders in effect told modern judges to pay attention to contemporary penal patterns and contemporary popular attitudes about punishment.").
11. Jonathan W. Still, *Political Equality and Election Systems*, 91 Ethics 375, 387–93 (1981).
12. 118 U.S. 356, 370 (1886).
13. 321 U.S. 649 (1944).
14. 517 U.S. 620 (1996).
15. 189 U.S. 475 (1903).
16. 88 U.S. (21 Wall.) 162 (1875).
17. 360 U.S. 45 (1959).
18. 395 U.S. 621 (1969).
19. 405 U.S. 330 (1972).
20. Memorandum from Justice Brennan's Law Clerks to Justice Brennan, Kramer v. Union Free School Dist. No. 15 (William J. Brennan, Jr., Papers, Manuscript Division, Library of Congress, Washington, D.C., Container I:192, Folder 2) (clerks' memo urging Justice Brennan not to use a compelling interest standard in

elections for minor elected officials because it would "unnecessarily restrict a state's ability to act flexibly in dealing with its problems" and noting that "[t]he Chief's law clerks recognized these dangers also, which is why they tried to find a middle ground by using the term 'important right.'"). Brennan rejected his clerks' advice, and advised Chief Justice Warren to change references from "important" interest to "compelling interest." Memorandum from Justice Brennan to Chief Justice Warren, Kramer v. Union Free School Dist. No. 15 (May 21, 1969) (William J. Brennan, Jr., Papers, Manuscript Division, Library of Congress, Washington, D.C., Container I:192, Folder 2). Warren made the changes.

21. 410 U.S. 719 (1973).

22. Frank I. Michelman, *Conceptions of Democracy in American Constitutional Argument: Voting Rights,* 41 Fla. L. Rev. 443, 469 (1989).

23. 531 U.S. 98 (2000).

24. 313 U.S. 299 (1941).

25. 418 U.S. 24 (1974).

26. *See, e.g.,* David L. Shapiro, *Mr. Justice Rehnquist: A Preliminary View,* 90 Harv. L. Rev. 293, 302–04 (1976).

27. Pamela S. Karlan, *Ballots and Bullets: The Exceptional History of the Right to Vote,* Stanford Public Law and Legal Theory Research Paper Series No. 45, at 22 (Dec. 2002), available for download at: http://ssrn.com/abstract_id=354702 (footnotes omitted). Karlan uses these statistics to argue that a lifetime voting ban for felons constitutes cruel and unusual punishment in violation of the Eighth Amendment.

28. 439 U.S. 60 (1978).

29. Issacharoff, Karlan, and Pildes suggest weighted voting to give nonresidents "'a bit of a say' but not as much influence over city policy as city residents." Samuel Issacharoff, Pamela S. Karlan, and Richard H. Pildes, The Law of Democracy 70 (rev. 2d ed. 2001).

30. Edward B. Foley, *Equal-Dollars-Per-Voter: A Constitutional Principle of Campaign Finance,* 94 Colum. L. Rev. 1204, 1211–12 (1994); Jamin Raskin and John Bonifaz, *The Constitutional Imperative and Practical Superiority of Democratically Financed Elections,* 94 Colum. L. Rev. 1160 (1994).

31. *See* Jac C. Heckelman, *The Effect of the Secret Ballot on Voter Turnout,* 82 Pub. Choice 107 (1995).

32. *See* Gary S. Becker, *A Theory of Competition Among Pressure Groups for Political Influence,* 98 Q.J. Econ. 371, 380 (1983); Sam Peltzman, *Toward a More General Theory of Regulation,* 19 J.L. & Econ. 211, 212–13 (1976).

33. *See generally* Mancur Olson, The Logic of Collective Action: Public Goods and the Theory of Groups (1971).

34. *See generally* Micah Sifry, Spoiling for a Fight: Third-Party Politics in America (2002).

35. 393 U.S. 23 (1968).

36. *Id.* at 31–32.

37. *Id.* at 32. The Burger Court decided a similar case along similar lines involving John Anderson's attempt to run as an independent presidential candidate in the 1980 election. *Anderson v. Celebrezze,* 460 U.S. 780 (1983).

38. 403 U.S. 431 (1971).

39. *Id.* at 442.

40. 446 U.S. 55 (1980).

41. *Id.* at 141 (Marshall, J., dissenting).

42. *Id.*

43. I provide greater detail on the Lebanese case in Richard L. Hasen, *Clipping Coupons for Democracy: An Egalitarian/Public Choice Defense of Campaign Finance Vouchers,* 84 Cal. L. Rev. 1, 57 (1996).

44. *See* Richard H. Pildes, *Is Voting-Rights Law Now at War with Itself?,* 80 N.C. L. Rev. 1517, 1525–36 (2002)(contrasting social science evidence of the extent of racially polarized voting in the 1980s and 1990s).

45. The case seems to have sparked little debate among the justices. Justice Brennan's conference notes on *Jenness* are quite sparse, with only Chief Justice Burger and Justice Stewart expressing any views. Burger stated that the case was "not like *Williams v. Rhodes.* There's no inherent right to be put on [the] general election ballot. . . . We abhor splinter parties [and] fraudulent candidacies. . . . I think 5 percent is not an undue burden." Justice Brennan Conference notes on *Jenness v. Fortson* (William J. Brennan, Jr., Papers, Manuscript Division, Library of Congress, Washington, D.C., Container I:229, Folder 4). Justice Stewart remarked that "context here is important. Even if 5 percent is high, other flexibilities about signing the [petitions] support this." *Id.* The files of Justices Brennan and Marshall reveal no substantive debates about the case among the justices through written correspondence (as was common with many of the important election law cases whose files I examined).

46. 403 U.S. at 442.

47. 460 U.S. 780 (1983).

48. 479 U.S. 189 (1986).

49. *Id.* at 194.

50. *Id.* at 195.

51. 520 U.S. 351 (1997). This paragraph and the next draw upon Richard L. Hasen, *Do the Parties or the People Own the Electoral Process?* 149 U. Pa. L. Rev. 815 (2001). For a more detailed description and criticism of the case, see Richard L. Hasen, *Entrenching the Duopoly: Why the Supreme Court Should Not Allow the States to Protect the Democrats and Republicans from Political Competition,* 1997 Sup. Ct. Rev. 331 [hereafter Hasen, *Duopoly*].

52. The Court accepted the state's argument that "a candidate or party could easily exploit fusion as a way of associating his or its name with popular slogans and catchphrases." 520 U.S. at 365. It also agreed that permitting fusion would

allow "minor parties to capitalize on the popularity of another party's candidate, rather than on their own appeal to the voters, in order to secure access to the ballot." *Id.* at 366. I criticize these rationales in Hasen, *Duopoly, supra* note 51, at 339.

53. 520 U.S. at 367.

54. *Id.* (citation omitted).

55. Although the ballot access cases typically have been cast as First Amendment cases, the underlying principle is one not only of political association (covered by the First Amendment) but also of the right to equal participation in the political process. At least early on, the Court viewed the two bases as somewhat interchangeable. At the conference in *Harper,* Chief Justice Warren said that the case should be decided "on equal protection grounds rather than [the] First Amendment." Justice Brennan's Conference Notes on *Harper v. Virginia Board of Elections* (William J. Brennan, Jr., Papers, Manuscript Division, Library of Congress, Washington, D.C., Container I:129, Folder 5). Justice Clark agreed, but Justice Black stated his view that the case does not "come within classification of equal protection." *Id.* Black did not endorse the First Amendment rationale either.

56. Daniel Hays Lowenstein and Richard L. Hasen, Election Law—Cases and Materials 71–72 (2d ed. 2001).

57. For additional analysis of the types of arguments that would be proper to make supporting antifusion laws, see Dennis F. Thompson, Just Elections: Creating a Fair Electoral Process in the United States 73–80 (2002).

58. Ronald Rogowski, *Trade and the Variety of Democratic Institutions,* 41 Int'l Org. 203, 209 (1987).

59. The Supreme Court recognized the point in *Federal Election Commission v. Colorado Republican Federal Campaign Committee,* 533 U.S. 431, 451–52 (2001). *See* Richard L. Hasen, *The Constitutionality of a Soft Money Ban After* Colorado Republican II, 1 Election L.J. 195, 203 (2002).

60. *See* Richard Winger, *The Supreme Court and the Burial of Ballot Access: A Critical Review of* Jenness v. Fortson, 1 Election L.J. 235 (2002).

NOTES TO CHAPTER 4

1. *See* Nixon v. Shrink Missouri Government PAC, 528 U.S. 377 (2000)(reviewing legislatively imposed contribution limits that became effective after a lower court struck down $100 limits passed by voter initiative).

2. *See* South Carolina v. Katzenbach, 383 U.S. 301 (1966).

3. *See* United Jewish Organizations v. Carey, 430 U.S. 144 (1977).

4. Julian Eule has argued that the Court should be *less* deferential to initiatives that may trample on individual rights, suggesting that the absence of legislative filters on initiative legislation requires the Court to take a "hard look" at such legislation. *See* Julian N. Eule, *Judicial Review of Direct Democracy,* 99 Yale L.J. 1503, 1549 (1990). Eule, however, noted that his hard look rule should not apply

to initiative measures aimed at regulating the electoral process. *See id.* at 1559 (where "the electorate acts to improve the processes of legislative representation, the justification for judicial vigilance is absent.").

5. *See, e.g.,* Citizens Against Rent Control v. City of Berkeley, 454 U.S. 290, 295 (1981).

6. Cass R. Sunstein, *Political Equality and Unintended Consequences,* 94 Colum. L. Rev. 1390, 1399 (1994); *see also* Ronald Dworkin, Sovereign Virtue: The Theory and Practice of Equality 354 (2000) ("[I]f we reject [the] majoritarian conception of democracy, in favor of a more ambitious one that understands democracy as a partnership in collective self-government in which all citizens are given the opportunity to be active and equal partners . . . [w]e should adopt instead a finer-grained and more discriminating, though still rigorous, test for deciding when government should be permitted to regulate political speech in the interests of democracy.").

7. L. A. Powe, Jr., *Mass Speech and the Newer First Amendment,* 1982 Sup. Ct. Rev. 243, 268–69.

8. Owen M. Fiss, *Free Speech and Social Structure,* 71 Iowa L. Rev. 1405, 1411 (1986).

9. 424 U.S. 1 (1976).

10. The FECA treated spending done in coordination with candidates as a contribution, not an expenditure.

11. *Buckley,* 424 U.S. at 16.

12. *Id.* at 21.

13. *Id.* at 26–27.

14. *Id.* at 46–47. The Court also remarked that expenditure limits could be circumvented easily, meaning that such limits would serve "no substantial societal interest." *Id.* at 45.

15. *Id.* at 48.

16. *Id.* at 48–49.

17. I provide a more detailed history of the drafting of the *per curiam* opinion in Richard L. Hasen, *The Untold Drafting History of* Buckley v. Valeo, 2 Election L.J. 241 (2003), relying upon the case files of Justices Brennan, Marshall, and Powell. Readers should consult that article for full citations to the quoted *Buckley* material in the next few pages.

18. On the media exception generally, *see* Richard L. Hasen, *Campaign Finance Laws and the Rupert Murdoch Problem,* 77 Tex. L. Rev. 1627 (1999).

19. Justice Brennan wrote:

At conference I indicated that contrary to my pre-conference view that [the provision limiting independent expenditures] was constitutional, conference discussion pointed up a possible fatal vagueness in the section, particularly since criminal penalties are imposed for violations. Potter's proposed construction does not wholly cure the vice of vagueness in my view [citation]; there remain a myriad of examples of its uncertain application even as construed.

In apparent response to Justice Brennan's concerns about the vagueness of the FECA's regulation of independent expenditures, the Court added the now-famous footnote 52 to *Buckley* that purported to draw a clear line between express advocacy subject to regulation and issue advocacy that was free from regulation. This footnote spawned the rise of "sham issue ads" and "soft money." *See* Hasen, *supra*, note 17.

20. *Buckley*, 424 U.S. at 266 (White, J., dissenting).

21. This position is a reversal of the position Justice Marshall took initially in conference. In a memorandum to Justice Marshall sent during the drafting of *Buckley*, one of his clerks argued that the limitations on expenditures from personal or family resources "*serve the vital governmental interest of equalizing access to the political* process. . . . If Congress can legislate absolute equality in economic wealth and overall ability to spend, I do not see why it cannot choose to act less drastically and simply legislate rough equality to spend in one particular area—an area in which there is a peculiarly strong interest in equalizing access." Other Marshall clerks disagreed with this reasoning.

22. *Buckley*, 424 U.S. at 287 (Marshall, J., dissenting).

23. 435 U.S. 765 (1978).

24. *Id.* at 789.

25. *Id.* Justice Powell's law clerk explained to Justice Powell that she added a footnote following this language with a citation to the broadcasting case of *Red Lion Broadcasting Co. v. FCC*, 395 U.S. 367 (1969). She did so "to communicate something of the notion that the government has an interest in keeping channels of communication open, and if a situation arises where people truly can't [hear] what other citizens think because corporations have taken over so much, then regulation might be permissible." Memorandum from law clerk Nancy J. Bregstein to Justice Powell (Feb. 9, 1978) in *First National Bank of Boston v. Bellotti* (Lewis F. Powell Jr. Papers, School of Law, Washington and Lee University, Lexington, Va., File No. 76-1172).

26. *Bellotti*, 435 U.S. at 790.

27. *Id.* at 809–10 (White, J., dissenting) (emphasis added).

28. 454 U.S. 290 (1981).

29. *Id.* at 299.

30. *Id.* at 308 (White, J., dissenting). Justice Marshall concurred in the result and stated he would have joined Justice White in dissent if he had found the record had contained sufficient evidence to support the California Supreme Court's conclusion about voter confidence.

31. 470 U.S. 480 (1985).

32. *Id.* at 499.

33. *Id.*

34. *Id.* at 521 (Marshall, J., dissenting) (quoting his earlier separate opinion in *Buckley* arguing for the constitutionality of the FECA's limits on personal and family funds).

35. 459 U.S. 197 (1982).

36. *Id.* at 207.

37. 479 U.S. 238 (1986).

38. *Id.* at 257–58 (citations omitted). Given his prior views, it is somewhat surprising that Justice Powell joined in this portion of the *MCFL* opinion. After Justice Brennan circulated a draft opinion containing the barometer equality language, Justice Powell's law clerk sent a memorandum noting this part of the draft opinion and stating that it stood for the principle that

> we permit regulation, i.e., the requirement that the organization form a PAC, to ensure that [the] amount of money spent in the political arena is a reasonable proxy for the degree to which the view is held in the country. Although complete equality in the ability to speak in the political arena is not required, Congress can at least require that all money spent in the political arena be intended by its contributor to be so spent. This would seem to be the principle from this opinion that will be applied to later opinions. It would appear to accord with your point of view, but if it does not, you should consider requesting alterations.

Memorandum from law clerk Leslie S. Gielow to Justice Powell (Nov. 6, 1986)(Lewis F. Powell Jr. Papers, School of Law, Washington and Lee University, Lexington, Va., File No. 85-701). Justice Powell wrote on the memorandum: "I'm inclined to join WJB" and four days after receiving the memorandum indicated to the other justices his intent to join the majority opinion.

It is also interesting that Justice Scalia, then new to the Court, enthusiastically joined in Justice Brennan's opinion in *MCFL* on this point. Justice Scalia wrote in a memorandum to the Court that he "would be delighted" to join in Justice Brennan's *MCFL* opinion. Memorandum from Justice Scalia to Justice Brennan (Nov. 21, 1986) (Thurgood Marshall Papers, Manuscript Division, Library of Congress, Washington, D.C., Box 413, Folder 5). This position is wholly at odds with his blistering *Austin* dissent issued a few years later.

39. 494 U.S. 652 (1990).

40. *Id.* at 659–60 (citation omitted).

41. *Id.* at 660.

42. *Id.* at 685 (Scalia, J., dissenting).

43. Austin v. Michigan Chamber of Commerce, First Draft from Justice Marshall, circulated Dec. 6, 1989, at 6 (Thurgood Marshall Papers, Manuscript Division, Library of Congress, Washington, D.C., Box 502, Folder 7).

44. Chief Justice Rehnquist wrote: "I would have considerable difficulty with the equal protection argument raised by the respondent if it were not for the fact that under our line of cases beginning with *Abood,* we have held that the First Amendment requires labor unions to permit dissenting members to 'opt out' from those portions of dues which might go to political campaigns." Letter from Chief Justice Rehnquist to Justice Marshall (copies to the Conference) (Dec. 11, 1989) (Thurgood Marshall Papers, Manuscript Division, Library of Congress, Washington, D.C., Box 502, Folder 7).

45. Letter from Justice Brennan to Justice Marshall (time stamped Dec. 18, 1989)(Thurgood Marshall Papers, Manuscript Division, Library of Congress, Washington, D.C., Box 502, Folder 7).

46. Austin v. Michigan Chamber of Commerce, Fourth Draft from Justice Marshall circulated Dec. 19, 1989, at 7 (Thurgood Marshall Papers, Manuscript Division, Library of Congress, Washington, D.C., Box 502, Folder 7).

47. Justice Stevens's proposed language that would have noted that in *Bellotti* the Court "recognized that a legislature might demonstrate a danger of real or apparent corruption posed by such expenditures when made by corporations to influence candidate elections." Letter from Justice Stevens to Justice Marshall (Dec. 19, 1989) (Thurgood Marshall Papers, Manuscript Division, Library of Congress, Washington, D.C., Box 502, Folder 7).

48. Austin v. Michigan Chamber of Commerce, Fifth Draft from Justice Marshall circulated Dec. 21, 1989, at 7 (Thurgood Marshall Papers, Manuscript Division, Library of Congress, Washington, D.C., Box 502, Folder 7).

49. Letter from Justice Brennan to Justice Marshall (Jan. 23, 1990) (Thurgood Marshall Papers, Manuscript Division, Library of Congress, Washington, D.C., Box 502, Folder 7).

50. *Austin,* 494 U.S. at 705 (Kennedy, J., dissenting).

51. *Id.* at 660.

52. Justice Blackmun's acceptance of the equality rationale remains a mystery as well, given his initial concurrence in the *Buckley* Court's rejection of the equality rationale for expenditure limits.

53. Colo. Republican Fed. Campaign Comm. v. Fed. Election Comm'n, 518 U.S. 604, 649 (1996)(Stevens, J., dissenting).

54. Nixon v. Shrink Missouri Government PAC, 528 U.S. 377, 402 (2000) (Breyer, J., concurring).

55. *Id.* at 400–401 (Breyer, J., concurring)(citations omitted).

56. 518 U.S. at 649–50 (Stevens, J., dissenting) ("Congress surely has both wisdom and experience in these matters that is far superior to ours.").

57. *Shrink Missouri,* 528 U.S. at 403 (Breyer, J., concurring).

58. *Id.* at 430 (Thomas, J., dissenting).

59. *Id.* at 390–94.

60. *See* William P. Marshall, *The Last Best Chance for Campaign Finance Reform*, 94 Nw. U. L. Rev. 335 (2000).

61. Emphasis added.

62. *See* Richard L. Hasen, Shrink Missouri, *Campaign Finance, and "The Thing That Wouldn't Leave,"* 17 Const. Comment. 483 (2000).

63. *See* Hasen, *supra* note 18, at 1645–46.

64. I develop this idea more fully in Richard L. Hasen, *Clipping Coupons for Democracy: An Egalitarian/Public Choice Defense of Campaign Finance Vouchers,* 84 Cal. L. Rev. 1 (1996); *see also* Bruce Ackerman and Ian Ayres, Voting with Dollars: A New Paradigm for Campaign Finance (2002).

65. 383 U.S. 301 (1966).

66. By this time, South Carolina's property qualification would have been held unconstitutional under *Harper*.

67. *Id.* at 323.

68. 17 U.S. (4 Wheat.) 316, 321 (1819).

69. South Carolina v. Katzenbach, 383 U.S. at 328 (footnote omitted).

70. *Id.* at 329.

71. Lassiter v. Northampton County Bd. of Elections, 360 U.S. 45 (1959).

72. South Carolina v. Katzenbach, 383 U.S. at 333.

73. *Id.* at 334.

74. *Id.*

75. *Id.* at 334–35. The Court also upheld the appointment of federal examiners to list qualified applicants who are thereafter entitled to vote.

76. *Id.* at 360 (Black, J., dissenting).

77. 384 U.S. 641 (1966).

78. *Id.* at 652.

79. *Id.* at 653.

80. *Id.* at 651 n.10.

81. 400 U.S. 112 (1970).

82. *See id.* at 133–34; *id.* at 144–47 (Douglas, J., concurring in part and dissenting in part); *id.* at 216–17 (Harlan, J., concurring in part and dissenting in part); *id.* at 232–36 (Brennan, J., concurring in part and dissenting in part); *id.* at 282–85 (Stewart, J., concurring in part and dissenting in part).

83. *Id.* at 239–50 (Brennan, J., concurring in part and dissenting in part). These justices further noted their view that there was "serious question whether a statute granting the franchise to citizens 21 and over while denying it to those between the ages of 18 and 21 could . . . withstand present scrutiny under the Equal Protection Clause." *Id.* at 240; *see also id.* at 135–36 (Douglas, J. concurring in part and dissenting in part).

84. 446 U.S. 156 (1980).

85. The Court addressed the issue in *City of Mobile v. Bolden*, 446 U.S. 55 (1980), decided the same day as *City of Rome*, and discussed in earlier chapters.

86. *City of Rome,* 446 U.S. at 177.

87. *Id.* at 210 (Rehnquist, J., dissenting) (emphasis added).

88. *Id.* at 215.

89. *Id.* at 211.

90. *Id.* at 193–206 (Powell, J., dissenting).

91. This revolution is described in Mark Tushnet, The New Constitutional Order (2003).

92. United States v. Lopez, 514 U.S. 549 (1995); United States v. Morrison, 529 U.S. 598 (2000).

93. *See, e.g.,* Seminole Tribe v. Florida, 517 U.S. 44 (1996) (holding Congress cannot use power under the Commerce Clause to abrogate a state's sovereign immunity in federal court); Alden v. Maine, 527 U.S. 706 (1999) (same result in state court).

94. 521 U.S. 507 (1997).

95. 494 U.S. 872 (1990).

96. *Boerne,* 521 U.S. at 514 (summarizing *Smith* holding).

97. The guarantee appears in the First Amendment, which the Court has held became applicable to the states through enactment of the Fourteenth Amendment. *See* Cantwell v. Connecticut, 310 U.S. 296 (1940).

98. *See* 42 U.S.C. § 2000bb-1 (2000).

99. *Boerne,* 521 U.S. at 519.

100. *Id.* at 520.

101. *Id.* at 527–29.

102. *Id.* at 530.

103. *Id.* at 532.

104. 527 U.S. 627 (1999).

105. *Id.* at 640.

106. 528 U.S. 62 (2000).

107. 531 U.S. 356 (2001).

108. *Id.* at 373.

109. *Id.* at 384 (Breyer, J., dissenting).

110. *Id.* at 386 (Breyer, J., dissenting).

111. Mississippi Republican Executive Comm. v. Brooks, 469 U.S. 1002 (1984). Chief Justice Burger and then-Justice Rehnquist dissented from the summary affirmance, though on grounds unrelated to the issue of congressional power.

112. 525 U.S. 266 (1999).

113. One thoughtful commentator called it "puzzling" that "*Lopez* pays little attention to the factors that have become increasingly important to establishing congruence and proportionality under the developing *Boerne* doctrine." Ellen D. Katz, *Federalism, Preclearance and the Rehnquist Court,* 46 Vill. L. Rev. 1179, 1202 (2001).

114. *Lopez,* 525 U.S. at 284.

115. 446 U.S. 55 (1980).

116. 478 U.S. 30 (1986).

117. *Id.* at 50–51.

118. Douglas Laycock, *Conceptual Gulfs in* City of Boerne v. Flores, 39 Wm. & Mary L. Rev. 743, 749–51 (1998). For arguments along similar lines aimed at proving the unconstitutionality of section 2 of the Voting Rights Act, see John Matthew Guard, Comment, *"Impotent Figureheads"? State Sovereignty, Federalism and the Constitutionality of Section 2 of the Voting Rights Act After* Lopez v. Monterey County *and* City of Boerne v. Flores, 74 Tul. L. Rev. 329, 359–363 (1999).

119. *See* Heather K. Gerken, *Understanding the Right to an Undiluted Vote*, 114 Harv. L. Rev. 1663, 1737 (2001).

120. Laycock, *supra* note 118, at 751–52.

121. Tushnet, *supra* note 91, at 78–79.

122. *See id.*

123. Pamela S. Karlan, *Two Section Twos and Two Section Fives: Voting Rights and Remedies After* Flores, 39 Wm. & Mary L. Rev. 725, 726 (1998).

124. *See* Philip P. Frickey and Steven S. Smith, *Judicial Review, the Congressional Process, and the Federalism Cases: An Interdisciplinary Critique*, 111 Yale L.J. 1707, 1734 (2002).

125. *See* Richard H. Pildes, *Is Voting-Rights Law Now at War With Itself? Social Science and Voting Rights in the 2000s*, 80 N.C. L. Rev. 1517 (2002).

126. Karlan, *supra* note 123, at 738.

127. *Id.* at 739–40.

128. *See, e.g.,* Missouri v. Jenkins, 515 U.S. 70 (1995).

129. Karlan, *supra* note 123, at 737–38.

130. David Cole, *The Value of Seeing Things Differently:* Boerne v. Flores *and Congressional Enforcement of the Bill of Rights*, 1997 Sup. Ct. Rev. 31, 70.

131. Michael W. McConnell, *Institutions and Interpretation: A Critique of* City of Boerne v. Flores, 111 Harv. L. Rev. 153, 194–95 (1997).

132. Evan H. Caminker, *"Appropriate" Means-Ends Constraints on Section 5 Powers*, 53 Stan. L. Rev. 1127 (2001).

133. Samuel Issacharoff, Pamela S. Karlan, and Richard H. Pildes, The Law of Democracy 564 (rev. 2d ed. 2001).

134. *See* Pildes, *supra* note 125, at 1559 n.116.

135. United Jewish Organizations v. Carey, 430 U.S. 144, 174–75 (1977) (Brennan, J., concurring in part).

136. *Id.* at 178.

137. *See id.* at 165 (White, J., joined by Stevens, J., and Rehnquist, C.J.) ("there was no fencing out of the white population from participation in the political process of the county, and the plan did not minimize or unfairly cancel out white voting strength"); *id.* at 180 (Stewart, J., and Powell, J., concurring) (clear purpose

of legislature in responding to the Justice Department under the Voting Rights Act precludes "any finding that it acted with invidious purpose of discriminating against white voters").

NOTES TO CHAPTER 5

1. Bruce E. Cain, *Election Law as a Field: A Political Scientist's Perspective*, 32 Loy. L.A. L. Rev. 1105, 1119 (1999).

2. Although Karlan has expressed general skepticism of academics' use of market models in election law, *see* Pamela S. Karlan, *Politics by Other Means*, 85 Va. L. Rev. 1697 (1999), she has not squarely applied her critique of structural equal protection analysis to the political market model of Issacharoff and Pildes discussed below.

3. Pamela S. Karlan, *Nothing Personal: The Evolution of the Newest Equal Protection from* Shaw v. Reno *to* Bush v. Gore, 79 N.C. L. Rev. 1345, 1346 (2001).

4. 509 U.S. 630 (1993).

5. Karlan, *supra* note 3, at 1351.

6. 509 U.S. at 647.

7. *Id.*

8. Easley v. Cromartie, 532 U.S. 234 (2001).

9. Richard H. Pildes and Richard G. Niemi, *Expressive Harms, "Bizarre Districts," and Voting Rights: Evaluating Election-District Appearances After* Shaw v. Reno, 92 Mich. L. Rev. 483, 506–07 (1993).

10. *Id.* at 507.

11. *Id.* at 509.

12. *Id.* at 510. Indeed, Professor Pildes has not directly confronted the question in his many articles on the subject.

13. Bush v. Vera, 517 U.S. 952, 984 (1996) (emphasis added).

14. Pamela S. Karlan, *All Over the Map: The Supreme Court's Voting Rights Trilogy*, 1993 Sup. Ct. Rev. 245, 282.

15. T. Alexander Aleinikoff and Samuel Issacharoff, *Race and Redistricting: Drawing Constitutional Lines After* Shaw v. Reno, 92 Mich. L. Rev. 588, 612–13 (1993).

16. Daniel Hays Lowenstein, *You Don't Have to Be Liberal to Hate the Racial Gerrymandering Cases*, 50 Stan. L. Rev. 779 (1998).

17. Guy-Uriel E. Charles, *Racial Identity, Electorial Structures and the First Amendment Right of Association*, 91 Cal. L. Rev. (forthcoming 2003).

18. Personal communication from Dan Lowenstein, December 2002.

19. *Compare* Richard H. Pildes, *Why Rights Are Not Trumps: Social Meanings, Expressive Harms, and Constitutionalism*, 27 J. Legal Stud. 725, 755 (1998) [hereafter Pildes, *Rights Not Trumps*] (under the view of expressive harms, "the meaning of a governmental action is just as important as what that action does.").

20. David T. Canon, Race, Redistricting, and Representation: The Unintended Consequences of Black Majority Districts 4(1999).

21. Richard H. Pildes, *Is Voting-Rights Law Now at War with Itself? Social Science and Voting Rights in the 2000s,* 80 N.C. L. Rev. 1517 (2002).

22. *See* Pamela S. Karlan, *Just Politics? Five Not So Easy Pieces of the 1995 Term,* 34 Hous. L. Rev. 289 (1997).

23. 531 U.S. 98 (2000).

24. Karlan, *supra* note 3, at 1364.

25. *See* Nathaniel Persily and Bruce E. Cain, *The Legal Status of Political Parties: A Reassessment of Competing Paradigms,* 100 Colum. L. Rev. 775, 788 (2000).

26. 50 Stan. L. Rev. 643 (1998). I provided a critique of the initial version of the argument in Richard L. Hasen, *The "Political Market" Metaphor and Election Law: A Comment on Issacharoff and Pildes,* 50 Stan. L. Rev. 719 (1998). The next few paragraphs draw on that critique.

27. Issacharoff and Pildes, *supra* note 26, at 645, 717.

28. *Id.* at 646, 648, 652, 655, 660, 690, 717.

29. This description follows Marcel Kahan and Michael Klausner, *Lockups and the Market for Corporate Control,* 48 Stan. L. Rev. 1539, 1540 (1996).

30. Daniel R. Ortiz, *From Rights to Arrangements,* 32 Loy. L.A. L. Rev. 1217 (1999).

31. 520 U.S. 351 (1997).

32. Issacharoff and Pildes, *supra* note 26, at 681.

33. *Id.* at 703, 706.

34. I summarize that literature in Richard L. Hasen, *Entrenching the Duopoly: Why the Supreme Court Should Not Allow the States to Protect the Democrats and Republicans from Political Competition,* 1997 Sup. Ct. Rev. 331.

35. 504 U.S. 428 (1992).

36. Daniel H. Lowenstein, *The Supreme Court Has No Theory of Politics—And Be Thankful for Small Favors,* in The U.S. Supreme Court and the Electoral Process 283, 301 (David K. Ryden ed., 2d ed. 2002).

37. Bruce E. Cain, *Garrett's Temptation,* 85 Va. L. Rev. 1589, 1600 (1999).

38. *Id.* at 1602.

39. Richard H. Pildes, *The Theory of Political Competition,* 85 Va. L. Rev. 1605, 1615 (1999).

40. *Id.* at 1607.

41. *Id.* at 1617–18.

42. *Id.* at 1616 (emphasis added).

43. *Id.*

44. Even Pildes's earlier writings on the structural approach recognized the inevitability of balancing in appropriate contexts. Richard H. Pildes, *Avoiding Balancing: The Role of Exclusionary Reasons in Constitutional Law,* 45 Hastings L.J. 711, 751 (1994) ("[R]ights play many roles, and no doubt many problems must

continue to be understood to involve direct conflicts between rights and state interests.") [hereafter Pildes, *Avoiding Balancing*]; *see also* Pildes, *Rights Not Trumps, supra* note 19, at 735 n.30.

45. Pildes, *supra* note 39, at 1625.

46. 530 U.S. 567 (2000).

47. For my own criticism of the case, see Richard L. Hasen, *Do the Parties or the People Own the Electoral Process?*, 149 U. Pa. L. Rev. 815 (2001).

48. Samuel Issacharoff, *Private Parties with Public Purposes: Political Parties, Associational Freedoms, and Partisan Competition*, 101 Colum. L. Rev. 274, 308 (2001).

49. *Id.* at 312.

50. *Id.* at 311.

51. Samuel Issacharoff, *Gerrymandering and Political Cartels*, 116 Harv. L. Rev. 593 (2002).

52. Samuel Issacharoff, *Oversight of Regulated Political Markets*, 24 Harv. J.L. & Pub. Pol'y 91, 100 (2000).

53. Issacharoff, *supra* note 51, at 600.

54. *See also* Nathaniel Persily, Reply, *In Defense of Foxes Guarding Henhouses: The Case for Judicial Acquiescence to Incumbent-Protecting Gerrymanders*, 116 Harv. L. Rev. 649, 667 (2002) (suggesting that Issacharoff's theory could be extended in many different areas, including the congressional franking privilege and ballot access regulation).

55. Martin Shapiro, *Gerrymandering, Unfairness, and the Supreme Court*, 33 UCLA L. Rev. 227, 228 (1985).

56. Issacharoff, *supra* note 51, at 627.

57. *Id.*

58. *Id.* at 626.

59. Persily, *supra* note 54.

60. Stephen Ansolabehere and James M. Snyder, Jr., *The Incumbency Advantage in U.S. Elections: An Analysis of State and Federal Offices, 1942–2000*, 1 Election L.J. 315 (2002).

61. Persily, *supra* note 54, at 673.

62. Issacharoff and Pildes, *supra* note 26.

63. Issacharoff, *supra* note 51.

64. For an argument along similar lines, see Luis Fuentes-Rohwer, *Doing Our Politics in Court: Gerrymandering, "Fair Representation," and an Exegesis into the Judicial Role*, 78 Notre Dame L. Rev. 527 (2003).

65. The parties certainly may be major players in the initiative process even if they do not overwhelm it. *See* Richard L. Hasen, *Parties Take the Initiative (and Vice Versa)*, 100 Colum. L. Rev. 731 (2000).

66. Richard H. Pildes, *Democracy and Disorder*, 68 U. Chi. L. Rev. 695, 714–15 (2001).

67. Nathaniel Persily, *Toward a Functional Defense of Political Party Autonomy,* 76 N.Y.U. L. Rev. 750 (2001).

68. Heather K. Gerken, *Understanding the Right to an Undiluted Vote,* 114 Harv. L. Rev. 1663 (2001).

69. *See* Heather K. Gerken, *The Costs and Causes of Minimalism in Voting Cases:* Baker v. Carr *and Its Progeny,* 80 N.C. L. Rev. 1411 (2002).

70. *See* Brian Barry, Sociologists, Economists and Democracy 166 (1978).

NOTES TO THE CONCLUSION

1. Harper v. Virginia Bd. of Elections, 383 U.S. 663, 672 (1966) (Black, J., dissenting).

2. *Id.* at 670. Memorandum from Justice Douglas to the Conference (Mar. 22, 1966) (John Marshall Harlan Papers, Seely G. Mudd Manuscript Library, Princeton University, Princeton, N.J., Box 249), notes the addition of this sentence.

3. 347 U.S. 483 (1954).

4. 384 U.S. 436 (1966).

5. David Strauss, The Common Law Genius of the Warren Court, University of Chicago Public Law and Legal Theory Working Paper No. 25 (May 2002), available at: http://ssrn.com/abstract_id=315682.

6. *Id.* at 33.

7. On Pareto superiority, see Richard A. Posner, Economic Analysis of Law 13–14 (5th ed. 1998).

8. For a similar view of judicial deal making, see Evan H. Caminker, *Sincere and Strategic Voting Norms on Multimember Courts,* 97 Mich. L. Rev. 2297 (1999).

9. Wells v. Rockefeller, 394 U.S. 542 (1969).

10. Opinions of William J. Brennan, Jr., October Term 1968 (Law Clerks Joseph Onek and Robert M. Weinberg), p. xv (William J. Brennan, Jr., Papers, Manuscript Division, Library of Congress, Washington, D.C., Container II:6, Folder 11).

11. 517 U.S. 620 (1996).

12. 478 U.S. 186 (1986).

13. *See* Jacobellis v. Ohio, 378 U.S. 184, 197 (1964) (Stewart, J., concurring).

14. *Compare* Brown v. Board of Education, 349 U.S. 294, 299 (1955) (noting that lower federal courts and local school authorities will need to craft solutions to end school segregation) *with* Swann v. Charlotte-Mecklenburg Board of Education, 402 U.S. 1, 6 (1971) ("This Court, in *Brown I,* appropriately dealt with the large constitutional principles; other federal courts had to grapple with the flinty, intractable realities of day-to-day implementation of those constitutional commands. Their efforts, of necessity, embraced a process of 'trial and error.'").

Index

About the Author

Richard L. Hasen is Professor of Law and William M. Rains Fellow at Loyola Law School, Los Angeles. He is coauthor of a textbook, *Election Law: Cases and Materials,* and co-edits *Election Law Journal.* He holds both a J.D. and a Ph.D. in Political Science, and his scholarship on election law and campaign finance issues has appeared in numerous publications, including the *California Law Review,* the *Columbia Law Review, Constitutional Commentary, The University of Pennsylvania Law Review,* and the *Supreme Court Review.*